WHY

[

NON-CHRISTIAN NONTRADITIONAL

RELIGIONS AND SECTS

04/02/06

Dear Queen,
"What a mighty
God we serve."

Love,
Dr. Joyce Henderson

WHY AFRICAN AMERICAN YOUTH ARE ATTRACTED TO NON-CHRISTIAN/NONTRADITIONAL RELIGIONS AND SECTS

by

Dr. Joyce T. Henderson

ISBN 1-58500-432-4

ABOUT THE BOOK

What is it that our African American youth apparently need which these non-Christian/nontraditional religions and sects provide that is not provided by the traditional church? By understanding why these young people join or follow such groups and leaders, then one can understand more meaningful and objectively how a Rev. Jim Jones can hold sway over a group forcing those individuals to submit to their will. One can more ably understand the needs of these youth and perhaps, in so understanding, see how the traditional churches have failed these youth in their endeavor to find God and themselves.

Not all groups in this study are characterized as cults or non-Christian religions. Some are independent while others are listed as studies.

Perhaps the traditional churches can embark upon programs to get young people involved in and offer them an avenue whereby they may find themselves and their God without losing their souls by following some leader like Jim Jones, into eternal damnation.

Understanding is the beginning of wisdom as one sage has said. And as such, if this work only serves to elicit understanding of the youth, their needs and their wants, then it is felt that we have begun to take the first step in rendering wisely a world safe and stable for your young people to find their way towards a meaningful Christian life and towards the God of their salvation.

TABLE OF CONTENTS

VI. THE ISLAMIC RELIGION

VII. THE JEHOVAH WITNESS

DEDICATION

I dedicate this work to my husband, John W. Henderson Sr., and my son, John Henderson Jr., and to a number of good friends, truly brothers and sisters in Christ, who greatly contributed to it getting done by their encouragement, prayers and the many special ways in which they helped me. May God bless them for the many wonderful ways they have blessed me.

I am most thankful to the Lord for all the grace He extended to me, enabling me to complete this further step of training and equipping for the ministry.

ACKNOWLEDGEMENTS

I am immensely grateful to the children who, in ways only they could mentor me through this process. The children I had the privilege to work with for thirty-two years at the various Recreation Centers throughout the Los Angeles areas will most likely never know of the tremendous impact they have had on my life.

I wish to thank the following persons for their helpful and kind assistance in granting me vital resource materials and interviews. They include Al Albergate of SGL Santa Monica, CA, Almeda Bailey, SGL Chicago, IL, and Miriam Wheeler, SGI of Los Angeles.

This book would not have been completed were it not for my devoted husband, John. While other marriages often suffer through the process of writing a book, mine reached new heights. His confidence in me was the driving force behind the entire project and it is because of this that I acknowledge my husband, John Henderson Sr.

FOREWORD

One of the most promising features of the modern religious scene is the proliferation of clamorous and vociferous cults. Many of them are variants from Christianity though some claim affinity with, and evident kinship to others of the world's living religions. Some of these bodies claim to be the only correct exposition of Christian truth, while others claim to present special items of a revelation nature which are said to be essential supplements of the Christian faith.

This book seeks to explain the nature of these groups and endeavors to outline something of their history and witness. It is an attempt to present any worthwhile and significant contributions these causes may be making to the well being of society or the advance of Christianity.

These studies are pointed to an evaluation of the relative Scripturalness and spiritual sensitivity of these people. It is recognized and pointed out that some are near Biblical truth than others and some present more points of divergence from the Scripture norm than others.

These lessons present an exposure of those points at which it is felt that these cults deny or distort basis Christian truth. This is not done in a spirit of bitterness, but in an attempt to warn earnest Christians of pitfalls to be avoided. The attitude taken in Abraham Lincoln expressed these lessons when he said: "While with malice towards none, with clarity towards all, with firmness in the right, as God gives us to see the right."

With a work involving so many intricate biblical, theological, and biographical materials it is impossible to believe that errors can be avoided entirely. Every attempt, however, has been made to be accurate. The spirit in which these cults are surveyed can be summed up in two quotations. One is from Othello, Act V, Scene 2. As Othello said, I have thought of these cults as saying: "Speak of me as I am, nothing extenuates, nor set down ought in malice." The other is from 2nd Timothy 2:19, "But God has laid a foundation and it stands firm and with this inscription: "The

Lord knows His own and everyone who takes the Lord's name upon his lips must forsake wickedness." (New English Bible).

[1]From the New English Bible, New Testament @ The Delegates of the Oxford University Press and the Syndics of the Cambridge University Press 1961. Reprint by permission.

I. METHODOLOGY

A. APPROACH TO THE STUDY

Over the past two decades and continuing into the new millennium — many of our young African Americans have been and are still being drawn away from the Christian Church into non-Christian religions. Overwhelming evidence exists that young African Americans have developed and are exhibiting a deep interest in the occult, as well as various satanic, pagan and witchcraft organizations. Just how much, if any, have Christian churches and denominations contributed to this mass defection among young African Americans?

This book purports to study the causes that lead young African Americans from the Christian Church into non-Christian/nontraditional groups. Used as source and reference material upon which my study is premised is the Holy Bible, along with the works of authors who are acknowledged as authorities in Christian theology. Included in the works are results from personal interviews, case studies, and field surveys conducted by the author.

A careful study of these non-Christian/nontraditional groups and sects will enable us to view them in their variety and their different degrees of approach to genuine New Testament Christianity. Based upon the findings in the study, the author will suggest what local churches may do to better connect with this generation of youth and some positive steps towards evangelism.

It is hoped that this book contributes to some understanding of non-Christian/nontraditional religions and sects; help churches, parents and communities to prevent such a mass exodus; assist to reclaim and restore to us our prodigal sons and daughters to their rightful place, as the children of God-in-Christ who have been granted life everlasting through the sacrifice for all of us by Jesus The Christ who paid for our sins.

B. DELIMITATION

Because of the enormity materials and scope of the subject consideration, along with the time constraints to which this work is to be completed, the author must curtail and restrict both, the focus and length of the book. The problems treated in this study are restricted to a consideration of how the churches and denominations have failed to meet the needs of young African Americans, thereby causing vast numbers within this population to reject Christianity. It should be noted from the start, that Christianity is not the problem, it has not failed our African American youth and young adults, although Christian churches and denominations have. Therefore, the author does not treat Christianity as contributing to the defection, although she does look at the basis tenets of Biblical Christianity, she only uses this standard for examining non-Christian religions.

This book also limits itself to the consideration of young African Americans. Therefore, this limits topics of churches to the African American churches and others in which our young African American brothers and sisters are members. It counsels only African American parents and the communities in which they live. While limited and addressing only one ethnic group, persons of ethnicities other than African Americans, who are involved with the problem of youth exodus from Christianity and youth entry into other than Christian organizations and churches may find the work useful.

Since the work handles only African Americans, the author has selected for study non-Christian/nontraditional religions that this group is most likely to channel into the personal search for relevance and meaning. Thus studies are: BUDDHISM — A New Discovery for African Americans; THE BAHA'I FAITH — An organization which strongly supports racial unity, oneness, equality of men and women, and interracial marriages; THE ISLAMIC RELIGION — An organization that holds a wide appeal and which siphons off a very large segment of the young African American population; and THE JEHOVAH WITNESS — A non-Christian sect who has produced its own translation of the Bible. In addition, a brief overview of several groups whom are on the horizon in the African American community which include THE HEBREW ISRAELITES — who claim that the African Americans are The Tribe of Judah, one of the twelve lost tribes of Israel and Amon-Rah — which espouses the knowledge of self.

Other such groups as Mormons, Hari Krishna's do not seem to exert the overwhelming pull that the above named do in causing young African American to flock to them. Accordingly, they have little part, if any, in this discussion. Additionally, the author looks into the group, which may or may not hold wide appeal but which have had tragic repercussions for its members; JIM JONES'S TEMPLE and consequently should be shared with any person who is considering uniting with any cult.

C. OVERVIEW OF THE WORK

Ten chapters make up this work: Chapter 1, Introduction is divided into three sections: Methodology is the author's approach to the work; Delimitations narrows the scope and focus of the work; and Overview is a summation of the content material.

Chapters II and III both deal with the issue that is the subject of the study. Chapter II, The Problem is divided into three sections: in Churches and Denominations the basic tenets of Biblical Christianity is set forth and churches and denominations are looked at in contemporary settings; Economic, Cultural, Identity, Social and Spiritual Needs of young African Americans are delineated from a standpoint of economic and class differences between groups of young African Americans, which is based in large measure upon a field survey conducted by the author, and how Christian Churches have failed to meet these basic needs are addressed; and Rejection of Biblical Christianity by young African Americans concludes Chapter II and this is where the word 'cult' as used by the author is defined allowing us to move into the next chapter of our study. Chapter III, Consequences is an elaboration or extension of the problem set forth in Chapter II. It is divided into four sections: Alienation and Separation the price for the severing of relationship with the Christian God and His Son, Jesus our Lord and Savior;

3

Alternative Options offered young African Americans for escape and flight via drugs, alcohol abuse, violent and antisocial behavior, cults, other non-Christian religions; Challenges to Biblical Christianity by non-Christian forces which result in an over emphasis on the self, giving rise to self-actualization/self-realization psychology's and the attempt to depersonalize Biblical Christianity; Choices opting for salvation — life everlasting and truth or opting for oblivion — death and deception are the two options open to young African Americans; a "yea" saying, to God-in-Jesus or a "nay" saying to life and truth.

Chapter II seeks to define the problem and establish the basic tenets of Biblical Christianity based upon the Word of God as the authority for truth and reality. Chapter III treats the failure of the churches which compounds the problem into a life-death crisis; salvation vs. damnation for young African Americans.

Chapter IV, Buddhism: A New Discovery for African Americans. Chapter V, The Baha'i Faith, Chapter VI, The Islamic Religion, Chapter VII, The Jehovah Witness and groups which are on the horizon in the African American community which include The Hebrew Israelites and AMON-RAH is chapters concerning various groups which young African Americans are likely to enter. Studies of their beliefs system along with their principles and practices. Various leaders in Chapters IV through VII of these movements are studied are studied as well as interviews from members and former members are included. Chapter VII also includes a brief discourse of Kwanzaa, a non-religious holiday which is the "CELEBRATION OF THE FAMILY, COMMUNITY AND CULTURE" in the African American community. Chapter VIII, "DISPELLING THE MYTHS — THE PSYCHOLOGICAL CONSEQUENCES OF CULTIC INVOLVEMENT" and "WHY SHOULD WE STUDY CULTS?" and "A CONSIDERATION OF THE PEOPLE'S TEMPLE" — A study of the dark side and tragic consequences that belonging to a cult may engender. This section is a wake up call to young African Americans who may consider exiting their church and at some point uniting with such groups to look before leaping into some organized cult that is non-Christian and conse-quently life affirming. This chapter also includes: "HOW CULTS

4

AFFECT THE FAMILIES" and "HOW YOUNG PEOPLE CAN PROTECT THEMSELVES AGAINST CULTS."

Chapter IX deals with an ex-member adjustment in: "REPAIRING THE SOUL AFTER A CULTIC EXPERIENCE." This chapter also includes: "COPING WITH TRANCE STATES: THE AFTERMATH OF LEAVING A CULT" and "INDIVIDUAL DIFFERENCES AFFECTING RECOVERY."

Chapter X includes: "WHAT CLERGY SHOULD KNOW," "CULTS: QUESTIONS AND ANSWERS," by: Michael D. Langone, PH.D "CONFRONTING CULTS VICTORIOUSLY," THE AUTHORITY OF THE BELIEVER" "MESSAGE TO THE CHURCH," Summary, Statement of Faith, and Author's Profile.

This concludes our focus on the problems of the Churches failures in ministering to young African Americans, their rejection of Biblical Christianity and their entry into non-Christian religious, sects and cults.

In conclusion, this book presents a social and cultural analysis from an evangelical perspective as it relates to religious challenges facing the family, church and community.

This book attempts to convey and at the same time meet the spiritual needs of people of all ages, ethnicities and economic status.

I believe this is the only book to date, which has been published, on the subject matter.

II. THE PROBLEM

A. CHURCHES AND DENOMINATIONS

There is an awful lot of controversy and misunderstanding among both authorities and lay persons over the question of what is meant by Christian Church. Many such groups defined as Christian churches by some authorities, e.g., the Church of Latter Day Saints, Jehovah Witnesses, Unification Church, Seventh Day Adventist and Christian Scientists in fact are groups that are not Christian Churches.[1] The majority of the members in such group's think of themselves as Christian, when in fact, they are really members of cults and other non-Christian groups although they may have their origin in Christianity. However these cults and non-Christian groups are outside of the pale of the Christian community of faith.

To be sure, there is widespread diversity and differences over doctrine and interpretation among the various Christian denominations which make up the population of the Christian community of faith. The Church, divided along these lines of differences is packaged as churches of various denominations. This division along doctrinal issues readily lends to the confusion as to definition of the *Christian Church*. However, despite the diversity in doctrinal perceptions and interpretations there are certain cardinal concepts and principles that all Christian denominations share with each other that makes them a Christian Church within the Christian community of faith. For the purposes of our study, so that we may have some criteria for determining what is a Christian Church and what is not, we review those cardinal concepts. In this way a standard for what is a Christian Church and a Christian denomination may be established. Any

---

[1]David Hunt, The Cult Explosion — An Expose of Today's Cults and Why They Prosper. [Eugene, Oregon: Harvest House Publishers, 1978]; p. 18

6

group that deviates on any of these basic tenets and concepts are non-Christian and are either cults or non-Christian religions that have the name "Church" affixed to it.

Christianity is Truth as opposed to Falsehood and is also Reality as opposed to Delusion. The Truth of Christianity has always prevailed from the time of Creation down to the present day. It has been transmitted to us through the Good Book, the Holy Bible. Authority for Truth and Reality of all Christian Church is the Holy Bible. All Christians hold the Holy Bible — both the Old and New Testaments as the Word of God. Each Church accepts "In the beginning was the word and the word was with God and the word was God. [John 1: 1, [NRSV]. Thus, the Holy Bible is the Word of God, inspired by and of God. For all Christian Churches this is the final and undisputed authority. Christian denominations housed in the Christian community of faith, both Catholic, Protestant, Orthodox, Fundamentalist accept all the Books and Prophets of the Old and New Testaments as God's Word. There is however one difference between Protestants and Catholics. Protestant Churches do not accept or allow the Catholic Deuterocanonical and Apocryphal as part of their Bible as these are not inspired of God but Catholics include these books as sacred treatises and canons which they attach to the end of the Old Testament. In between Malachi and Matthew there is not intervening books in Protestantism wherein Catholicism there is. The addition of such words to the Catholic Bible does not altar the concept of Biblical Christianity creating a theology that differs from Christianity, as these books are only historical elaboration of the Old Testament. Thus, Catholic Churches are viewed as legitimate institutions in the Christian community of faith.

All Christian Churches accept the Truth and Reality that God Almighty is the Creator who created this world and all that are in it. God created man in his own image and breathed into man the breath of life. The first created man was Adam. God sat this crown of his creation in the Garden of Eden. Perceiving that man needed a helpmate, God created woman from the rib of man. Her name was Eve. Adam was given the run of Eden. And he could eat anything that he wanted in this paradise except for one thing: "but of the tree of knowledge of good and evil you shall not eat, for the day that you shall eat, you shall die" [Genesis 2: 17, NRSV].

All churches in the Christian community of faith accept the concept of the fall of man. The serpent in Eden tempted Eve to eat of the fruit that was forbidden to them. The serpent stated that she would not die; Instead her eyes would be opened and she would be like God. She ate of the fruit and prevailed upon Adam to eat so that he also partook of the fruit. This was man's disobedience to God and the price of such disobedience was the fall of man, the exile from the Garden which was seated by a flaming sword such that man could never return to his original home. Death then entered the world.

Christians are all unanimous in the concept of covenants between God and men of great faith that God thought worthy as covenant partners such as Noah in which God said that never again would he destroy mankind by flood and Abraham because of his great belief and faith in God? God promised Abraham that his seed would be as numerous as the stars in the sky and that they would become a great people and nation. They would be his people and he would be their God. This covenant with the patriarch Abraham was renewed with Isaac, and later with Jacob whose twelve sons would comprise the twelve tribes of Israel. The Patriarchs of the Old Testament are in integral part of the Christian belief. Also the fine of God's chosen people is a continuum through the patriarchs, especially Jacob whose son Judah who was the progenitor of David. This genealogical line reached its zenith in the New Testament with the virgin birth of our Lord Jesus Christ. Thus, the Old Testament and New are connected by the bloodline of Jesus back to David, Judah, the Patriarchs, Noah and Adam.

The nature of God is reflected in the Old Testament. God remained true to his people: the majority who were not true to him. They were insistent on exerting their own will rather than God's will which resulted in their being punished or expunged for God the Creator was a righteous and just God. But God was also merciful and compassionate. When God heard the cries of his people lifted to him over the oppression and hardship their Egyptian overlords had exerted on them, God sent Moses to demand of Pharaoh to "let my people go". Moses was assigned the task of leading his people out of Egypt land into the wilderness and finally leading them to the threshold of the Promised Land which was barred to Moses for entry as result of his transgression against God. Moses was also assigned the task in the wilderness to give to God's people God's law as set down by God on two stone tablets which were dropped by Moses and shattered when he observed the people worshipping the idol of the golden calf, a blatant sin against their God. Idolaters lost their lives. Moses pleaded for the saving of the remnants that were not destroyed. God spared them. The Ten Commandments that God had given Moses were God's law for the conduct of his people. It was God who led and fed his people during their years of wandering through the wilderness. Upon reaching the Promised Land as forbidden by God, Moses did not enter. God had fulfilled his Promise to Abraham and his descendants. He had made them a great nation and was their God. However, the people lapsed at times and did not keep their part of the Covenant and the acceptance of God as their God.

Once Joshua had led the Israelites into the Promised Land as God had so commanded, they took possession of it. The Land was divided between the eleven tribesmen sons of Jacob and the twelfth and the tribe of Levi was given the role of the priesthood. The nation had become powerful. It reached its zenith under the of reign of King David. After Solomon, because the people insisted time and time again after promising God to be faithful and to do God's will, they would turn from God and do as they so willed, thereby incurring God's wrath. God's punishment resulted in the fall of the Kingdom of Israel, and later that of Judah. They were subject to foreign rule and many were shipped to other parts of the world. During these long years of nationhood, God remained true to his people who did not remain true to him. He worked through his prophets to warn the people of impending dangers if they continued to disobey God. These prophets exhorted the people to return to the God of their Fathers, They also foretold of the coming of one who would be sent by God as their Savior — the Messiah.

This promised Messiah was Jesus Christ. All denominations in the Christian community believe that God So loved his creation that he sent his only begotten son to offer salvation and life everlasting. Unlike the first Adam who did not remain true to God, the Creator, this Son did as God so willed, even unto death on the Cross. So begins the New Testament with its central focus upon the divinity of Christ who came down from Heaven to enter into human history by his earthly birth to a virgin mother, Mary who was come upon by the Holy Spirit. The name of the child was Jesus, descended from the fine of David.

The Messiah was born of humble birth in a stable. Shepherds who saw a star witnessed this birth heralding the arrival of our Lord and Savior. He was visited and presented gifts by three wise men who were led by the heralding star to his place of birth. His cousin John baptized him the Baptist. He began his active ministry at about ages thirty. He had selected and surrounded himself by twelve apostles who accompanied him as he preached the Good News, performed miracles and preaching God's Word. He and the Father was one. Betrayed by the apostle Judas, he was condemned to death on the cross by crucifixion. After his burial, he descended into hell but on the third day, he arose from the dead. He was seen by Mary first and then sojourned with his apostles for fifty days when he ascended into heaven to be united with his Heavenly Father. In his absence, he left for humankind the Holy Spirit as Advocate. At the end of time he will return to establish God's Kingdom.

All Christian Churches and denominations believe in the virgin birth of Jesus Christ and in the Trinity of God — Three Persons in One. There is but one God and this God is God the Father, God the Son, and God the Holy Spirit. They believe that God is righteous, just and holy and that God is Love. They also share belief in the Resurrection and the atonement of sin. Jesus Christ gave his life so that we may have everlasting life — our victory over death. This salvation can only be gained through Christ. We cannot have salvation or know God unless we accept Jesus as our Savior.

The New Testament is the authority for all truth in the Christian community of faith. Its theme is the Incarnation and the work of Jesus Christ who redeemed mankind. God has widened his people to include all humanity who will accept him as their God arid commanded Paul to bring the faith to the Gentiles. The Golden Pule is established as "Do unto others as you would have them do unto you." Justice is based upon the concept of reaping what you sow. The proper moral standard for Christians, those, who accept Christ, is love.

With the Old Testament and New Testament scriptures the Word of God has been completed. Nothing is to be added or changed. The Word stands for all times arid encompasses all Truth and Reality. 2 John 4 says that "Everyone who does not abide in the teaching of Christ, but goes beyond it, does not have God" [NSRV]. Revelation 22: 18-19 adds: "I warn everyone who hears the Words of this book: if anyone adds to them, God will add to that person the plagues described in this book if anyone takes away from the words of the book of this prophecy, God will take away that person's share in the tree of life and in the holy city, which are described in the book" [NSPV]. Taken together, these passages make it clear that the Holy Bible is complete as it stands and is written thus containing within it all truth, reality and authority. The truth and reality is that no one can come to the Father save through Jesus Christ and that we have all been redeemed of our sins through Jesus' sacrifice. We may have life everlasting in Jesus Christ.

In summary all of the institutions in the Christian community subscribe to:

1. The doctrine of the Holy Bible as the Word of God
2. The Doctrine of the Creation and Fall of Man
3. The Covenants between God and man and God's promises to Abraham
4. The doctrine of the Trinity — there is one God who exists in three persons[2]
5. The doctrine of the deity of Christ - Jesus Christ is God who became man

---

[2]C.Michael Cooris, Cults: Deception or Denomination, [Los Angeles Thomas Nelson, Inc., 1982], p. 4

11

6. The doctrine of atonement — he died as a substitute for sinners and bodily arose from the dead[3]
7. The doctrine of salvation by faith — a person is righteous when he trusts Jesus Christ and him alone for salvation[4]
8. The doctrine that the Word of God is complete in the Old and New Testaments. Nothing is to be added or taken away.

It should be noted that the above are concepts and the foundation upon which Christian Churches and denominations are based. Any deviation from these norms of what constitutes Christian Churches and denominations are not part of the Christian community of faith.

B. THE ECONOMIC, CULTURAL, IDENTITY, SOCIAL AND SPIRITUAL NEEDS OF YOUNG AFRICAN AMERICANS

Growth into a wholesome human being of any ethnicity is dependent in large measure on certain basic needs that individuals have being adequately met. The primary need of all of human kind is an economic need. From the time of birth, the human being must be provided with food, clothing, and shelter. Without fulfilling these needs the human cannot survive and will die both physically and spiritually.

There are also primary social needs that must be fulfilled — the need to belong and to be loved. The infant is socialized through a frame of family be it natural or foster. The family provides a bond of security and love by which the infant is nurtured from birth. Without this need, the infant will either wither away or become warped in its social development. These needs trigger in the human cultural and identity needs which are inculcated through a process of socialization and induction into the group and society into which the person transacts his/her life.

---

[3]Cooris, Ibid.
[4]Cooris, Ibid.

Finally, there is a special need that must be fulfilled. The kernel of spirituality is strong in the infant from birth. The person is a human life, a creation of God in the image of God.

Sought from the moment of birth on a subconscious level is the drive for a union with God through Jesus Christ as a "child of God". This kernel of aspiration within the human does not easily fall prey as other needs do to destruction but rather remains present in the human awaiting nurturing to grow into the realization of its truth and reality as one of God's children. However, without nourishment and correct guidance this spirituality will degenerate until it becomes closed to growth and development such that the person is not able to discern his kinship or ties with God the Father. Instead, this person is left to the ravages of Satan and becomes devoid of conscience, compassion, and love.

Needs to be fulfilled are met by parents/providers in various ways. Some are not met at all in which case the infant generally does not survive. Some are met so marginally at a rate so that the infant may survive but be damaged emotionally and sometimes physically. In some instances, needs are met a little below the adequate level so that the individual may be troubled, but is able to function and cope in society. Those whose needs are adequately fulfilled have a chance of wholeness and health, both physically and spiritually.

Also needs are not all met equally; economic needs may be met adequately, while social and identity needs may be neglected. Perhaps all physical needs may be provided but spiritual needs and nurturing needs are neglected. In the fulfilling of needs, a lot is really depended upon the individual's background and out look who provides the needs. Providers, whether parents or others, tend to raise their young as they were reared and if they were victims of abuse and neglect; there is the great possibility they may likewise rear their young as they were and subject them to the same abuse and neglect that they experienced. Also needs are dependent upon the ability of the family/provider to be in a financial position to see that the needs are met. A family in poverty is unlikely to provide the child with adequate clothing, shelter or food necessary for healthy growth as is the family who is in a better financial situation and can provide these needs more readily. Evils, such as drug addiction, alcoholism and gambling that undermine a family's financial resources also adds to one's inability to adequately provide for the needs of their family which is usually secondary to the securing of drugs, alcohol or gambling. The one parent household is not only penalized by the cost that adequate fulfillment engenders but also in its failure to provide good role models of a father-mother image to their children.

In attempting to discern what the needs of young African Americans are, I found the needs to vary among differing groups along something of class delineation. In the African American groups I observed three classes into which African Americans were divided: the poor, the middle class, and the affluent. It was noted that this division into socioeconomic classes were roughly based upon which income bracket into which a parent/s/provider fell. This in turn largely determined how and what needs were met. It is apparent that needs rail parallel to the class group into which one fell.

For purposes of this book, the poor are those persons who have an income of $12,000 or less yearly; the middle class are those with an annual income of between $15,000-$40,000; the affluent are those with an income of $45,000+ yearly. These figures vary from what is thought of as the poverty level and also the median yearly income of middle class and affluent. Undoubtedly the middle class and affluent could be thought of as the poor middle, middle-middle, high-middle in terms of total population numbers. Why these figures are used as basis of class determination is because African Americans earns less than their white peers are and consequently cannot be easily categorized into their class groups.[5]

There is disparity between the poor and middle class as well as the middle and the more affluent in African American

---

[5]The figures I use fit are accurately the African American economic structure into classes of poor, middle class and affluent class which takes into consideration the disparity between African Americans and white in terms of income earnings and distribution.

communities. The majority of the poor are project dwellers though some may live in homes in poor sections. Some of the middle class may be apartment dwellers; however, it seems that the vast majority are owners of modest homes, bordering on either poor sections or affluent sections. Some of the affluent are condo residents but most live in upscale luxury homes in areas as Baldwin Hills, View Park and Ladera Heights. The poor are housed in south central Los Angeles as are some of the middle classes. However, many of the middle class live on the fringe of Los Angeles in homes in such communities as Lynwood, Carson, and Compton.

In order to determine what the needs of young African Americans are and how they are met, contact was established whereby members of these three distinct groups could be reached through church where their parents attended. For the poor, I attended two churches along the 10000-11400 blocks of South Wilmington Avenue; and one located on 103 Street east of Wilmington Avenue in the Watts area of Los Angeles. For the middle class, I attended two churches along West Adams Boulevard, two along South Wilmington area in Compton, and one on West Rosecrans Avenue west of Central Avenue. To reach the affluent, I attended one church on West Adams Boulevard, another on Don Felipe Drive in View Park and one on La Tijera Boulevard, all in Los Angeles. Of these thirteen churches, three were churches of Christ, two were United Methodist, two were Missionary Baptists, two were Presbyterians, two were Assemblies of God, one was African Episcopal Methodist and one was Holiness. This constitutes a fair sampling of churches and denominations in the Christian community of Faith and was adequate for the purposes of my study in during interviews and field study.

I attended service at each of these thirteen churches three times. On the first visit, I introduced myself and mingled with the congregation after service. On my second visit, I talked to the Senior Pastor of each of the thirteen churches. They were given an overview of my study and my needs were related. Then their cooperation was requested. All of these Pastors were very cooperative and supportive. In churches where there were Youth

Ministers, I met with them as result of the Senior Pastor's request to them that they assist me, and in those churches that did not have a Youth Minister on staff, I was introduced to the appropriate person to help me secure young African Americans and other persons needed for this study.

The persons selected for the study were mainly drawn from church school groups and in a few instances from the congregation of several of the thirteen churches. Some of the churches ranged in numbers of congregants from 50 members or less, others from 100- 150 members and still others from 200+ members. Young African Americans were arranged for the three categories according to age levels: 5-7; 8-11; 12-15; 16-19. Five individuals for each age level classification was selected. From the poor class 8 mothers of these 20 children were selected and interviewed; and from the middle and affluent classes ten mothers from each group were selected. These age group subjects and their mothers were interviewed and surveyed; at times only children, at other times mothers/parents; and at times both. These interviews were conducted on four different occasions. Children were interviewed in both church school and home settings; mothers/parents were interviewed at church and also at home with and without their child/children being present. These twenty eight mothers and 60 children between ages 5 through 19 make up this group. Some of the mothers had more than one child spread among the various age ranges which allowed me to perceive different levels of development and behavior at different ages in young African Americans.

One of the unexpected things that was found was that rigid lines of class based upon economic stratification is not the case in regard to attendance in churches, which primarily service the poor, middle, and affluent classes. This suggests that church membership be not based exclusively upon class affiliation. One of the children and that child's parent who are in the poor socioeconomic category attend a church in an affluent neighborhood that caters to the more affluent in the African American population. The mother of the child as well as the child was baptized in this church. The mother's membership has been in this church all of her life. This mother's parents are members of this church as were her grandparents. In the case of the middle class several held membership in churches that primarily serve the poor and in the poor neighborhood. In another church whose membership is primarily poor; there is a member from the affluent class. Her parents were members of this church for as long as she was able to recollect. She grew up in this church and has remained part of it. She and her daughter attends regularly even if she has moved from the poor socioeconomic into the affluent group.

Thus, while most people tend to be members of churches which serve primarily their own class, some people are members of churches that are made up of people of another class, which indicates that family background and social mobility play a role in determining church membership. Mother and daughter mentioned above who are of the poor socioeconomic class but members of an affluent church are there because of the mother's background. This mother's parents are of the affluent class and their daughter was also until she dropped out of school in her teen years because of pregnancy. In her early adult years, she found herself in the economically poor and disadvantaged class. However, her attachment to her early childhood church and her connection to her family was never severed. Thus, she kept her membership and is raising her daughter in the church that has been "home" to her from birth. In the case of the affluent member of a church in which are the congregation is predominantly poor, this person related that her family was poor and the church she grew up in was so much part of her life that she decided to return to it after attempting to find other churches closer to her home to meet her spiritual needs. She had climbed the ladder of social mobility from the poor into the affluent class. The only church that offered her the comfort she was seeking was the church of her childhood and it is where she finally settled. Accordingly neither women felt any discomfort with the churches of their choice. They are well accepted by the membership despite their being of another class. Very little distinction seems to be made along class lines in churches.

Another surprising observation, which was made during this study, was the amount of financial support given by each of the groups to their particular churches, especially in regard to the poor. While the poor seemed unable to give as much in dollars because of the limited amount of available funds as either their middle class and affluent peers, the percentage that they dropped into the church pot was on par with the other two groups. In some instances, they gave more percentage-wise. The poor also gave a lot of their time, in some instances, even more than the other two classes. Their main preoccupation seemed to be fund raising — the raising of needed monies for their respective church. Their various choirs were robed in choir attire that appeared just as costly as those of middle class and affluent churches. They were generous in seeing that their pastor and first lady lived in comfort, if not in luxury. Circumstances of the pastor in terms of economic stability and income was far above those of the congregants in most instances.

There were very few programs among the poor outside of church activities, fellowship, visitations and fellowship with other churches. All had a church school program for various age levels. Some were very elementary and others well developed. There were evangelistic campaigns in which members canvassed their neighborhoods and also revivals to bring others into the fold. Church services were held longer than in middle class and affluent churches. There generally was fellowship after church service on Sundays of one sort or another. Sunday was a day almost exclusively reserved for the member's worship, fellowship and other church-related activities. The preferred music was that of spirituals, gospels with a spiritual rock beat. In a few of these churches there were other instruments than organ and piano. None of the churches of the poor seemed concerned or involved in social and community issues. As a matter of fact, it seemed that congregants were suspicious of leaders, the government, and the police. They tended to personify Satan as very active in the daily lives of individuals. He certainly was present and active in their lives. They had to be on their toes to be on the lookout for Satan lest he would entrap and ensnare them. All of their woes were laid at the feet of the devil who inflict pain and misery in their lives. Their only salvation was Jesus Christ.

Such is not the case in most middle classes and all the affluent churches that were observed. These churches had outreach programs that sought to address social ills. Members tended to see racism, corruption and drugs as the greatest ills of the time. Although they believed in Satan and the powers of evil, they did not personify the devil such as the devil himself was leading the forces of evil against good as did their peers who were of the poor class. For the poor the evils of the world were result of man's inability to love and his desire for power, control riches. He had closed his heart to God and turned away allowing Satan and satanic forces to enter his life. It was unfair and unjust laws as well as a corrupt establishment that championed such institutions as racism. The affluent and middle classes believed in some cases, those in power may have good intentions but are powerless to act. Christians and people of good will were needed to challenge the system to bring about social justice and the kind of just society that was voiced and envisioned by Dr. Martin Luther King, Jr. For the poor the world was seen as black or white with no ands in between. Either a thing was good and of good or of evil and of the devil. The individual's task was to keep him away from the entrapment of the devil and allow God to exert God's will; not to exert any energies to reform or transform.

A different world view held sway over the affluent and middle classes as was asserted in the prior paragraph. Thus their programs are geared to enable the disabled. Included are substance abuse programs, programs for teen mothers, employment counseling and training, social justice and civil rights issues as well as those of women's liberation, the homeless, tutorial programs to help children educationally, parenting classes, literacy programs to teach those without reading skills and ability to read.

Unlike the poor, most middle and affluent class persons see the causes of pain and alienation from God as the result for evils generated by an unjust and ungodly system. They see as their duty the marshaling of forces to lobby for passage of just and moral laws, to elect public officials who are responsible and incorruptible, and to work toward the ushering of a new order in which all of God's children are equal, free, and treated justly. Their work is as Kingdom Builders here on earth within their own community. They are God's labor forces who have been chosen to proclaim the Good News and to transform this world into one that God so ordained it to be.

Their poorer brothers and sisters on the other hand feel that the world is so corrupt and contaminated that it is Satan's principality. They tend to withdraw from active participation in any organization that is not church based and do not subscribe to any cause except that of remaining free of the devil's influence by staying under the grace and mercy of God in Jesus. They forged a personal union with Jesus Christ through prayer and worship. All evils of the world — racism, murder, rape, drugs are all work of the devil. As such, little can be done except to be born again in the Spirit. They tend to renounce the world and their energies are not expended in improving the world but in resisting the devil and remaining faithful to their Lord and Savior. Any hardships or difficulties are seen as a means of God's testing their faith and trust as He had tested Job. Despite their sins and shortcomings as well as backsliding, they know that they have a merciful and loving God who forgives all who call on the name of Jesus, their Lord and Savior who died for their sins and gives them eternal life. Their goal is to join the Lord and Savior in his kingdom which is not is not of this world. So they place little hope and are concerned about changing or transforming this world in which Satan is sovereign. Their hope and future is in a heavenly realm distinct and not part of the world in which their lives are transacted on a daily basis.

In interviews and observations during the course of this study, it became evident that there are these two differing world views that are held between the poor and middle and affluent groups. It seems that these two different views shape how one and one's offspring perceives the world in which the individual lives. If one views the world as a place in which to carry on the Lord's enterprise of kingdom building and transforming the world into an order that is just and righteous, then one is open to the world and does God's work in the Here and Now. They spread the Good News along with their work to minister unto the world making it more conducive to human life. Their concerns are of the world in which they seek to do God's will. If one holds the view that the world is a principality lorded over by Satan, then one sees the world as a threat and becomes closed to the world. The world can only be changed by the will of God; thus there is very little hope in the world. Their role is to steer free of Satan and prove themselves worthy of being God's children through their faith and belief in the name of Jesus. The world is a testing ground for their faith. Their hope is above and beyond this world in the realm of God's Kingdom; namely Heaven. There they will seek their reward for withstanding the trials and tribulations of their earthly life. They are mainly concerned with their church, keeping faithful, and with their eventual homeward journey. Which world view one holds will effect one's choices, and also tends to predict which choices an individual is likely to make.

Of the 8 women who are of the poor class making up subjects of this study and members of churches ministering to the poor, one has five children ranging in ages from 7 to 11; 2 have three children each; and 4 have two children each. They may have other children — those given are children who attend church along with their mothers. All 8 women belong to the poor group and all 20 children except one are children of these 8 mothers. The child not of the poor group is the child of a woman from the affluent group. She and her mother commute from the affluent neighborhood in which the live to attend their church in a poor neighborhood. They are very active and supportive of their church. Thus there are only 7 women in the poor category that are members of the church of the poor. The other is in the affluent class but she and her child are counted here among the congregants of the church of the poor.

Five of the seven women who are poor live in project dwellings, another in a privately owned apartment complex and the seventh in a single house dwelling. 2 of the seven are high school dropouts; 3 have no high school experience at all — dropping out at the junior high school level; one has a high school diploma and some college training; the seventh holds an AA degree and is pursuing a Bachelors. She is the only one of the seven who has a job. None of the other six have ever been employed except for the high school graduate who had a relatively good job until the birth of her second son and subsequent birth of her other children made working impossible. These seven women are relatively young, the youngest 20 and oldest 37. Four have significant others[6] with whom they share their lives. They consider themselves a couple. In two incidences these significant others are the fathers of their children. Two of the seven women have grandchildren. These women for the most part are educationally disadvantaged and consequently cannot help their children effectively in any of their educational endeavors. They engage in very little activity other than church, socializing with their friends, and making themselves available to their caseworker. The one woman listed in this category that is of the affluent class has one daughter who attends a church of the poor with her. This woman is married and is 39 years old. She was a member of this church since early childhood along with her mother and siblings. Her mother is no longer living. She is one of the few who have escaped the poor neighborhood through her mobility. After high school, she attended and graduated from Dominquez Hills. She moved up the education ladder from teacher into administration. She married a man who is a medical doctor. Their wise budgeting and investment of earnings have made them very secure. They own 4 apartment houses and a few pieces of commercial property, which augment their income. This woman attempted to find a church home in the various neighborhoods she had resided in once moving up the scale. Her husband is not a very religious person and so does not attend church, although he may go on special occasions when his wife or daughter has a featured role in some special program. However, she had deep need for church. The various churches

---

[6]A "significant other" is a person who lives in the household in a common law type marital arrangement who shares in the head of the household's life. In most instances he is not the blood father of her children although he could have fathered several of them. It is rare to find a 'significant other' who is the father of all of his "woman's" children. He may help support the family if he is employed or may just live off support and aid his "woman" receives. He most often is not on the case record as a member of the household.

that she attended seemed very cold and without too much Christian spirit. She was looking for a church home for herself and her daughter, who is now a young adult, that would fill her with the same peace of mind and spirit as the church of her youth. About ten or eleven years ago, while her mother was still living, she attended a revival meeting with her mother at the church of her youth. She was so moved by the spirit that she reunited with her church and has been a member since. Her daughter is also very active in the church. She is a member of the Young Adult Choir and is very much respected by her peers. Both hold their pastor and first lady in high esteem and are very close to their fellow sisters and brothers. They give heavily to the church and support all its activities.

Because these women are Christians, they are exceptional in their behavior. All of the poor sisters who are church members avoid alcohol and drugs. They are not promiscuous and attempt to give their children right direction and guidance. In some instances a few of these women were involved with drugs and alcohol as well as neglected their children prior to their being saved and uniting with the Church. However, since Jesus had entered their lives they have been free of these toxic influences. As a result their small financial resources are not squandered on drugs and other such things and their children are not neglected as are those of their peers who have not embraced Christianity and some who abuse drugs and alcohol.

Thus, their children eat better than most of the peers; especially among project dwellers. However, I observed that the diet is full of fatty, unhealthy food — high in sugar, starches, and cholesterol. Beans seem to be a staple as well as greens and other canned foods. During some months nearing the end of the period prior to check arrival food may run out or become scarce so there is a lean period until check arrival and food stamp time comes around. WIC vouchers help out and shopping for food is a big and engaging event. In between purchasing food, paying bills, some household goods and appliances may be purchased, Some small toys for the children as well as a needed pair of shoes, personal grooming necessities, some needed item of clothes. Some of these women shop at second hand stores for their younger children. The older children revolt and reject such apparel that they are not on their mother's shopping list for Goodwill.

Among the poor mothers that I interviewed, their main complaint was not having enough resources to take care of their children. They had to cut corners and their children go without. Also they feel that they are looked down upon by such people as social workers, poorly serviced and looked down upon by the staff of the medical facilities where they receive medical treatment, and are also mistreated by school officials and teachers when summoned on some matter involving their children. Surprisingly, mixed emotions were expressed about policemen. Some of them saw their presence as a blessing. They felt protected against violence of the gangs. Others saw them as trouble markers and bullies whose main activity was arresting their children for "doing nothing." They looked negatively on schools as places where administrators and teachers picked on their children for no good reason other than not liking their child. They saw their children for the most part as being good. Children influenced any wrong they did who were bad. They tend to take their children's side in all issues. Someone else is at fault. It seemed that the mothers I talked to seemed to be most concerned with their sons rather than their daughters. In some instances they actually deferred to their sons. They could overlook the bad behavior of their sons as mischievous pranks but would not tolerate any identical behavior from their daughters. I saw one mother take away a toy from her daughter to give it to her son upon his whining. They talked of their sons and expressed concern over his/their future and seemed to have some type of hope he would be blessed by God to deliver the family from their impoverished circumstances. Very little was said about daughters except perhaps they were obedient and less of a problem than the boys.

Some of these mothers were having problems with their sons concerning church attendance. Some did not want to go any longer and some had stopped attending all together. There were some daughters, who rebelled but for the most part if their mother went, they also went until they have completely broken with the mother. In the cases of the poor who were members of a Christian church, daughters remained in the house more than their brothers, performed chores did and were more closely watched than sons especially at the age when they began to develop sexually. They could invite friends over and play. They had to be in at a certain time and were warned about all that boys wanted. Some mothers lamented at length about their sons running with bad company and becoming increasingly more difficult to manage. Satan was waging an earnest campaign to recruit him into his ranks The sons were being influenced to do wrong by his friends. Most spoke negatively about gangs and expressed a belief that their children were not gang affiliated and involved. Others did not see gangs as threats but as children with nothing to do and no place to go; that liked to hang out and pass the time away. They were not dangerous. They only sought to protect their members and the community. These young males seemed to be exempt from household chores. About the only activity performed for the house was going to a nearby store for Moms for a needed item or two.

On one occasion during a home visit to a mother who was having problems with her son and who maintained that he was not gang affiliated and involved, I noticed her son come in with a few of his friends — so called "homeys". All of their pants drooped well below their buttocks. They made themselves at home in front of the TV while the mother and I talked in the dining area that was an extension of the living room. Everything about these youths seemed to indicate gangism. In interviewing one of the women's other children who was younger than the particular son who had come it at a later time, I asked if the brother had any gang affiliation. The sibling told me that everyone in the neighborhood belonged to a "posse" and therefore were gangs members. His brother was no exception. In fact, there was nothing wrong with gangs or membership in them. They were just a group of friends who "hung out" and who watched each other's back. His brother would bring friends over to watch TV and sometimes share a meal with them. They were friends his mother knew and like. What "Moms" failed to understand was they all were into gangism. "Moms" saw nothing wrong with them even though some had dropped out of school and a few have gone to camp.

They treated her respectfully and she knew their parents. The sibling went on to say that "Moms" seemed not to notice her son's new source of wealth — his new clothes, shoes, jewelry, things he bought for himself and on occasion for his other brothers and sisters, as well as the few dollars he gave his mother to help ease her financial burdens. She was told he had a job and just accepted his word. She had warned him about getting into trouble and informed him she did not want anything from him if it was not earned legally. She did not know exactly where he worked or what he did but knew he had a job for he had told her so. Because she was a Christian and did not tolerate fornication, she would not allow girls to come to the house and then disappear into his bedroom or anywhere else alone with him. So he went to his girl friend's house, and if her mother did not allow them to play bedroom games, they would go over to another friend's house whose "Moms" was not at home or didn't care what happened behind closed doors. The sibling looked up to his brother and friends and loved his mother. However, to this sibling the mother was old fashioned and just not with it. However, out of respect for her, they never let her know too much about their gang activity and just what type of job her son had. This young male spoke of trouble he was having with school. He also related his hate for all police and for whites that he blamed for any and every act of evil. There were negative comments made about church as well as other people, generally outside the projects who thought of themselves as being better than he was. Asked what his future plans were, the response was to be like big brother, and to make it in the world, which meant a nice set of "wheels, nice home, nice wife and children". The youngster was very happy and satisfied with his surroundings. There was nothing wrong with using drugs or alcohol if that is what one wanted. Jobs in the drug economy was dignified and paid well compared to low paying McDonald's jobs. This youngster had witnessed several killings and a number of beatings and felt they were justified. He had not taken active part in it since he was too young. However, these incidents did not bother him. His expressed view on the matter was "we all got to go some kind of way." He said he felt he could kill another person if necessary and although he did not want to die, he was not afraid of dying. The only reason that the subject was not involved with gang activities was his young age, the control his mother still was able to exert over him, and most importantly the gang telling him when he was a little older they would "jump" him into their gang. So when a little older, this youth would become part of the cult of gangism.

I really felt for this mother, her being unaware that one of her sons was a gang member and another would be in a matter of time. She is under the impression that her sons and his friends have nothing to do with gangs and would resist them. Her hope is all based upon God and God's will. If he allowed her son to fall prey to gangism then it must be punishment for some sin or some type of test of faithfulness. This she can accept. Her son's lives are in the hands of the good Lord and he will deliver her sons by his will in his way or to punish them for allowing Satan to tempt them and their consequent faithlessness and unbelief.

This interview and other such interviews point out the need of adequate amount of monies to provide for necessary food, shelter and clothing are a basic necessity poor African American young people are not able to secure. In the above discussed case, the mother did provide food of a subsistence. Her funds like so many of her other peers were not depleted by the need to support a substance habit or to support a significant other in addition of her children.

This mother is head of the household in a single parent household. She does not belong to any community or school groups and is not interested in anything outside of her children and the state of her church. Her children although attending church are rebelling against attending it. The church was fun for them as small children in which they thought of God and Jesus as their friend. They have come to believe the whole thing is a myth created by the white men to keep African Americans down and out. They still have a great deal of respect and love for Moms but believes she just wasn't with it and doesn't understand. However, if she wants to attend church and believe in some hocus-pocus God and a goodie, goodie Jesus, then let her do so. Why cause her more stress and take away her only comfort? Her son's models and heroes are negative gang members who provides them an image of what a real "dude", a man, is all about. He protects his turf and all that reside in it against intruders, other rival gangs, the police; he protects his family which includes extended family or other gang members; and he does whatever is necessary by what ever means available to provide for himself and others. Their model is one who talks that talk and walks that walk that they understand and do. From a love of school and learning at the outset of their induction into the educational system, most of these children become gradually closed to school and learning by grade three or four. Increasingly, they find school boring, their attention span becomes short and they find teachers and administrators oppressive. They begin cutting classes by the end of their elementary years so by junior high and grade 9 a large percentage of these children are drop outs or on their way to become so.

This and other such interviews pointed to the need for more financial resources in order to fulfill physical and other basic needs of poor young African Americans: enough money to provide nutritional foods that foster healthy growth, enough funds to provide adequate clothing and shoe apparel, enough to buy hygienic items and other such necessities along with other aids to help children in their educational endeavors. The best that a poor mother can do is to secure these needs at a subsistence level. All such aides to enhance the child's education and learning is out of the question. Some needed, essential items go lacking because there are not enough funds to purchase all this is needed.

In the above mentioned case the mother did provide food to feed her children. This mother is a single head of household whose total resources are well below the poverty level.

Aside from food, clothing and shelter, there are monies needed for utilities, laundry and transportation. She demonstrated amazing ability in her management and even managed to support her church through the monies she was able to put aside and contribute for herself and her children. This is a very devout Christian, who through sacrifice and faith has been able to handle funds wisely and in making her few dollars count where most needed.

Unfortunately such is not the case with the majority of her peers, especially those with a substance habit or a significant other to care for. In such situations, children are usually very neglected, deprived, and abused. They often go hungry for days at a time and are malnourished. They are lacking in basic clothing and shoe ware apparels along with having no personal hygiene items. They go around dirty and unkempt. They have to fend for themselves from a very early age and must depend upon themselves and others to get by. In instances where the courts place children, they are shifted from foster home to foster home receiving but little better care by foster parents who are just in the business of taking in such children just for the money. They are lost at a very early age becoming very closed to the world which is a very frightful place.

Although this mother I have discussed goes to church and makes sure her children attend, as well as provide her children with some measure of security, neither she nor the church seem able to provide good role models that her children are willing to accept. The only acceptable models that her child often encounters are the Gangs. Few other models exist outside of this image. Gang members are usually generous and protective of the child if he is hungry, some member usually feels sorry and will get him something to eat, share with the child some of his own food and sometimes will get his Mom to allow the child to eat a meal with them. Some "Moms" feel sorry for such a neglected child and will provide him a meal now and then. Sometimes a gang member may give him a dollar or two for doing small chores and errands. They will protect him for bullies and get others to leave him alone. Thus the gang usually become a surrogate parent or some family member for the child. They give him some measure of validation and a sense of belonging. Small kindness by the gang, which may be the only kindness he gets, are never forgotten. Who better to model after than a trusted person who is there for you?

Because of this serious need in the lives of the poor in developing a positive self image and cultural identity by the lack of such image, a negative self-image emerges that fosters a negative cultural identity — as being dumb, stupid, nonproductive and unworthy. The child takes on a defiant, non-caring, non-valuing attitude. He tires of school and other "put-downs" from those with whom he comes into contact. While maintaining a relationship with "Moms," siblings and "homeys" all others are severed. His life becomes pointless, aimless and directionless except for "hanging out" and "doing his thing.

10 parents and 20 children of the middle class were studied and interviewed. 8 of the ten were female and 2 were male. Of the 8 women, 4 are married — two of these have spouses who attend church with the family on a regular basis; 3 are divorcees who live alone with their children; 1 has never been married but lives with a significant other who is not the father of her child. 1 of the 2 males are divorced whose ex-wife has visitation rights, and with whom the child stays at various times, and the other is a widower whose spouse died who went home by way of public transportation or walked to school are latch key children. They let themselves in their homes and wait for their parent's arrival. At any rate, once home, the parent busies herself with the evening meal and while the child does homework tasks or watches TV. They then went to bed and early the next morning the same routine is enacted. During the holiday season they stayed home most of the time. Their weekends are busy with activity. In the summer children generally attend some type of camp — Vacation Bible School or some summer camp. A few went on vacations with their parents.

In my transaction with parents, I noted that most of them are self-centered to the point of being locked in which is especially true in the affluent group. They are totally absorbed in their own interests; their work, relationships, and standing in the community. Their children seem to take a second to these interests. As long as the children's needs are adequately met and they are constructively preoccupied, there is really very little communication between parent and child especially after age 13. After this age, whatever reason, the child seems to have come into his/her own and is allowed to make certain basic decisions without much parental interference.

There appears to be at a distant however subtle and polite, between child and parent that was not observed in the relationship between poor parents and their children where there is a very close bond between both and a love shared that is rather unconditional, "good or bad, you are mine and I love you" type of bonding. The poor child may think the parent ignorant and "not with it" but accepts this parent with unconditional love. Neither poor parent nor poor child act to manipulate the other. Also their rage is not directed at one another; perhaps a little at one's self but mainly outward at those they regard as their enemies. However, there is reason. Especially among the affluent was this rage more noticeable. Why, I asked myself as I sought to understand the dynamics of such rage.

It seems that the middle and affluent class individuals are more self-centered than are poor people. They certainly are involved in more things. A great deal of their time and energies are spent in advancing their careers. Their status is a matter of importance to them. They think of themselves as industrious, creative, organized and intelligent. Their children are often lost in the things vying for their attention: their careers, activities and friends. To be able to transact their lives smoothly, they often are highly organized and compartmentalized.

If it is a two parent home, both are generally part of the work force and in a one parent setting the mother is part of the work force so that very little time is spent at home, whether it is or is not a two parent home. Soon after birth, in some instances a month or two, the child is entrusted to the care of another while the mother returns to her work place. The Mother is away from home and the child for about an eight to ten hour period. Upon her return from work if the care provider does not transact her job in the house, the baby must be picked up and transported home. There is little quality time spent with the child before it is time to prepare and eat dinner. Dishes must be done and perhaps there are other children who need attention. There is little time to spend in unwinding, catching a little of TV or communicating with friends or one's spouse before it's time for bed.

The same routine is enacted for five days out of the week generally. Saturday and Sunday are likely to be breaking from the work routine. This is the only time marketing, visiting, entertaining can be done. Saturday is the time to get one's hair done and one's nails groomed. For males its time for a visit to the barbershop. Some parents have maids or hired service to do the main job of cleaning during a day or two throughout the week. There is the laundry, the shopping and household chores to perform. It is also the time for going out with hubby or share recreation and company with a friend or friends. It is the time to take in a seminar or attend some club meeting. Sunday is usually church, perhaps dinner out and a visit to grandmas. The child does have a few more hours with you on Saturday and Sunday. However, it must also compete for your attention in your itinerary of things to do places to go. Vacations and outings, while they may fill a void caused by separation, does not overcome or heal the effects of the separation. Thus as the child grows and is separated from the first care provider to be enrolled in nursery, then elementary, and finally high school, the separation gap is never successfully bridged. The child is passed from hand to hand. Basically, you and your child are strangers to one another. There is not much you know about the other. Your expectations of the child and his of you are at odds. The common denominator that binds you together is physical: the biological fact of birth and the sharing of a residence. The child's sense of identity and belonging is never satisfactorily developed. He feels that he comes in second to all the things going on in your life. He needs someone there for him — to care, to understand, to love, and just to be there. His going back and forth from home to school and other places implants in him the idea of abandonment. He may play out his sense of aloneness by attention getting antics as temper tantrums or just may withdraw keeping his anger in. Whatever the case, there is a rage within aimed generally at the parent. The child does not feel loved or wanted. You on the other hand feel that the monies you spend on the child are affirmation and expression of your love. Sometimes you feel guilty at not spending or making enough time for your child, so you soothe your guilt by indulging in the child — giving him an elaborate treat, buying him an expensive present, or giving him money to spend however he desires. With your busy agenda, you fail to see the emotional problems your child has and can't understand what more the child could want you've been a loving, devoted and sacrificing parent. If the problem escalates, you may involve your child and self in counseling but dropped out before coming to any satisfactory resolution of the estranged relationship with your child.

Unlike the poor parent, you have the power of control over your child: control of the purse strings. The child is dependent upon you for its support. The child is ill prepared to fend for itself on the streets and in the community in which he lives. There is not a support system as in the poor neighborhoods and projects. He is isolated with no where to turn, and in most instances no one to whom to turn. He blames all of his pain and frustrations on you. You are "full of yourself" to him. You don't care about anyone or anything except having your own way. You push aside his concerns as being "much ado about nothing" and childish. You think you have all the answers and know your child. In the meanwhile the child feels you do not love him or understand him. You don't even pay attention to him; you shove him aside and out of sight. To get you to pay attention, he develops attention getting devices including manipulating you. In some two family situations, each parent is played off against the other, especially in cases where there is little communication between the spouses or where the parents are in conflict and each is vying for the love of child against the other. He counts you out of his life as someone he loves, admires, or aspires to be like. His friends at an early age is the lone computer set or TV and peers he generally meets at school who share the same problems he has.

The little time that the child does get to spend with you are times you are generally at your worst. In the morning, you are in a frenzy to get to work on time, drop the child off to school and do all the things leading up to your leaving the house. It's a rushed situation in which time is of the essence. In the afternoon he encounters you after you have been on your job all day long and are drained. If you are stressed out or angry, unconsciously you make take your frustrations out on your child. He sees you and if there is a father in the home, involved in disputes over one thing or another; if you're separated, as a contributing factor in the break-up; and if there is a significant other, then you are seen in a very bad light in which you love and care more for this person while rejecting him. Your child does not see the best of you — you at work, your creativity, your sensitivity and he does not share in these things so that he really can't understand you and all you may be going through to provide and maintain a comfortable life style. He just sees you preoccupied with things that do not concern or include him and the complaints and mean spiritedness after a stressful day in which he is unfairly attacked by you for something he does not deserve. He feels abandoned by you doing much of the day and weekends so that you can indulge in yourself. He takes all of this as your selfishness, shallowness, and your caring only for yourself. If you are sacrificing, he is that which you are sacrificing for your own self aggrandizement. You're really monstrous. Many children of this class see parents as deadly enemies. They do not want to listen, they do not care nor do they love. They certainly are a negative image once the child is rejected as a model.

Such children as a rule are well educated. They are primarily the products of private schools. They generally are open to what interests them and can extend this basic knowledge via the Internet. They submit to what they perceive as your tyranny because of powerlessness and rootlessness. They are depended upon your good graces. Thus they obey and do your bidding until such time they can make their own decisions. Being insecure and unsure of their decision making capabilities, they tend to defer their departure from the nest by devising a life style their own outside of the home and living your life style when at home. Parents go about their daily routine as usual being free of the burden of decision making for the child who goes his own way living in his own private, secret world which is free and apart from that of the parent. All runs smoothly as long as there are no problems at school and with the law. At a certain age, the children drop out of church without too much opposition from the parent(s) who honor the decision as being a legitimate choice of the child.

The results of my observations and interviews with the affluent seems to point out that as the child reaches the mid teen years, the more the rage lessens. The parent/s have distanced themselves from the child's overall activities, while the child had devised a life style separate from his parent's, whether still at home or away. Their relationship seems to shift to one of accommodation in which both coexist under the same roof.

From a very early age, there is the need of the child for validation by the parent. Unable to get this validation, the child becomes enraged and angered turning away from the parent. However, he is not able to make a clean break because he is dependent upon tile family and unsure of himself. Into his mid teens as he approaches young adulthood, this need for parental validation is resolved by the youngster impressing upon his family that he is a person worthy of love and respect by some accomplishment and recognition usually in athletics, the arts, educational endeavors. Doing well and showing signs of making it justified to the parent/s that the spending of monies on their child has been well worth the effort, signifying to the parent/s that they have been very successful in this role. Thus, the child is given the validation and respect so long sought after. The child in turn comes to understand the parent/s struggle and accepts that he was loved after all. The love that exists between the two is depersonalized type of love. The relationship that bonds the two together is that of parent as provider or the means and child as the provided or the end. It is when this validation and recognition transpires that another kind of relationship begins to merge; one of mutual self-interest, respect, and admiration. Whatever their differences may have been, they are now resolved and each set about discovering what is best in the other.

In summary, it seems that in the poor all the basic needs for wholeness are inadequately met, and in the instances where the parent is not church connected, the youth is more than seriously disabled. Those who have been extremely neglected, abused and forgotten have very little chance of becoming whole, as their spirit has been broken. They grow up, if at all, persons without conscience, incapable of love, and bent on destruction in retaliation for crimes against him during his life time. This is a born killer psychopath. However, there is one positive thing among the poor and that is the relationship between mother and their children, the male child in particular, in families where the mother provided some type of care and protection. There is a very close bonding and love that is genuine and real in which mother and child accepts the reality of their circumstances to tend to blame the system although they are dependent upon the system for their very survival.

In case of the middle and affluent classes, it seems that their basic economic needs are more than adequately met. However, all other needs seem to be blocked because of the differing perceptions and expectations from the parents of the children and from the children of their parents. The children are in spiritual shambles. Parent(s) and child are virtually strangers whose common bond appears to be the sharing a roof and a blood relationship. The parent/s believe that money spent in the caring and nurturing of their children is affirmation of their love while child sees the parent(s) as non-caring, nonunderstanding, non-loving. I felt that children of these two classes were more seriously disabled in forming warm and rewarding relationships than the poor and had just as many, if not more, emotional problems.

C. REJECTION OF BIBLICAL CHRISTIANITY

In the above section of this chapter, we have taken a very extensive look at the needs of young African Americans and how these needs are provided for or go wanting. We looked at 60 young African Americans, the children of 28 parents we talked to in thirteen churches selected for this study. This focus gave us some ideal about the child and the world view, which shaped his perception of his world. It also suggested that at some point, mostly, if not all of these young people would leave the church based upon need deprivation.

We noted that poor parents basically do not have many interests or affiliations outside of the church and their homes. Poor mothers and their children bond more closely than other classes whose parents are part of the work force. Mother and child display more genuine feeling and concern for the other. The mothers interviewed were able to provide minimal requirements in meeting their children's physical needs. These children attended church with their parents. They also took part in church school. However, both mother and the church failed to provide their children with a satisfactory image for a role model. The image the children patterned themselves after even while in church was that of the gang. While in church, children were introduced to and taught about God and our Lord Jesus Christ. They were also warned about Satan of whom they were afraid. They enjoyed Church School and were opened to the tenets of Biblical Christianity until about age 10 or 11. Thereafter many became disenchanted with going to church preferring the company of their homeys. They began to whine about going to church pointing out so-and-so's mother does not go to church nor do her kids. Why should they? Nevertheless, they continue to go as long as "Moms" has some control over them. However, in "rapping" — dialoguing — with their "homeys", a negative and erroneous picture of the church emerges.

The initial rejection about church being boring and others not made to go becomes a rejection of basic teachings of the church itself. Some come to accept the gang's premise that God is an invention of "the Man" to keep them in a subservient position. It there really was a God, then why did he subject them to a life of misery and poverty with no means of escape? And Jesus, if he did die, then it was for himself because he certainly has not come back bringing any salvation. If there is a God, then God is a Black man and it is a Black man through which Black salvation will be effected. The poor young African American determination to drop out of church was realized over his mother's protest. When approached by the pastor or a church member, he had excuses for not attending. He was aware of his mother's deep commitment and generally did not argue with her against the church or convince her and his younger siblings to follow him from the church. To him, it was the "Man" who was the enemy; the devil. All of those inside the church, including the preacher were just dupes — harmless and pathetic. There certainly was nothing wrong with the church — it just wasn't his cup of tea and had nothing to offer him by way of deliverance. It was the gang that was most necessary and relevant and to which his faith and belief were given. So while "Moms" could do nothing about his break with the church but pray for his soul, he bartered that soul to an ungodly body. His rejection of Christianity meant rejection of Christian's ethics and morals.

However, there were those who remained who did not reject Christianity in favor of the sect of gangism. Most generally, their rejection occurred at an older age. They were persuaded by non-Christian groups as the Black Muslims who canvassed their turf and sold them on the false idea of the godliness of Allah and his prophet, Elijah Muhammad. The Jehovah Witnesses also canvassed the neighborhood and were able to convert some members into their watching kingdom of God.

A few remained with the Church. They have fared better than those who had dropped out have. They had managed to stay out of trouble and in school and have been able to secure employment. Some still live at home and others moved away. They still communicate openly with siblings and friends who are in gangs as well as their mothers. Those who remain in the church are active as members of the choir, church schoolteachers, officers, and other church functions. Those who have moved a distance from the church have found membership in other churches or commuted to church.

Thus there is not total rejection of biblical Christianity by poor Africans Americans. The patterns and rationale for rejection is also varied; the church is important and is an invention for control. The gang is where truth and reality reside; some non-Christian groups are more godly and not realizing that some groups who claim to be Christian are cults. Rejection is achieved by rebellion and defiance of the parent's wishes but is reluctantly accepted, if not approved, by the parent who at that point leaves the child in the hands of the Lord.

In the case of middle and affluent class children, defection from the church come generally a little later than the poor, about age fourteen do. There is not the whining, protest prelude. These children attend church and are very active when about age thirteen or fourteen, expresses his desire to no longer attend on the pretext of needing this time slot for some other activity of importance or to check out other churches and groups. Their parent(s) accept this as legitimate cause and are not adverse to their children's departure. In fact, in an interview with on parent who had a son no longer involved in church, the parent felt that the son's departure was a sign of maturity. He needed time out to find himself. The parent felt that young person now heavily into Buddhism would eventually return to the church; "after all he was raised in the church," was the basis for this parent's prediction about the son's eventual return. Not as many middle class youth defected, as did youth from the affluent classes.

The spiritual needs of young African American youth plunged them into chaos and began an odyssey in search of a world view and belief system to replace their Christian world view which they rejected and opened them up to cults and non-Christian religions.[7]

I use cults and non-Christian groups interchangeably in this book making little distinction between the two unless to clarify a point. So any belief system that teaches anything contrary to the basic tenets of Christianity as set forth under Churches and Denominations is considered a cult.

Any group that does not support any one of the eight tenets on pages 11-12 of this book is a cult for the groups rejecting biblical Christianity. In so doing it denies the sovereignty of God the creator, the doctrine of the Trinity, the doctrine of the deity of Jesus Christ, the doctrine of the Trinity, the doctrine of the Holy Bible as the Word of God as final authority which cannot be added to or taken from. As such cults are ungodly organizations that are not part of the Christian community of faith. Cults are non-life affirming. They deny the individual salvation and eternal life as these gifts come only in Jesus' name, name cultists deny.

Some cults have their origin in Christianity — Christian Scientists, Jehovah Witnesses, Church of the Latter Day Saints but have in their development rejected some basic tenet of biblical Christianity; others have their origin in non-Christian religions — Hinduism, Buddhism; still others are based upon non-Christian

---

[7]See Enroth's and Melton's dialogue in <u>Why Cults Succeed Where the Church Fails</u> for a better insight and understanding of the meaning of cults, a very ambiguous term and Hunt's <u>The Cults Explosion: An Expose of Today's Cults and Why They Prosper,</u> I share the same understanding of cults that Hunt has and stand closer to Enroth understanding of cults than that of Melton.

philosophies and psychology's — EST, many self-consciousness and awareness groups, and much of gangism; while some others are founded by persons who are bent on usurping the cloak of God as Creator and Jesus as Lord and Savior e.g. Jim Jones and his People's Temple. All of these movements or cults lead God's children into disbelief, unfaithfulness, and sin and into the valley of death where they are become hopeless with no hope for salvation and everlasting life in Jesus. The cult is the house that shelter evil and brings damnation to those who have strayed away from their shepherd. Some find their way out and back to be forgiven by a compassionate and merciful God while others never find their way out of the hell they have chosen by their defection from God's house.

III. CONSEQUENCES

A. ALIENATION AND SEPARATION

The causes of alienation and separation from church by young African Americans are varied. They stem from some needs generally that have not been adequately fulfilled. This causes disaffection and finally rejection. The pattern of alienation and separation also differ along class lines. The consequence of alienation and separation are seriously life threatening. Such consequences may result in many of these young people becoming involved in a life of violence, criminal activities, and drugs. It also opens the door for incursion and invasion by non-Christian groups and cults vying for their allegiances and their loyalties. The quality of their lives diminishes. They become restless, hopeless, without faith and believe in nothing. This causes serious emotional and personality problems. They are constantly at war with themselves and the love and peace of God-in-Jesus alludes them.

My observations point out that young African Americans of the poor class tend to separate from the church somewhat earlier than their middle and affluent peers. Their separation is an act of willfulness, disobedience, and rebellion. There are warning signs to be sure — the protests, the whining about being made to go to church when so many of their friends are not in church and how boring they find church, or how they don't believe anymore. Their parent reluctantly accepts the child's separation as fact after realizing she no longer has control over the child to further see that her child is in church. However, she does not approve of her child's behavior. She is powerless to change his dropping out of church. She cautions him about the devil stating how she feels about his turning his back on the church. She then steps back leaving the problem in God's hand for resolution.

The alienation that drove him from the church is most like peer pressure exerted by his "homeys" and older gang members who persuade him that religion is an invention by the "Man" to keep African Americans poor and powerless. "There is no God", as he had been taught because if there were, then God certainly would not have created a world of misery and poverty. Perhaps, he was worshipping the wrong God — the white man's God and should worship the true God who is Black. Some are convinced that prayer is not effective. They feel that they have been brainwashed and will no longer tolerate such degradation.

However, the poor/young are not completely closed to church although he rejects it. His growing up in it offered fellowship and activities that he found enjoyable. God and Jesus had some meaning for him. He even had respect for the pastor and others in the church. His separation from the church is more it is not his "cup-of-tea" type of excuse. From time to time he can be persuaded to attend some church function, especially a funeral for one of his "hommies."

Poor young African Americans do not attempt to influence their parent or even their siblings that they should leave the church. If it is helpful to them, then they should remain. They have nothing against the church or even the Pastor. They feel that members and the Pastor have been duped or are blind. They are not bad or evil and the experience of the church for them has not hurt them much. It is just that God is meaningless and there are more important things for them with which to be concerned. If they are to find salvation then it will have to be by their own doing. And salvation — meaning enough money to get the things they find important — they intend to secure by any means necessary.

Poor, young African American females are likely to remain in church longer than their brothers. They do not have as much freedom as their brothers and tend to better obey their parent more than their brothers. They also do not leave in as great of numbers as do the male members of their family. I found that most of the young females of this class who were interviewed and observed tended to be unsure of themselves and also very shy. They were busy with household chores or looking at television. They did not leave home very much and so church offered a welcome change. School was also another chance to get away from the house during the day. Thus, they did not reject the world outside their "turf", as did their brothers. Thus, their experience on the outside however limited was greater than that of their brothers who rejected both schools by dropping out and church by no longer attending. Brothers did not have the need that their sisters had, as they were not subject to being in the house in the same manner as their sisters.

Separation of the middle and affluent classes occur generally at an older age and without an act of rebellion. Female as well as male tended to separate at the same age and with an equal number. The decision to drop out of church was sanctioned and approved by the parent when told by their child of their desire to no longer attend church. The parent(s) felt this was their child's right and so approved it. They felt their child was showing some maturity, needed some time out and eventually will return to the church.

Why African American Youth Are Attracted To Buddhism

Why African American Youth Are Attracted To Buddhism

1. *Their strong emphasis in the youth and development of youth.*
2. *Chanting Nam-myoho-renge-kyo gives one the power of taking control of ones life.*
3. *Chanting calms ones hearts and mind and dispels depression, anxiety and it brings about peace.*
4. *Provisions of spiritual happiness.*
5. *Opportunity to successfully deal with life issues and to view oneself through their own eyes.*
6. *It brings about a great discipline in one's life.*
7. *It produces a state of unshakable happiness.*
8. *Because it is a universal philosophy based on reason and common sense.*
9. *Its ability to awaken in practitioners a commitment to serve society.*
10. *It provides a living example to follow a mentor.*
11. *It provides diversity and unity in membership.*
12. *Its commitment to peace, culture. and education.*

Why I Was Attracted To Buddhism
By: Practicing African American Buddhists

I recently spoke by way of long distance to Almeda Bailey, who is the administrator at the SOKA Gakkai International of the Chicago Buddhist Cultural Center which is the North Side to 1455 S. Wabash in Chicago, Illinois.

During our conversation, I discussed my intention to write a book which pertained to **"WHY AFRICAN AMERICAN YOUTH ARE ATTRACTED TO NON-CHRISTIAN/ NONTRADITIONAL RELIGIONS AND STUDIES."**

I requested her assistance in becoming one of the contributors regarding the reasons as to why she was attracted to Buddhism and possible recommendations of other African Americans who practice Buddhism in the Chicago area; in hope that they would share the same.

I understand that the African Americans who practice the sect of Buddhism which is based on the teachings of Nichiren Daishonin, a 13th Century Japanese Philosopher.

Ms. Bailey, a practicing Buddhist, was raised in a devout Christian home; has been chanting for twenty-three years and believes that it strengthens the inner self and enlightens the practitioners to their "life condition."

Statistics indicate that there are over 5,000 practicing Buddhists with SOKA Gakkai in the Chicago area. Approximately one third of them are African Americans. Soka Gakkai has about 1.6 million members in 128 countries and regions outside Japan, where there is about 8 million member families.

I am grateful to Ms. Bailey for her helpful and cordial assistance in this area. I am also grateful to the following contributors who are African Americans and members of the SGI-USA, of Chicago, who wrote why they were attracted to Buddhism. They include Michael M. Townsend, Alice Quaye, Kente Johnson, Gyasi Kress, Irma Bogan, Michael Ewing, and Yvonne Wade-Bey.

August 1, 1998
To: Dr. Joyce Henderson:

Dr. Henderson, my name is Michael M. Townsend Sr. I have been an active practicing Buddhist with the SGLUSA organization since April 1987. I am a Senior Management Consultant for the Illinois State Board of Education We monitor and regulate the entire educational system, K-12, for the great state of Illinois. My professional educational background consists of BA in Psychology, MA Human Services, and currently completing my Doctoral Degree in Educational Administration (ABD. 1998).

The child of a young single parent, I remember being Catholic during the early years of my life (five-seven years), but later my grandmother insisted on raising me, so for the next 12 years I became or shall I say was forced to become Southern Baptist in Memphis, Tennessee. As I reflect back, I remember so vividly attending the Mass services with my mother and how terrified I was of these white men in these ugly looking robes, and I never understood why I had to bow and fall on my knees so much. I also never understood the language they were speaking. My mother never quite explained it to me. I had a strong sense that people just mimicked everything that each other did. (I was taught to never question the priests.) When I lived with my grandmother, the process was about the same. The ministers simply wore the officiant sort of show robes, they preached much louder and there was always good music from the church band or choir. There were also a lot of things that I never quite understood in the church, like: why do people shout and scream. Again I was taught never to question, just to believe in something known as an almighty God, Master, Savior, etc.

As I grew older, I began to really question ministers and members, why and how could I improve my personal and financial situation. I was always told to just pray and wait on the Lord; don't move ahead. He knows when it's your time. He would make a way. I continued to feel confused, frustrated, and over-whelmed. As usual, I felt so helpless having to wait on the Almighty to make a way for me.

A few years later, while still an active Christian, I became married. I was so determined to have the very best for my family, that I worked night and day and contributed financial resources to my church. However, I was still unhappy with my spiritual results. I always seemed to be in the same spiritual rut, helpless and no way out, praying for a power to change my situation, a power to let me open a business for myself, a power to let me become successful in whatever I desired. Shortly afterwards, a SGI-USA member strongly suggested that I should consider chanting "Nam-myoho-renge-kyo" and that whatever I desired, chant and take the personal action myself My life seemed to unfold overnight, as I began to chant these powerful words. Nichiren Daishonin's Buddhism has been my dream come true. This practice has provided me with so much spiritual happiness, and most important, the power of taking control of my life, understanding the significant of cause and effect in our lives, and how to change my destiny (Karma), not next year but right now. The SGI-USA organization has been a lifeline to me. Our members have always been there offering so much positive support. We learn through the Buddhist study materials and the lives and experiences of each other, in the here and now.

Our Buddhist's three key requirements of faith-practice-and study have been the contributing source not only in my personal career success, but also to my family's as well. My wife, Minnie, will be completing her BA Degree this year. Our son, Michael Jr., just graduated with honors from Georgetown University and will be entering the University of Illinois School of Law in August 98, our daughter Kellie (also an active SGI Young Women's Division leader), a high school honor grad. May 98, will be attending The University of Iowa as a pre-law major.

I don't mean to brag, but I believe in giving credit where and when it's due and to give deep appreciation to the leaders of this outstanding Value Creating organization known as the SGI-USA. The organization is committed to World Peace and developing Global World Class Citizens, (it's free).

Should you need more information, please contact me.

Sincerely,

Michael M. Townsend Sr.

Alice Quaye
August 6, 1998
Ilinois

Hello, my name is Alice Quaye, and I reside in Chicago, Illinois.

I am determined to deepen my faith so that I can manifest a life condition so high and so strong that I will affect every situation that I encounter in a positive way from the moment I arrive at each job assignment everything must become peaceful, must end peacefully, with no violence, and everyone must be happy and satisfied with the outcome: including the victim, the perpetrator, and myself.

Even before I started reciting this specific prayer, I enjoyed the protection of Gohonzon on my job. In the fifteen years that I've been a police officer I've never gotten hurt, never seriously injured anyone else and only broken a fingernail once. It is a tremendous feeling knowing that I can go into the most dangerous, hostile and violent environments and not only come away unharmed but actually create some happiness in the situation. I love it.

The area where I work is predominately African American. As an African American police officer I feel that it's important that people respect police officers. Often this is not the case. Many people hate and fear police officers because their encounters with police officers have always been negative. I see it as my responsibility as a Buddhist to challenge and improve police officer's relationships with African Americans. I work very hard to accomplish this. Sometimes when I go to court I'm actually embarrassed (professionally) at the way the arrested and I smilingly greet each other. There's such a warm and friendly feeling between us that people often stare at us and ask me if I am the "arresting officer." They don't believe the rapport between us. It is only through my practice of Nichiren Daishonin's Buddhism and my activities with the SGI that I'm able to create such remarkable relationships with people under unpleasant conditions.

49

I began practicing Buddhism twenty-three years ago. I had lost all hope of ever having a happy life — up to that time. I had tried all of the traditional religions, from Catholicism to Islam. None of them worked for me. Even though I prayed sincerely, with my entire being, I never got anything that I prayed for, ever. I had been chanting for two weeks — not sincerely — when I realized some great changes had occurred in my life. I was no longer stressed out, no longer depressed. I felt good. I was happy. I decided to continue and have grown and matured because of my practice, realizing many of my dreams.

In 1980, my husband and myself, he's from West Africa and also practices Buddhism, lost our five-month-old daughter to a liver disease. I was devastated, yet it was at this point that I determined to assume full responsibility for my life. Finally accepting the fact that the law of cause and effect governs the universe, just as postulated by Nichiren Daishonin's Buddhism. I needed to put out more causes to end my suffering and create happiness, and I have. I've never looked back — only forward. I don't have any regrets. This is what I try to instill in the people that I meet on my job; that each person is responsible for their own life. We all make choices. As African Americans, who are ostracized in probably every country on earth, we have lots of issues to deal with. Practicing Nichiren Daishonin's Buddhism affords me the opportunity to successfully deal with these issues and to view myself through my own eyes, not through the eyes of others. Thus, I am very aware of my value and worth as a human being. This awareness developed through my practice of True Buddhism.

With an attitude of respect for each person's life, again predicated upon True Buddhism, I try to encourage a sense of hope, the spirit to never give up and the desire to fight for their happiness in everyone I meet. We don't have to suffer endlessly; not do we have to fall short in our own eyes. I try to communicate the understanding that as we start to assume responsibility for each of our actions our lives will open up. Each of us must become responsible. A happy life demands that we do so.

Gyasis Ayo Kress
August 1998

Hello my name is Gyasi Ayo Kress. I am a 17-year-old high school graduate living in the Chicago area. I plan to attend the University of the Arts in Philadelphia this fall to major in theater.

My mom, who had been chanting five years before my birth, raised me. So I had the great fortune to be born into Nichiren Daishonin's Buddhism. My mom, Kanika Kress, was the lead blues singer in a band. Despite her tours of Europe, performance at the Taste of Chicago, and the Chicago blues circuit, as a family we remained financially poor. We struggled constantly with rent; therefore, we had to move frequently. My two older brothers and I transferred from school to school while my mom, in the midst of, being a female with her own band, a homosexual with parental problems with my father, violent tension between her lover and our extended family, tried to raise three young men.

During her second tour of Europe, Mom got sick. Years later, I learned that besides one of her kidney's failing; she also had a heart attack. Even though she received two years of successful dialysis at home, she ultimately passed from a heart attack. She died in 1993 when I was in the 7th grade.

Although the freedom always existed, at this time is when my religious exploration began. It seemed inevitable with such a drastic switch in lifestyles. I first moved in with my mother's mom, a household with strong Christian beliefs and a dislike for Buddhism because of "what it did to my mother." My father, Roy Cherry, though not a Muslim, supported Minister Farrakhan. That encouraged my understanding of the "black man in America" which in itself affected my religious beliefs. Above all these factors, however, I was now more open to America, which affected me the most. At home, in school, with fiends and just in daily existence I was confronted with religion and God.

Wanting to discover the "truth" I began to take note on the lives of the people around me. I thought of my mom, who through many storms was my strength in every instance, and the wisdom that gave her the ability to keep a genuine smile on her face. My grandmother, though very strong, seemed to be fundamentally

51

unhappy. Surrounded by family that acted like enemies she was unable to change her situation. I remember the times that my brother and I chanted to get or accomplish things and how we were able to achieve them. My father had overcome many difficult times, but lacked the bright spirit and freedom my mom instilled in me. I realized that I only experienced the energy when I visited the SGI (Soka Gakki International Buddhist Center.)

So I began to learn more about this Buddhism and to chant again. The difference in perception between my family and myself become boldly apparent. I met a peer who also chanted. Together we began to strengthen our practice and the effects were phenomenal. At school and at home we were and still are a source of inspiration and hope in our environment. The inherent optimism in Nay Myoho was enough to stick with it. There is no need to preach the validity of chanting Nam-myoho-renge-kyo. It changed my life and therefore my Mom's.

"Kente" (Johnson-Taylor)
August 1998

My name "Kente" (Johnson-Taylor) refers to the unity and togetherness of all people. Therefore, it makes the perfect sense for me to be a part of a religious society that pray night and day for peace throughout the world and the happiness of all people.

I was three years old when my mother chose the path of Nichiren Daishonin's True Buddhism in 1983. I have vague memories of the Baptist Church and Sunday School, but most of my childhood experiences with religion involved running around the Buddhist center and occasionally sitting in on prayers and lectures.

I was extremely fortunate to be raised in an environment that promoted self-empowerment and self-reflection, while recognizing, praising, and strengthening the interconnections of all human beings. I could not have hand picked a more bright and nurturing environment.

In the past four years, as I have gotten older, I have delved into the deep philosophical and humanistic studies of Nichiren Daishonin's True Buddhism. Through unwavering, tenacious conviction, and consistent faith, practice, and study, I have experienced the tremendous benefit and boundless joy of chanting Nam-myoho-renge-kyo.

To share an experience, for the last months of 1997 up until the middle of 1998 my family and I were under horrendous attack by the negative forces of the universe. We went four months without heat, electricity, or phone. My mother and I were told that I would not graduate high school because we didn't have the ransom that my previous school demanded for my transcripts, my serious girlfriend of two years broke up with me, and I was denied acceptance from all five of the universities to which I applied.

Despite all of our hardships, we continued to awaken every morning with brilliant smiles and pray earnestly to the Gohonzon, rejoicing at this great opportunity to polish our character and strengthen bur faith. We remembered the words of Nichiren Daishonin, "Suffer what there is to suffer, enjoy what there is to enjoy" regard both suffering and joy as facts of life, and continue chanting Nam- myoho-renge-kyo, no matter what.

As winter always turns to spring, our gas, electricity, and phone were reconnected. I successfully graduated from high school with more than enough credits and I have been accepted to Temple University in Philadelphia, PA. Also, my soul mate and I have tapped a new and more powerful level of true love through our separation than we have ever known.

For everyone to realize and utilize the power inherent in their own lives and experience true happiness is my dream, and this is why I practice.

Irma Bogan
August 1998

My name is Irma and I began my practice of Nichiren Daishonin's Buddhism in February 1973).

My sister was hosting a party for a friend of hers and asked me to help her with the preparations.

I arrived at her townhouse with the expectation that I would be rewarded for a little work by having a good time at the party. At this time my sister, a very private person, had been chanting for less than a year and had not told anyone in the family of her practice. She realized though that a good number of the people expected to attend the party that night were members and, once discovering that I did not know about Nam-myoho-renge-kyo, would seize the opportunity to share it with me. She gave me one of those, "Oh, by the way ... "We can discuss it further, later."

My upbringing in terms of discipline, housekeeping, and religion was very strict. My parents were very hard working and made sure that my three sisters, one brother, and I did not need for anything. They were very pessimistic about society and did not trust our safety and delicate minds to the influence of anyone. We attended school because the law said we had to and church because religious teachings were a must.

I was born after World War II, so I did not experience any of its horrors. Yet in the late 50's I found myself quite frightened by the possibility of war with China, and in the early 60's, Cuba. The air-raid drills at school and the storage of food in case of any emergency at home validated my fear. Along with the fear that a bomb from the sky would kill me, was the fear that God would strike me dead. In my search for peace of mind and heart I would read the Bible. I simply wanted someone to explain it all to me so I too could love and have faith in God, but was only made to feel bad, because I questioned too much. I wanted to feel safe and whole.

My total dissatisfaction came when I told myself I was okay, that I was not bad, or evil, or blasphemous just because I wanted to know more and understand. I knew there was more to my life than keeping a clean house, being a good cook and nurturing mother. I knew I fit into the scheme of the universe in some significant way; for some unknown reason. I was alive; a human being; more specifically, a female and Black. I was awed by the scope of the universe: the sun, moon, stars, planets and even the depth of the earth's core.

On that February day in 1973, when I was told about chanting Nam-myoho-renge-kyo, I did not think too long or hard about it because I was busy making preparations for the party that night. As the people began to arrive and we were introduced, the members made sure that I had been told as much about the practice as they could impart to me before the night was over. I had a crash course in Nichiren Daishonin's "Buddhism 10 10."

The members did a thorough and effective job. All I could think about the next morning was that I was not stuck with my life as it was. Whatever unhappiness and misfortune I had experienced or was experiencing could be transformed into joy, happiness and benefits. If I really wanted something, I could have it without fall. It was all up to me and no one but me; not some Omnipotent deity I could not relate to.

I chanted that day for several hours and asked a member for a liturgy book. The next day I did morning and evening prayers, again chanted for several hours.

After twenty-five years of practice, do I always feel this way? No. Do I always follow Nichiren Daishonin and "Suffer what there is to suffer and enjoy what there is to enjoy [No] — chant Nam-myoho-renge-kyo without fail [Yes]." I feel happy and joyful more often and for longer periods of time and dismayed less frequent and only briefly.

Why do I chant? Nam-myoho-renge-kyo nurtures my life. It caresses my soul. It calms my heart and mind. Be still my foolish heart ...!

Michael Ewing
August 1998

My name is Michael Ewing. I am the oldest of ten children and the first in my family to practice Nichiren Daishonin's true Buddhism. My wife and I began this practice together over 26 years ago. I have five children, three boys and two girls. Four of them were born into Buddhism. Today all of them practice Buddhism. Currently we are "Home Alone." Our children are successful, living in different parts of the United States. We have just come proud grandparents, and the third federation of our Buddhist family is blossoming.

Regarding my religious upbringing I would have to say that it was atypical. I never belonged to a large church and I never got baptized. I did, however, meet Christian missionaries while quite young. These two ladies ran a mission out of a home and garage on the West Side of Chicago. Through them I learned of the Christian faith. I was not only a student; I influenced many other young people to become involved.

My activities continued throughout grammar school and high school, ending when I went to college. In college I did not practice any form of religion.

After graduating from college, I married my wife, Valerie. We had difficulty getting along very early in our marriage. A harmonious relationship seemed impossible. I was becoming a hopeless situation and the likelihood of our marriage continuing lessened. Intuitively I knew that there was something "out there," something that could enhance my life and enable me to fulfill my dreams. I searched for that something in forms of spiritual exploration. It wasn't until a fellow fraternity brother of mine told me about Buddhism that I began chanting; therefore, becoming a truly happy person and creating a happy family.

Initially my parents did not support my practice of true Buddhism. They became skeptical and resistant. Were it not for the actual proof, confidence and joy derived from chanting Nam-myoho-renge-kyo, I don't think I would have been able to withstand the opposition. I am truly appreciative of this practice. Over the years there have been many instances where we as a family demonstrated the actual proof this practice guarantees. While challenging the many obstacles of developing a happy family, in the Urban Jungle of a large inner city, it was our practice of Nichiren Daishonin's True Buddhism and the SGI that we relied upon.

Initially my wife, who suffered from various illnesses, was informed that she would never have children. But through practicing of Nichiren Daishonin's True Buddhism she conceived. Each of our children have become splendid and accomplished young adults with a long list of honors and achievements in society. Even though our college friends chose us as the couple most likely too not succeed my wife and I have been able to complete 27 years of marriage, aiming towards 50. My dream of a happy family indeed is a reality.

Although chanting Nam-myoho-renge-kyo to the Gohonzon is a choice for a person born in the United States, I am so glad I made the choice. As an African American, meeting Buddhism on the south side of Chicago in the 70s was indeed a rare find and for that I feel so fortunate. I believe deeply that becoming a member of the SGI-USA and practicing true Buddhism was the wisest choice I have ever made.

Yvonne Wade-Bey
August 1998

My name is Yvonne Wade-Bey and I am a 55-year-old African American woman. A single parent with two adult sons, I have been practicing Buddhism for 10 years. I was introduced to Buddhism after practicing Islam for 11 years.

I have, as an independent African American woman, to make choices and be directed through this Johnson, the realization of change within one's self overcoming the karma we carry once we are born, the acceptances of self and the responsibility for your karma. You can't blame any one else for your choices, mistakes, or errors.

I have never felt better about doing something in my whole life. I feel so profoundly moved. Once I discovered Buddhism, all I needed to do was nurture it through practice for others and myself.

Those 11 years that I practiced Islam. I never learned formal prayers. In the morning 5 prayers are done, in the evening there are 3 and chanting Nam-myoho-renge-kyo are the major parts of the practice that require the great deal of discipline it has brought into my life.

This philosophy has helped me to understand how to reeducate myself in the area of religion. I know and understand the statement "taking responsibility for your life."

Even though my parent's taught me values and respect when I was a child, it was not until I began to practice Buddhism that I learned the real meaning of creating value and respect for another person the world and myself. Facing the struggles of life, I found it necessary to break the chains of the traditional way of Christian thinking. The decision to practice Buddhism was the action that turned my life 360 degrees.

August 31, 1998

TO: Dr. Joyce Henderson

FR: Marion D. Wheeler (age 32)

RE: Responses to Questions re: **Buddhism (The SGI)**

Q: WHAT ATTRACTED YOU TO BUDDHISM?

My mother! From the tender age of 5, she had encouraged and nurtured my faith in a spiritual practice called Religious Science (or the "Science of Mind" Church). Our belief was that God was a "Divine Force" or "Truth" that permeated the universe. As human beings, we were expressions of that truth, and therefore, endowed with the qualities of God or truth if we could "awaken" to this oneness, which we strove to accomplish through daily prayer.

During my childhood, my mother and I did not always live together. It was our faith in this teaching that got us through some very difficult times and kept us bound together at the heartstrings. Also, observing my mother struggle to put her beliefs into action as she underwent hardship after hardship for 15 years engendered in me a deep respect and admiration for her and provided me a wonderful example of how to live a upright, disciplined life based on faith.

So when, at the age of 40, my mother began practicing Buddhism, I was shocked and dismayed. I had heard about the practice of chanting "Nammyoho-renge-kyo" and was convinced that it was just another shallow, LA "trend". I waited for her to snap out of it. But 3 months went by and she was still chanting so, after repeated refusals, I finally agreed to attend a meeting with her. Two things convinced me: 1) She seemed happier 2) Ultimately, I trusted her judgment. At the time, I was 21 years old and a senior at Occidental College in Los Angeles I was feeling very unsure of myself and My future, so although I went to the meeting wearing the face of a skeptic (I told my mother I was only attending to make sure she hadn't joined a cult), secretly I hoped that this religion was something that could help me renew a sense of hope within myself.

(In order to give you a more complete picture of my religious background, I would like to note here that for a two-year period during my childhood — from ages 8 to 10 — I lived with relatives who were very devout members of an African Methodist Episcopal Zion Church (A.M.E.Z.) which we attended as a family every Sunday).

Q: WHAT DOES IT OFFER THAT OTHER TRADITIONAL OR OTHER NONTRADITIONAL RELIGIONS DO NOT?

1) A universal philosophy based on reason/common sense.

Because I began practicing Religious Science at such an early age (5 or 6), I could never completely relate to the explanation of events as told in the Bible. My perception of Good was more that of a "universal force" *or "entity", whereas the Bible seemed to portray God as a "Him" — a "man-like" figure with omnipotent power. I had been taught to believe that God existed within me and I needed only acknowledge this and make efforts to bring out the God-like qualities within myself. The traditional Christian church seemed to view God as something outside of me that I had to beseech for help.*

The philosophy of the Buddhism of Nichiren Daishonin (also known as "True Buddhism") was similar to the one that I had grown up with: it taught that there was a "universal Law" or "ultimate Truth" that existed both in the universe and within us ("God", if you will). If we could fuse our lives with this "Law" or "Truth", then we could attain a state of unshakable happiness.

In Religious Science, you tapped into this "Truth" within through 0 affirmations" in which you conditioned yourself or believe that you were an expression of God, and thereby, entitled to happiness and fulfillment But True Buddhism went much deeper.

It taught that life was eternal — that we are born, we die and then we are reborn again and this process continues forever.

During the course of these many lifetimes, we made "causes" that led us to receive "effects" — some positive, some negative, depending on the cause made. The accumulation of theses causes (known as "karma") carried over into each lifetime and determined our present circumstances (from things like our gender and ethnicity to the type of relationships we attracted, our financial situation, etc.).

For me, this was the first time any religion offered an explanation that made sense as to why some people came into the world with tremendous suffering and why others did not. Or why two people with the exact same circumstances could lead lives with such incredibly different outcomes. I just didn't buy that God (again, this "outside force") had a master plan for everyone and we just had to learn to accept. To me, this made people seem like helpless victims.

But here's what sold me on True Buddhism. It taught that chanting the words "Nam-myoho-renge-kyo" gave you the ability to actually eradicate your negative karma and thereby transform your entire destiny. By chanting, you could establish within yourself a state of <u>absolute </u>happiness — happiness that was completely independent of outside circumstances. Now that was appealing.

Another plus was, that you didn't have to wait until after death to experience this wonderful transformation. It began as soon as you started chanting! I was told that by continuously polishing my inner life through faith activities (studying the philosophy, sharing it with others, and supporting other practitioners along the way), that I would begin to see immediate results in my daily life ("actual proof"). These results would be both conspicuous and inconspicuous in nature. But most importantly, through these actions, I would I be making the ultimate "good" cause and would receive the "good" effect of becoming unshakably happy within this lifetime.

2) **Its ability to awaken in practitioners a commitment to serving society.**

Another aspect of the philosophy that makes this Buddhism different from my previous religious experiences is its ability to awaken in its practitioners a genuine commitment to serving society.

True Buddhism teaches that life and the environment are one and the same. The environment is a mirror reflection of the people's inner state of life. The reason that there is so much suffering and unhappiness in the world is because people are suffering and "happy and this is due to the fact that people, in general, lack a solid philosophy by which to live". When people are able to transform themselves from within, there will be a corresponding change or "effect" in society. The goal of the SGL USA organization is to bring about this transformation of society by spreading the humanistic ideal of True Buddhism, the most fundamental principle being the importance of respecting the dignity of each human being.

Now when I first started practicing, I was not so interested in this larger objective of realizing world peace. Though I was a very sweet and considerate person, my main focus was on my own happiness. But through the activities of the SGI, I began to learn that by devoting my energies to helping others, I could actually light the way toward my own happiness. I learned that what really matter is the heart — what kind of human being you are. I learned that when you work hard to improve yourself first, you become the kind of person that others want to be around and become a more valuable member of society.

I have found through my own personal experience! That the strength of True Buddhism lies in the fact that it actually changes your life from the <u>inside-out</u>. So though you may start out a self-centered person, with a strong determination to emulate the spirit of our founder, Nichiren Daishoni (prayer), coupled with dedicated efforts to care for others (action - and the SGI provides lots of opportunity for this), you can literally transform into a person whose personal happiness derives from helping others. In fact, that is the sole purpose for why the SGI was established — to awaken this sense of responsibility and mission in people (and in young people in particular) so that they could go out into society and devote themselves to the welfare of humanity, a commitment sorely lacking in our world leadership today.

With the Church of Religious Science, quite honestly, there was no focus whatsoever on helping others become happy. All that mattered was your own personal salvation.

3) A living example to follow — a Mentor.

I have become the person that I am because as SGI members, we are fortunate to have a wonderful teacher by the name of Daisaku Ikeda (he also happens to be the President of the SGI) who provides a living, tangible example of what caring, altruistic Buddhist behavior is all about. From extremely humble beginnings, he has gone on to create an incredible life solely dedicated to the service of humanity.

He founded an entire educational system from pre-school to post-graduate school. He founded a museum as well as a cultural performance association to promote understanding among diverse people through cultural exchange. He has personally engaged in dialogues with some of the world's most respected academics and intellectuals sharing ideas about how to create world peace and foster better understanding among people. People like President Nelson Mandela and Mrs. Rosa Parks consider him a friend and true comrade in the struggle for human rights. He has received numerous awards and recognition from universities and nations around the world for his efforts to promote peace.

On top of all this, he still works tirelessly to inspire the SGI membership throughout the world through various writings and speeches, managing to make you feel as though he is composing it just for you. Through his example, I remain constantly rejuvenated about the limitless possibilities of my life. His leadership of our organization over the past 51 years has been unparalleled. He is my mentor.

4) Diversity and unity in the membership.

Another thing that makes the SGI so different from other religious bodies is our diversity and our unity. Blacks Whites, Jews, and Mexicans. The elderly, children, wealthy, poor — all praying and taking action side by side together for one clear purpose: world peace through individual happiness. When I went to my first meeting, I remember being so struck by this. And everyone looked so happy and joyful. The atmosphere was very relaxed. It gave you the sense that you could be yourself and you would be accepted no matter what.

True Buddhism, like Christianity, stresses the idea of tolerance based on the concept that there are no distinctions among human beings, We are all equal, But because SGI members are human and full of pre-conceived notions, we, too, face many problems in trying to work together. However, because True Buddhism is a teaching that focuses on personal growth first (and we have so many activities to help each person achieve this), the membership is able to rise above differences of race, class, and gender in a way that I have not seen in other religious groups.

For instance, though I was raised to be open-minded and unbiased , I nevertheless, joined the SGI with many prejudices regarding other people. However, over the past 11 years of practice, I have developed unbelievable life-long bonds of trust and friendship with people that I would never have thought it possible to do this with. One of my closest friends is a White male. There are things that I can share with him. That I cannot share with my African American girlfriend of 20 years I can tell you, honestly, that 11 years ago, I would never have sought out a close friendship with a White male. I am by no means completely "bias free" 'today, but I am much less likely make such superficial distinctions in my relationships and. I now have the desire to, work through. These limitations in my heart.

My previous religious experiences were not so diverse. The church of Religious Science was almost all White middle-class and the A.M.E Church was all African American.

I feel that the main reason this Buddhism attracts such a diverse group is the broadmindedness of the philosophy. Next, there is the simplicity of the practice itself (though it requires serious dedication and effort!). Also, there is something incredible about the sound of chanting. It is very powerful, resonant and harmonious. It sounds like unity!

5) A strong emphasis on the growth and development of youth.

One other thing about the SGI that differs from others religious bodies that I have encountered is its emphasis on young people. President Ikeda puts extra effort into encouraging; young people because he knows that they are the leaders of the 21st century. They hold the key to the victory or defeat of humanity. Consequently, our organization is very "youth-oriented" and "youth-driven". Young people are encouraged to take on tremendous responsibility and give free reign to their unlimited potential. As a result, there is a tremendous energy and vibrancy to our organization; it is more apt to be fresh and progressive. That is, one of the key elements that convinced my mother that she should get me involved in this Buddhism. She had concerns about the direction I was headed in and felt that the SGI might influence me in a more positive direction. Her hopes were realized.

In the Church of Religious Science, there were virtually no young people at all and. they made no effort to attract them. This proves that they didn't really care about the future of humanity.

In the A.M.E. Church, there were lots of young people, mostly the children of the parishioners. But there were not that many activities to stimulate us. The only options were Sunday school and the youth choir. The energy seemed more centered on the minister and his sermon.

Q: WHAT IS THE GROWTH PATTERN OF YOUNG AFRICAN AMERICANS JOINING BUDDHISM IN THE LOS ANGELES AREA?

I'm not aware of these kinds of statistics, but if I could give a "personal impression" based on my observation, I would say 'that in the part of the organization for which I am responsible (from Sherman Oaks westbound to Pasadena), of the youth, maybe 30-33 percent are African American. I do not know the "growth pattern", though, of young African Americans joining the SGI.

Q: WHAT PERCENTAGE LEFT THE CHRISTIAN CHURCH TO JOIN BUDDHISM?

As stated above, I am not aware of those kinds of statistics, but I can give a "personal impression" based on my observation. I would say that at least half of these young people left the Christian Church to join Buddhism.

Q: CAN A PERSON BECOME A MEMBER OF BOTH?

Buddhism seeks to make people free and independent and the truest sense, therefore, in our SGIc-nganization, there are no rules or formalities stating that one must "give up" one's previous religion. It is up to the individual. I will say, though, that although Christianity and True Buddhism share very similar aims, they differ significantly in how to get there. In order for an individual to truly get the full benefit of practicing Buddhism, eventually, he or she will need to reconcile these fundamental differences in their hearts. For the sake of that person's happiness, this reconciliation is patiently encouraged.

"What's Love Gotta Do With It?"

This being the movie title that portrays Tina Turner's life of abuse with Ike Turner. According to an American Buddhist movement, and not only Buddhism, love has everything to do with it, the love of self, mankind, and nature. This movement promotes peace and personal happiness. Something we all strive to attain. We exercise this in the arena our faith. In exercising the faith of Buddhism, near the end of the movie, the then, Mrs. Turner is introduced to the element of chanting by a friend, therefore she is enabled to change her life. After some investigation, it was found that her involvement is with Soka Gakkal International-USA, an American Buddhist organization. Tina Turner and a small number of African Americans have found their freedom in this vast sect of Buddhism that is based on the 13th Century Japanese philosopher Nichiren Dalshonin.

Who they are and what they believe...

Approximately, a 2,500 year old religion that began in India by Gautama Siddhartha, the original Buddha, who is without roots in Africa and North America. Their core belief is fixed in the concept of human revolution, an inner transformation process that focuses on the thought that every action we partake of has an influential extension beyond the moment that will affect the whole of life. This inner transformation will lead one to pursue the course that will enable personal fulfillment and assist one in a personal contribution to the development of mankind. The Buddhist have a world view of dependent origination, which is the basis for these ideals, a belief of inter relatedness where nothing exists in isolation, from the realm of mankind or all of nature. When human revolution takes place; we become cognizant to self-responsibility with our circumstances and environment. SGI-USA enhances peace and personal happiness based on the philosophy and practice of the Nichiren School of Mahayaria Buddhism. This American branch is part of an association with 75 other SGI movements which members reside in more than half the countries of the world. The activities of SGI-USA are governed by their understanding of the definite connection between personal happiness and the peace and prosperity of our diverse people. Their religious teachings place considerable emphasis on the sacredness of life. Over 700 years ago, the Buddhist reformer Nichiren wrote, "life is the most precious of all treasures." Their members strive through faith, to improve their lives by accepting the challenge to care for their families, to live free from fear, to engender value, to be accountable for their circumstances, and to always be compassionate with others. Almeda Bailey shared that the attraction to Buddhism for her was that it assisted her in breaking free of the struggles that black people face in many aspects of life.

This decade, the SGI — international organization — adopted a Charter to make known the organization's philosophical doctrines and to offer guidelines for its future actions. The Charter sets out a number of purposes and principles that can be summarized as follows:

- contribute to peace, the culture, and education of our communities
- embrace an unconditional respect for the sacredness of human life
- foster the virtues of wisdom and compassion
- respect and protect the freedom of religious expression
- promote tolerance and respect for human rights
- pursue nonviolent social change through inner reformation and dialogue — **Commitment to Peace, Culture and Education....**

The contribution to peace in society and the good of mankind by cultivating culture and education while challenging any form of violence are the intentions of SGI -USA. Their belief is that peace begins within, grounded in the Buddhist idea that with all people lies this endless skill to create value in society and accomplish harmony between themselves and their world. Being that culture is the voice of this human potential, while education is the necessary vehicle for its development.

What they do...

Buddhist fundamentals are applied through a nationwide network of local activities. The value of every person living meaningfully and contributing to society is emphasized. Neighborhood discussion groups, youth activities, educational seminars, exhibitions and conferences, are used to address the urgent issues facing individuals and humanity as a whole. Their activities have included: "Nuclear Arms Threat to Our World" Exhibition — developed by the SGI and sponsored by the United Nations Department of Public Information. This exhibit was initially shown at the UN Headquarters in New York in 1982 and subsequently toured cities worldwide.

- "Ecology and Human Life" Exhibition — developed by the SGI-USA Culture Department and cosponsored by a number of federal, state and community organizations; it explored the environmental crisis, encouraging a shift in consciousness toward a recognition of our interconnectedness with the natural world.
- "Socially Engaged Buddhism and Christianity" Conference of the Society of Buddhist-Christian Studies (SBCS), held at DePaul University, Chicago, 1996 and cosponsored by SGI-USA. The SBCS supports the comparative study of and interaction between Buddhism and Christianity. "Friendship Through Knowledge" Project — sponsored by the SGI-USA Youth Peace Conference (YPQ, which collected and shipped more than 16,000 much needed books to eight institutions of higher learning, including five universities in three African nations. "Treasuring the Future: Children's Rights and Realities" Exhibition - created by the SGI-USA Youth Peace Conference, to mark the 50th anniversary of the United Nations Children's Fund (UNICEF). An interactive and child-friendly exhibit to focus public attention on the need to safeguard children's rights *__Their Heritage.__*

The educational theory of Tsunesaburo Makiguchi is the basis for SGI, whose search to understand the profoundest meaning of life eventually led to his encounter with the Buddhism of Nichiren. He learned a philosophy that acknowledged and endeavored to develop the wisdom inherent in all humans. In 1930 when Makiguchi published his Insightful "Value Creating Educational Theory," the term soka gakkai (value-creation society) was first used.

A study group under the appellation "Value Creating Pedagogical Society" or Soka Kyoiku Gakkai was formed by a small number of young educators and scholars interested in Makiguchi's reformism views. With face to face dialogue and group discussions that started approximately 70 years ago, as an educators group has flourished into an international fellowship of member organizations around the world that share the philosophy of Nichiren Buddhism.

As Japan moved forward into the war in the 1930's, Makiguchi denounced this direction his nation headed and was outraged by the governments endeavor to infringe upon the freedom of religion by imposing Shintoism as a national religion. Makiguchi continued to organize community-based discussion groups where religious and moral views were openly communicated as the government restricted one by one the people's freedoms. He held fast to his convictions as the pressure mounted to compromise his beliefs and lend support to the war effort. Arrested in 1943, Makiguchi and other organizational leaders were incarcerated as "thought criminals."

At 73, Makiguchi was dead from malnutrition and privations he endured in prison. This occurred within 18 months of his imprisonment. Josei Toda, his closest associate, weathered the ordeal, was released on July 3, 1945, just prior to nuclear weapons being used for the first time. A war torn Japan was to us reality at his release from prison. Immediately he began to rebuild the organization, which he renamed Soka Gakkali, maintaining his resolve to develop Makiguchi's ideals beyond the arena of education for the improvement of mankind. His hope was to experience a world in which justice and humane values would be granted universal respect. The exceptional initial growth of the

Soka Gakkai sprang from its commitment to assist the relief of people's suffering in the postwar chaos. In 1957 Toda reinforced the Soka Gakkai's pacifist stance by taking a strong, pioneering, public position against nuclear weapons development.

Daisaku Ikeda became the organization's third president on May 3, 1960. He established associations in the United States and South America within six months. Organizations were established in nine European countries the following year. SGI-USA makes its headquarters in Santa Monica, CA, with more than 60 other centers throughout the USA.

SGI-USA members are a reflection of a cross-section of American society. Practitioners from all walks of life make up a full spectrum of ages, races, religious backgrounds, education, geographic distribution as well as cultural and political persuasions.

An Ages Old Tradition

The teachings of the historical Buddha, Shakyamuni, who lived approximately 2,500 years ago in what is now Nepal, are the founding roots of SGI-USA world-view. He was born Gautama Siddhartha, and abandoned the noble life that shielded him from human suffering outside the royal palace. In a quest to understand the inescapable stands almost a unique figure in the history of Buddhism, not alone because of his persistence through hardship and persecution ... and eloquent speaker, a powerful writer, and a man of tender heart.

My functioning of the universe is an expression of a single principle or Law — Nam-myoho-renge-kyo according to Nichiren Buddhism. One can unlock their hidden potential and achieve creative harmony with this Law. Nichiren Buddhism illustrates a vehicle of personal empowerment — being that each person has the power within to transform the certain sufferings of life, and furthermore to be a positive influence in the community and society at large. Nichiren teachings were swayed by a strong empathy and compassion for peoples in pain and sorrow; being steeped, to speak in contemporary terms, in the universality of human rights.

72

Permission granted for:

A *Buddhist* Movement for <u>Peace, Culture and Education</u> (Soka Gakkai International — USA, 1966).

Why African American
Youth Are Attracted
To
The Baha'i Faith

Many African Americans are attracted to the Baha'i Faith because of their 12 principles which characterize the Baha'i cause. These are:

1. *The Oneness of the world of Humanity.*

2. *Independent investigation of truth.*

3. *The foundation of all religion is one.*

4. *Religion must be the cause of unity.*

5. *Religion must be in accord with science and reason.*

6. *Equality between men and women.*

7. *Prejudices of all kinds must be forgotten.*

8. *Universal peace.*

9. *Universal education.*

10. *Solution of the economic problem.*

11. *An International Auxiliary language.*

12. *United States of the World.*

AFRICAN AMERICAN BAHA'I COMMUNITY OF LOS ANGELES
By Mary Helen Berg

THE FOLLOWERS OF BAHA'I

Founded 50 Years Ago, the Faith Preaches Unity through Diversity and promotes a Progressive Agenda of Social and economic Justice. Its Central Message of a Peaceful World Without Borders, Followers Say: "Has Special Resonance in Racially Divided LA."

On a cool, breezy evening in Chinatown beneath a soulful black and white portrait of a man wearing a turban and white bard, weekly visitors trickle into the comfortable living room of Lourdes and Valid Sanei. An unemployed secretary, a computer programmer, a full-time mother, a flower shop owner, a building supervisor. White, black, Latino and Iranian. Some murmur an Arabic greeting: Allah' u Abha: God is most glorious.

Most have embarked in spiritual quest to arrive here, at a Baha'i "fireside," an informal educational gathering that mingles believers in the Baha'i faith with prospective followers and the merely curious. Under the photographic gaze of one of the faith's leaders, Baha'is talked about their independent religion.

"Los Angeles needs the Baha'i faith," said Bob Hopper, 58, a Baha'i and a city tour guide who regularly attends firesides. "Other religions have brought similar principals, but they need to be renewed and looked at again, and that's what the Baha'i faith does."

Founded 150 years ago by a Tehran-born nobleman bow called Baha'u'llah, the Baha'i faith preaches unity through diversity and promotes a progressive agenda of social and economic justice and racial and gender equality. For believers, it is the means to accomplish what no war or political movement has-a peaceful world without borders uniting all peoples, all religions and gods.

Baha'u'llah's central message. "The earth is one country and mankind its citizens," followers say, has special resonance in Los Angeles, a city so recently shattered by racial divisions.

"We're pioneers in living in unity and diversity." Said Amin Banani, a Baha'i and UCLA historian. "Los Angeles is becoming a multiracial, multicultural place and we are a people who have practiced living as a unified people and a have a (systematic) plan for doing it".

In Los Angeles, that plan has included launching an institute on healing racism, a multiethnic youth theater group and an after-school enrichment program and a **multicultural gospel choir all based** out of the Baha'i headquarters in Baldwin Hills.

One of those groups, the Baha'i Youth Workshop, founded in 1974 by Oscar and Freddie DeGruy in their living room, has worked toward encouraging youths to find common interest. The traveling theater troupe, which has toured nationally, has included black, white, Latino, Asian, Iranian and about 10% non-Baha'i performers.

As workshop members, "they can be together from different religions and different cultures and different races and the can find a point of unity," Oscar DeGruy said.

The group visits schools, community centers and other sites and uses hiphop, rap, jazz and other styles to address topics such as peace, equality, education and social ills.

"We're brought up to believe that if you don't fit, we don't want you," Oscar DeGruy said. "We're all different for a reason and now it's time to share those differences with each other ... The Baha'i faith gives (the youths) the opportunity to come together."

The Los Angeles Baha'i community's aim is to triple its active members from its base of 1,500 in the next two years. There are 5,000 active Baha'i members in Southern California and about 110,000 nationwide.

Already, the Baha'i community in Southern California is one of the largest in the country. Its hub is the Baha'i Center, located at the edge of Baldwin Hills at Rodeo Road and La Cienega Boulevard. Thornton Chase, an insurance company executive who became the first American Baha'i, is buried in Inglewood

Park Cemetery and his grave site is considered a holy place of pilgrimage. Los Angeles is also home to a Baha'i radio show and Kalimat Press, one of three Baha'i publishers in the country.

The Los Angeles Baha'i community formally organized in 1909, making it on of the country's earliest multiracial religious communities, said Muhtadia Rice, public information officer for the Baha'is of Los Angeles.

The religion forbids missionaries and Baha'is are not allowed to proselytize, so the informal firesides held every week across the city are the foremost way believers spread the faith. Perhaps because of this low-key approach, the faith is relatively unknown, despite an 85-year presence in Los Angeles.

"We're confused with B'nai B'rith, we're confused with Buddhists, or people have never heard of us at all," Rice said. "It's critical for us that we are accepted as credible and very mainstream."

Islamic fundamentalist have called the Baha'i heretics. Other critics dismiss the religion as a cult. Scholars still view the faith as somewhat new, small and exotic, and there are few non-Baha'i specialist in academia.

Nevertheless, said Diana Eck, a professor in comparative religions at Harvard University, the Baha'i faith is a world religion in the sense that, "though it is neither very ancient nor very large, you can find Baha'is all over the world today."

With 5 million members in 233 countries and territories worldwide, it is among the widest spread and fastest growing religions by percentage increase in the world, according to Baha'i researchers.

This modern faith has attracted followers ranging from entertainers Dizzy Gillespie, Jim Seals and Dash Crofts of the singing duo Seals & Croft, to jurist Dorothy W. Nelson, a U.S. 9th Circuit Court of Appeals judge and her husband, retired state Judge James F. Nelson. The Nelsons have hosted weekly firesides in their home for 36 years, some of which have drawn more than 200 people.

"At first we went to firesides (in the early 1950's) to see if (the Baha'i religion) was just one of those "California things," admitted Dorothy Nelson, an elected member of the Baha'i

National Spiritual Assembly who was raised an Episcopalian. By 1954, the Nelsons had left their traditional Christian backgrounds for the Baha'i faith.

Baha'is believe racism is the greatest challenge facing Americans today. The faith demands that followers work together to abolition of prejudice and encourages intermarriage to overcome racial barriers.

In 1969, Gloria Haithman-Ali, now a USC administrator, realized that Baha'i principals of unity and racial equality gave a spiritual name to her personal beliefs. As a young black woman in Greensboro, NC, she had protested and demonstrated against discrimination during the civil rights movement. Later, as a mother in New York, she recalls seeking a home for her family and being shut out of trailer parks and neighborhoods because of her color. One day she was invited to a Baha'i retreat in Teaneck, NJ.

At one point I looked around (the multicultural group) and said:"These are the true Christians," and at that point, in my heart, I knew I was Baha'i," recalled Haithman-Ali, who is vice chair of the Los Angeles Baha'i Spiritual Assembly.

After the riots, a group of Baha'is formed the Institute for the Healing of Racism, and began offering nine-week courses in how to cure what the faith considers a moral and social disease.

"There has really been a demand for (the classes)," said Haithman-Ali one of the institute's founders. "At the end (of the session), hopefully people realize it's really the beginning."

What may distinguish the Baha'i faith most from other religions is the belief that all religions are part of one religion and that each faith's prophet has provided humanity with updates for God.

Baha'u'llah (1817-1892) is considered the most recent in a line of holy messengers sent by God to guide men on earth. Another messenger is expected in 1,000 years, according to Baha'i teachings.

"The Baha'i have a real perspective on the unique contributions of all the different religions," Eck said. "Other religions don't do that, especially the Western, monotheistic religions."

In Islamic Iran, where orthodox Muslims believe Mohammed to be the last prophet. Baha'is have been tortured and killed for their beliefs. Since the 1979 Islamic revolution more than 200 Baha'is have been executed and Baha'i scholars report that slayings occurred as recently as last year. Baha'is are Iranian immigrants.

That fact that the Baha'i encourage openness and investigation of other religions appealed to Lourdes Sanaei, 37. Sanaei spent 14 years in Catholic school and always wondered by, as a young girl, her church taught that sinners — everyone, including even children who were baptized — would be doomed to eternal hell.

"I had all these questions and the priests would say "Oh, don't ask that. Have faith"' recalled the mother of three. "Then I started to read the Baha'i writings and the answers I'd looked for were there. This is a religion that is very clear and there are no dogmas. It's like there were veils before my eyes and they fell away."

Angelica Huerta remembers how her Catholic family became alienated from the church after the charges of Vatican 11. Now 44, she spent her early 20's investigating other religions and even traveled to Jerusalem in search of answers. Then she discovered the Baha'i community in Los Angeles.

Services, such as Catholic Sunday Mass, although members can attend "devotional," or informal prayer meetings in most communities.

Perhaps the most important Baha'i gathering is known as the area feast, held every 19 days at the end of each Baha'i month. (The Baha'i calendar is based on 19 months of 19 days each. The number 19 is significant among Baha'is because in 19th Century Persia, the numerical Abjad system gave each letter a standard value of 19.) The Nineteen-Day feast is a community gathering that combines prayer, administration and socializing. It is the only Baha'i activity that is closed to outsiders.

The faith has on clergy and little ritual and is governed by a nine-member Local Spiritual Assembly elected by residents of that city. Campaigning and nominations for positions on the assembly are forbidden. Local members elect the National Spiritual Assembly, which in turn helps elect representatives to the Universal House if Justice, the nine-member international body based on Haifa, Israel, whose decisions on spiritual matters are considered to be infallible and guided by God.

Fiona Missaghian, a 22-year-old German-born USC master's student remembers being harassed for her beliefs by other children in her hometown near Cologne, Germany.

"As a child, sometimes it was difficult because you're different." Saud Missaghian, who, in jeans and a backpack looked very much like every other student on campus. "I remembered in sixth grade a kid called me 'Miss World Peace,' but eventually they all began to realize (unity is) something we have to achieve."

"At first we went to firesides (in the early 1950s) to see Baha'i religion) was just one of those "California things" admitted Dorothy Nelson, an elected member of the Baha'i National Spiritual Assembly who was raised an Episcopalian. By 1954, the Nelsons had left their traditional Christian backgrounds for the Baha'i faith.

Baha'is believe racism is the greatest challenge facing Americans today. The faith demands that followers work toward the abolition to prejudice and encourages intermarriage to overcome barriers.

Permission granted for reprint by The Los Angeles Times, Oct. 9, 1994. City Times page 14. By Mary Helen Berg. Copyright 1994. The Times Mirror Company.

THE BAHA'I FAITH

"The earth is one country, and mankind its citizens."
– Bahau'llah

One religious group to originate in the past two centuries that has not received enough attention from Evangelical Christians is the BAHA'I FAITH in just over 100 years. The Baha'i Faith has grown from an obscure movement in the Middle East to the second most widespread of the independent world religions, embracing people from more that 2,100 ethnic, racial and tribal groups, it is quite likely the most diverse organized body of people on the planet. Its unity challenges prevailing theories about human nature and the prospects for our common future.

The Baha'i Faith began in the mid 1800's and is today a world's religion with over 5 million members in 235 countries and territories. Baha'u'llah, Prophet/Founder, who proclaimed in 1863 that he, was the manifestation God for this current age. He taught that only one God exists who progressively reveals his wife to humanity.

Each of the great religions brought by the messenger of God — Krishna, Moses Zoroaster, Buddha, Jesus, Mohammed, and Baha'u'llah represent successful stages of the spiritual development of civilization.

Baha'u'llah, the most recent messenger in the line, has brought teachings that address the moral and spiritual challenges that address the modem world.

It is important to not that this religion is attracting many African Americans because of its stand on racial unity, interracial marriages, oneness of humanity, equality of men, women and men, the elimination of prejudices, wealth and poverty, the independent investigation of truth, universal education, religious tolerance, to harmony of science and religion, a world Commonwealth of Nations and an universal auxiliary language.

Baha'is follow the moral code of the Ten Commandments and more.

Baha'u'llah forbids:

Killing, stealing, lying, adultery and promiscuity, gambling, alcoholic drinks, drug abuse, gossip and backbiting.

Baha'is strive to uphold a high moral standard. Baha'u'llah stressed the importance of. honesty, trustworthiness, chastity, service to others, purity of motive, generosity, deeds over words, unity and work as a form of worship.

NOT A SECT BUT AN INDEPENDENT RELIGION

In the past, scholars sometimes refereed to the Baha'i Faith as a "sect" of Islam -owing to the fact that it's Prophet and early followers emerged from an Islamic society.

Today, religious specialists recognize that such a reference would be equivalent to calling Christianity a "sect" of Judaism, or referring to Buddhism as a "denomination" of Hinduism.

Although Christ was indeed Jewish and Buddha was born a Hindu, their religious messages were not merely reinterpretations of the parent religions — but went far beyond them.

In the same way, Baha'u'llah laid entirely new spiritual foundations. His writings are independent scripture, and His work transcends that of a religious reformer. As historian Amold Toynbee noted 1959:

"Bahaism [sic] is an independent religion on a par with Islam, Christianity, and other recognized world religions. Bahaism is not a sect of some other religion; it is a separate religion, and, it has the same status as the other recognized religious."

THE SECOND-MOST "GLOBAL" RELIGION

The Baha'is have established "significant" communities in more countries and territories than any other independent religion with the exception of Christianity.

According to the *1992 Encyclopedia Britannica Book of the Year*, the Baha'i Faith is established in *205* sovereign countries and dependent territories

This point was first made in *1982*, in the *World Christian Encyclopedia* That volume reported on the work of some *500* scholars, demographers and statisticians who conducted the first comprehensive survey of religious believers worldwide.

BAHA'IS AND RACIAL UNITY

WHY DO BAHA'IS WORK FOR RACIAL UNITY?

"All humanity are the children of God; they belong to the same family, to the same race." This is the foundation of all Baha'i belief "This truth compels the abandonment of all prejudices of race, color, creed, nation and of class — of everything which enables people to consider themselves superior to others." Baha'is believe that "the world of humanity is a composite body" and that "when one part of the organism suffers all the rest of the body will feel its consequences. Thus, "personal salvation is linked to the salvation, security and happiness of all the inhabitants of the earth."

Our goal is to create vibrant communities enjoying unity in diversity; havens of justice, interracial worship, and service to humanity: and places for genuine fellowship and raising prejudice-free children.

> *"The diversity in the human family, should be The cause of love and harmony..."*
> *Baha'i Scripture*

HOW DO THE BAHA'I WRITINGS HONOR PEOPLE OF AFRICAN DESCENT?

Baha'u'llah is the Prophet-Founder of the Baha'i Faith. He once compared people of African descent to the "black pupil of the eye surrounded by the white. "In this black pupil is seen the reflection of that which is before it, and through it the light of the spirit shineth forth."

"The spirit of the African believers is very touching, very noble, and indeed presents a challenge to their fellow-Baha'is all over the world. It seems that God has endowed these races ... with great spiritual faculties, and also mental faculties which ... will contribute immensely to the whole, throughout the Baha'i world."

HOW ARE WHITE BAHA'IS OVERCOMING RACISM?

Baha'i teaching gives challenging instructions: "Let the white make a supreme efforts in their resolve to contribute their share to the solution of this problem, to abandon once for all their usually inherent and at times subconscious sense of superiority, to correct their tendency towards revealing a patronizing attitude towards the members of the other race, to persuade them through their intimate, spontaneous and informal association with them of the genuineness of their friendship and the sincerity of their intentions, and to master their impatience of any lack of responsiveness on the part of a people who have received for so long a period, such grievous and slow-healing wounds."

"Casting away once and for all the fallacious doctrine of radial superiority and welcoming and encouraging the intermixture of races and tearing down the barriers that now divide them, they should each endeavor, day and night to fulfill their particular responsibilities."

DO I HAVE TO GIVE UP MY "BLACKNESS" TO BE A BAHA'I?

No way! People of African descent have "a great contribution to make to the advancement of world civilization." "Unity in diversity" is the standard. "We hold in contempt every attempt at uniformity or at complete separateness." Baha'is are "Encouraged to preserve their inherited cultural identities, the music, culture and spirituality of African Americans are promoted, celebrated and honored in the diverse Baha'i community. "The perpetuation of such cultural characteristics is an expression of unity in diversity."

HOW LONG HAVE BAHA'IS BEEN WORKING
ON RACIAL UNITY?

American Baha'is have over one hundred years of hard-earned experience in community building. We are not perfect but continually strive toward our goal: "to create through the power of the Word of God, genuine love, spiritual communion and durable bonds among individuals." We invite you to share in the experience.

WHY IS RACE UNITY SO URGENT TO BAHA'IS?

"Racism is the most challenging issue confronting America. To ignore the problem is to expose the country to physical, moral and spiritual danger .... America's peace, prosperity, and even her standing in the international community depend on healing the wounds of racism and building a society in which people of diverse backgrounds live as members of one family."

We strive to walk the walk with "genuine love, extreme patience, true humility, consummate tact, sound initiative, mature wisdom, and deliberate, persistent, and prayerful effort."

Baha'is believe that the unity of the entire human race is the will of God for this day.

'ABDU 'L-BAHA ON RACISM

According to the words of the Old Testament, God has said, "Let us make man in our image, after our likeness." This indicates that man is of the image and likeness of God — that is to say, the perfection's of God, the divine virtues, are reflected or revealed in the human reality. Just as the light and effulgence of the sun when cast upon a polished mirror is reflected fully, gloriously, so likewise, the qualities and attributes of Divinity are radiated from the depths of a pure human heart. This is evidence that man is the noblest of God's creatures ....

Let us now discover more specifically how he is the image and likeness of God and what is the standard or criterion by which he can be no other than the divine virtues which are revealed in him. Therefore, every man imbued with divine qualities, who reflects heavenly moralities and perfection's, who is the expression of ideal and praiseworthy attributes, is verily, in the image and likeness of God. If a man possesses wealth, can we call him an image and likeness of God? Or is human honor and notoriety the criterion of divine nearness? Can we apply the test of racial color and say that man of a certain hue — white, black, brown, yellow, and red — is the true image of his Creator? We must conclude that color is not the standard and estimate of judgment and that it is of no importance, for color is accidental in nature. The spirit and intelligence of man is essential.... Therefore, be it known that color or race is of no importance. He who is the image and likeness of God, who is the manifestation of the bestowals of God, is acceptable at the threshold of God — whether his color be white, black or brown; it matters not. Man is not man simply because of bodily attributes. The standard of divine measure and judgment is his intelligence and spirit ....

A man's heart may be pure and white though his outer skin is black; or his heart is dark and sinful though his racial color is white. The character and purity of the heart is of all importance.

— Excerpts from a talk given by "Abdul-Baka" at the fourth Annual Conference of the National Association for the Advancement of Colored People, 30 April 1912, Handel Hall, Chicago, Illinois.

SOCIAL AND MORAL TEACHINGS

A BLEND OF THE PROGRESSIVE AND THE TRADITIONAL, WITH AN EMPHASIS ON UNITY

The central theme of Baha'u'llah's writings is that humanity is one single race and the day has come for this unification into one global society. Through an irresistible historical process, the traditional barriers of race, class, creed, faith and nation will break down. These forces will, Baha'u'Rah said, give birth in time to a new universal civilization. The crises now afflicting the planet face all its peoples with the need to accept their oneness and work towards the creation of a unified global society.

Baha'ullah outlined certain fundamental principles upon which this new world civilization should be founded. These include the elimination of all forms of prejudice; fill equality between the sexes; recognition of the essential oneness of the world's great religions; the elimination of extremes of poverty and wealth; universal education; high standard of personal conduct; the harmony of science and religion; a sustainable balance between nature and technology; and the establishment of a world federal system, based on collective security and the oneness of humanity.

Covering questions pertaining to the role of women, race relations, economic justice, environmental degradation, and world order, these principles illustrate the concerns that have fueled the century's most dynamic movements. And, accordingly, they have come to head the social and political agenda of humanity.

There has never been a futurist, a forecaster, or a prophet, whose vision has so accurately foreseen the critical features of the social landscape. Far from fading, a century after He lived, the issues Baha'u'llah focused on have come to dominate the collective life of humanity.

UNITY THE THEME

The Baha'i Faith's progressive approach to human society originates with Baha'u'llah emphasis on unity. Indeed, if one were to characterize His teachings in a single word, that word would be unity. Throughout His writings, Baba'u'llah emphasized the importance — and the reality — of unity and oneness. First, God is one. All of the world's great religions are also one. They represent humanity's responses to the revelation of the world and will of God for humanity by successive Messengers from the one God. These understandings lie at the heart of the concept of unity in Baha'u'llah teachings. From this fundamental concept of divine and religious unity, other principles emerge. Baha'u'llah teaches that all humans, as creations of the one god, is also one people. Distinctions of race, nation, class or ethnic origin are ephemeral when understood in this context. Likewise, any notions of individual, tribal, provincial or national superiority are discarded 'in the Baha'i Faith. Speaking through Baha'u'llah, the voice of God proclaims:

"Know ye not why we created you all from the same dust?" That no one should exalt himself over the other. Ponder at all times in your hearts how we were created. Since we have crated you all from one same substance it is incumbent on you to be even as one soul, to walk with the same feet, eat with the same mouth and dwell in the same land, that from your inmost being, by your deeds, actions, the signs of oneness and the essence of detachment may be made manifest."

THE ONENESS OF HUMANITY

The idea that all humanity is one race forms the foundation for the other principles of social justice in the Baha'i Faith.

Baha'u'llah condemned racial and ethnic prejudice, urging: "Close your eyes to racial differences, and welcome all with the light of oneness."

"Women and men have been and will always be equal in the sight of God."
– Baha'u'llah

Baha'u'llah also unequivocally proclaimed the equality of the sexes — at a time when the women's movement was only beginning its fight for suffrage in the West and such ideas were unheard of in the Middle East — thus becoming the first Founder of a world religion to explicitly uphold strict equality for women and men.

Indeed, girls should receive priority in education — if by some circumstance a family (or a society) cannot afford to educate its children equally. "Until the reality of equality between men and women is fully established and attained, the highest social development of mankind is not possible," the Baha'i scriptures state.

This challenge for full equality does not ignore natural differences between the sexes. Baha'u'llah emphasized the importance of motherhood, fatherhood, and family life.

Baha'u'llah's call for economic justice also reflects His central theme of human oneness. He wrote extensively about the necessity of promoting economic justice and proposed specific remedies to help control the extreme inequalities of wealth in human society. The redistribution of wealth through a tax on income for example and the concept of profit sharing are both promoted in His teachings.

Education is given a special emphasis, as humanity is considered capable of tremendous progress and advancement. "Regard man as a mine rich in gems of inestimable value," wrote Baha'u'llah. "Education can, alone, cause it to reveal its treasures, and enable mankind to benefit therefrom."

Education, accordingly, should be universal and should incorporate positive spiritual values and moral attitudes. Baha'is envision a future in which even "basic education" goes beyond rote learning and the teaching of simple skills. Students must be given the tools to analyze social conditions and requirements themselves, to take part in community planning and action, and to investigate truth on their own. The oneness of humanity is an essential element of every Baha'i curriculum.

WOMEN: UNAMBIGUOUS EQUALITY

For the first time in history, the Founder of a major world religion has explicitly stated that women and men are equal. The Baha'i writings also state that:

Girls should be given preference over boys when educational opportunities and resources are limited. In Baha'i marriage, neither the husband nor the wife has a dominant voice. Any apparent inequality between the capacities of women and men is due solely to the lack of educational opportunities so far open to women.

SCIENCE AND RELIGION

The theme of unity also emerges in Baha'u'llah teachings on science. His writings portray science and religion as different yet harmonious approaches to the comprehension of reality. These two paths are essentially compatible and mutually reinforcing.

Scientific method is humanity's tool for understanding the physical side of the universe. It can describe the composition of an atomic nucleus or the molecular structure of DNA. It is the key to new technologies. Science cannot, however, guide us in the use of such knowledge. The revelation of God offers to humanity a basis for values and purpose. It provides answers to those questions of morals, human purpose, and our relationship to God that science cannot approach.

The independent investigation of reality, whether scientific or religious, is strongly encouraged in Baha'u'llah's Writings. Individuals should strive He said, to free themselves from prejudices, preconceptions, and reliance on tradition or traditional authorities. Consultation is a critical tool for discovering truth.

Baha'u'llah also called for the adoption of a universal auxiliary language as a means to promote unity. "The day is approaching when all the peoples of the world will have adopted one universal language and one common script," He wrote. "When this is achieved, to whatsoever city a man may journey, it shall be as if he were entering his own home. The term "auxiliary" is important. Baha'u'llah's injunction is not a mandate for cultural uniformity. Indeed, the Baha'i teachings both value and promote cultural diversity.

When first outlined by Baha'u'llah more than 100 years ago, these principles were as radical as any social program ever drafted. The fact that they have not only borne the passage of time, but indeed, become ever more widely proclaimed and recognized is a testimony to the vision that produced them.

Baha'u'llah's moral code for the individual and His pattern for marriage and family life is wholly consonant with the genuine needs of modem society. As with the social principles, the laws of Bahau'llah on individual morality and family structure are aimed at the promotion of unity and well being for society at large.

91

"They whom God hath endued with "insight will readily recognize that the precepts laid down by God constitute the highest means for the maintenance of order in the world and the security of its peoples," Baha'u'llah wrote.

"The well-begin of mankind, its peace and security, are unattainable unless and until its unity is firmly established."
– Baha'u'llah

This insight — that the standards for social justice and individual conduct outlined by Baha'u'llah offer an integrated and distinctive approach to the apparently intractable problems faced by humanity today — underlies the essential optimism of the worldwide Baha'i community. Whether considering the threat of environmental degradation, the cancer of racism, or the erosion of the family, Baha'is believe firmly that answers are available in the writings of Baha'u'llah. Their commitment is to share these insights with the world.

MARRIAGE AND FAMILY LIFE

Baha'is understand that the family is the basic unit of society. Unless this all-important building block is healthy and unified, society itself cannot be healthy and unified. Monogamous marriage stands at the foundation of family life.

Baha'u'llah said marriage is "a fortress for well-being and salvation. "The Baha'i writings further state that married couples should strive to become "loving companions and comrades and at one with each other for time and eternity ...

Baha'is view preparation for marriage as an essential element in ensuring a happy marriage. The process of preparation includes a requirement for parental approval of the choice of a spouse. This does not mean that Baha'i marriages are arranged. Individuals propose marriage to the persons of their own choice. However, once the choice is made, the parents have both the right and the obligation to weigh carefully whether to give consent to, and thus guide their offspring in one of life's most important decisions.

Baha'is believe that this requirement helps to preserve unity within the marriage and within the extended family. As did previous Messengers of God, Baha'u'llah asks His followers to honor their parents. Obtaining parental permission for marriage reaffirms the importance of the bond between child and parent. It also helps to create a supportive network of parents in the often difficult first years of marriage.

SIMPLE VOWS AND CEREMONY

Once parental permission is obtained, the marriage takes place, requiring only the simplest of ceremonies. In the presence of two witnesses designated by the local Baha'i governing council, the couple recites the following verse: "We will all, verily, abide by the will of God." For Baha'is, that simple commitment to live by God's will implies all of the commitments associated with marriage, including the promises to love, honor, and cherish; to care for each other regardless of material health or wealth; and to share with and serve each other.

Beyond these simple requirements, Baha'is free to design their own marriage celebration. Depending on personal tastes, family resource, and cultural traditions. Baha'i ceremonies fan the gamut from small to large, including all manner of music, dance, dress, food and festivity.

As in most religions, the marriage vow is considered sacred in the Baha'i Faith. The partners are expected to be absolutely faithful to each other.

The Faith's emphasis on the equality of women and men, however and its promotion of consultation as a tool for problem solving means that the roles of husband and wife within a Baha'i marriage are not the traditional ones. Women are free to pursue careers that interest them; men are expected to share in household duties and child rearing.

So-called "interracial marriage" is also encouraged in the Baha'is teachings, which stress the essential oneness of the human race.

DIVORCE IS ALLOWED BUT DISCOURAGED

If a Baha'i marriage fails, divorce is permitted, although it is strongly discouraged. If Baha'is choose to seek a divorce, they must spend at least one year living apart and attempting to reconcile. If a divorce is still desired after that year, it is then granted, dependent on the requirements of civil law. This "year of patience," as it is known to Baha'is, is supervised by the local Spiritual Assembly, the local Baha'i governing council.

The key purpose of Baha'i marriage — beyond physical, intellectual and spiritual companionship — is children. Baha'is view child-rearing not only as a source of great JOY and reward, but as a scared obligation.

While stating firmly that women must enjoy fill equality with men, Baha'u'llah's teachings also recognize explicitly the innate differences between the feminine and masculine natures — both physical and emotional. Baha'is understand, accordingly, that mothers have a special role to play in the early education of children — especially during the first few years of life when the basic values and character of every individual is formed.

Since Baha'is believe that the soul appears at the moment of conception, the parents pray for the well-being of the unborn child while it is still in the womb.

Education in general, and Baha'i education in particular is of paramount importance in Baha'i families. From their earliest years, the children are encouraged to develop the habits of prayer and meditation, and to acquire knowledge, both intellectual and spiritual.

WHILE SOCIALLY PROGRESSIVE, THE BAHA'I TEACHINGS ON PERSONAL MORALITY ARE UNCOMPROMISING

Baha'u'llah teachings on individual morality start with the notion that there is only one God. Although religious teachings in relation to society at large must change to fit the needs of the times, there are certain fundamental moral and ethical teachings that are common to all faiths. Baha'is understand that these teachings are fundamental to the happiness and well being of the human species and they do not change.

The moral code of the Ten Commandments, with its condemnation of murder, adultery, theft, lies, covetousness and disrespect for parents, can be found in all religions. Likewise, those commandments that define the individual's relationship with God have steadily emerged in the succession of Divine revelations.

Baha'u'llah reaffirmed these laws and elaborated them. He not only condemned murder and lying but also particularly censured backbiting. Gambling, assault, and trespassing are interdicted. So are alcoholic drinks and narcotic drugs — unless prescribed by a physician.

Honesty and trustworthiness are extolled in Baha'u'llah writing. "Trustworthiness is the greatest portal leading unto the tranquillity and security of the people," Baha'u'llah wrote. "In truth the stability of every affair hath depended and doth depend on it."

Although the world's ever-shifting moral climate has led some modernists to reject or modify elements of God's historic moral code, Baha'i believe that an unbiased survey of contemporary conditions leads inescapably to the conclusion that society will only suffer if human morality is not revitalized. Worldwide corruption in business and government, the epidemic of sexually transmitted diseases, and the dissolution of family life provide concrete examples of the need to return to a high standard of individual conduct.

SPIRITUALS BELIEFS OF THE BAHA'I FAITH — WHAT BAHA'U'LLAH TEACHES ABOUT GOD, RELIGION AND HUMAN NATURE

There is only one God, the Creator of the Universe. Throughout history, God revealed himself to humanity through a series of divine Messengers — each of whom has founded a great religion. The Messengers have included Abraham, Krishna, Zoroaster, Moses Buddha, Jesus and Muhammad. This succession of divine Teachers reflects a single historic "plan of God" for educating humanity about the Creator and for cultivating the spiritual, intellectual and moral capacities of the race. The goal has been to prepare the way for a single, global and ever advancing civilization. Knowledge of God's will for humanity in the modem age was revealed just over 100 years ago by Baha'u'llah, who is the latest of the divine Messengers.

That is the essence of Bahau'llah's teachings about God, religion and humanity. Baha'is often express these beliefs simply by speaking of the oneness of God, the oneness of religion, and the oneness of humankind. Unity is at all times the overarching theme of Baha'i belief, in theological terms, it manifests itself in the understanding that the sole Creator has a single plan for the one humanity.

Coupled with these ideas is an understanding that human nature is fundamentally spiritual. Although human being exists on earth in physical bodies, the essential identity of each person is defined by an invisible, rational, and everlasting soul.

The soul animates the body and distinguishes human beings from the animals. It grows and develops only through the individual's relationship with God, as mediated by His Messengers. The relationship is fostered through prayer, knowledge of the scriptures revealed by these Teachers, love for God, moral self-discipline, and service to humanity. This process is what gives meaning to life.

Cultivation of life's spiritual side has several benefits. First, the individual increasingly develops those innate qualities that lie at the foundation of human happiness and social progress. Such qualities include faith, courage, love, compassion, trustworthiness and humility. As these qualities are increasingly manifest, society as a whole advances.

Another effect of spiritual development is alignment with God's will. This growing closer prepares the individual for the afterlife. The soul lives on after the body's death, embarking on a spiritual Journey towards God through many "worlds" or planes of existence. Progress on this journey in traditional terms, is likened to "heaven." If the soul fails to develop, one remains distant from God. This, in traditional Christian of Muslim terms, is "hell."

The coming of new Messengers from God represent pivotal points in history. Each releases a fresh spiritual impulse, stimulating personal renewal and social advancement. Baha'u'llah's revelation, and the spiritual impulse accompanying it, is especially significant because it coincides with the maturation of humanity.

Baha'u'llah teaches that humanity as a whole, has today entered a new stage in its collective existence. Like an adolescent entering adulthood, new levels of accomplishment are now possible. Global undertakings, once considered impossible, can now be achieved. Such undertakings include the realization of world peace, the attainment of universal justice, and the furtherance of a harmonious balance between technology development, human values and protection of the natural environment.

THE UNKNOWABLE ESSENCE

In elaborating how Baha'is view the relationship between God, religion and humanity, the best place to start is with the Baha'i concept of God. And that concept begins with the realization that God is unknowable.

Baha'u'llah taught that God is the Creator of the universe and its absolute ruler. His nature is limitless, infinite and all-powerful. It is therefore impossible for mortal men and women, with limited intellect and finite capacities, to directly comprehend or understand the Divine reality, Its motives or the way it operates.

While unknowable in His essence, God has chosen to make Himself known to humanity through a series of divine Messengers.

These Messengers have been the only way to knowledge of God, and their number includes the Founders of the world's great religions: Moses, Krishna, Zoroaster, Buddha, Christ, and Muhammad — to name those Messengers who are best known. Baha'is also include other prophets in this group, such as Noah and Abraham.

"A new life is, in this age, stirring with in all the peoples of the earth ...
– Baha'ullah

97

The Messengers, in Baha'u'llah's words, are "Magnification of God." The Manifestations are perfect mirrors of God's attributes and perfection, providing a pure channel for the communication of God's will for humanity.

This idea — that God has sent a succession of Messengers to educate humanity — is called "progressive revelation." An analogy is the process of schooling. Just as children start with simple ideas in the primary grades, and are given increasingly complex knowledge as they move on through secondary school and college, so humanity has been "educated" by a series of Manifestations. In each age, the teachings of the Messengers of God has conformed not to their knowledge but to the level of our collective maturity.

A TWOFOLD STATION

The Manifestations of God have a twofold station. On the one hand, they are Divine beings, reflecting perfectly God's will. On the other hand, they are humans, subject to birth, disease, suffering and death. They have different physical identities and they address humanity at different stages in history. These differences give rise to cultural distinctions between religions that sometimes conceal their inherent unity.

> *"The Word God hath set the heart of the world afire; how regrettable if ye fail to be enkindled with its flame!*
> *– Bahau'llah*

"Every Prophet Whom the Almighty and Peerless Creator hath purposed to send to the peoples of the earth hath been entrusted with a Message, and charged to act in a manner that would best meet the requirements of the age in which He appeared," Baha'u'llah said.

Fundamentally, however, the spirited message of God's Messengers has been universally the same. Each has stressed the importance of love for God, obedience to His will, and love for humanity. Although the words have varied, each has taught the "Golden Rule" — that individuals should treat others as they would like to be treated themselves.

"Know thou assuredly that the essence of all the Prophets of God is one and the same Baha'u'llah wrote. "Their unity is absolute. God, the Creator, saith There is not distinction whatsoever among the Bearers of My Message ..."

The manifestation of God communicates God's will to humanity through the process of divine revelation. This process of revelation has been recorded in the world's great holy books — books that range from the Torah to the Qur'an, and which include Hindu, Buddhist, Christian and Zoroastrian scripture. These writings represent humanity's record of God's revealed Word.

Baha'u'llah says that the Word of God is the "master key" for the whole world.

HEAVEN AND HELL. A BAHA'I VIEW OF LIFE AFTER DEATH

As in the world's other religions, the Baha'i concept of life after death is deeply integrated into teachings about the nature of the soul and the purpose of this earthly life.

Baha'u'llah confirms the existence of a separate, rational soul for every human. In this life, He said, the soul is related to the physical body. It provides the underlying animation for the body, and is our real self.

Although undetectable by physical instruments, the soul shows itself through the qualities of character that we associate with each person. The soul is the focal point for love and compassion, for faith and courage, and for other such "human" qualities that cannot be explained solely by thinking of a human being as an animal, or as a sophisticated organic machine.

The soul does not die; it endures everlastingly. When the human body dies, the soul is freed from ties with the physical body and the surrounding physical world and begins its progress through the spiritual world. Baha'is understand the spiritual world to be a timeless and placeless extension of our own universe — and not some physically remote or removed place.

Entry into the next life has the potential to bring great joy. Bahau'llah likened death to the process of birth. He explains: "The world beyond is as different from this world as this world is different from that of the child while still in the womb of its mother."

The analogy to the womb in many ways summarizes the Baha'i view of earthly existence. Just as the womb constitutes an important place for a person's initial physical development, the physical world provides the matrix for the development of the individual soul. Accordingly, Baha'is view life as a sort of workshop, where one can develop and perfect those qualities which will be needed in the next life.

"Know thou, of a truth, that if the soul of man hath walked in the ways of God, it will, assuredly return and be gathered to the glory of the Beloved," Baha'u'llah wrote. "By the righteousness of God! It shall attain a station such as no pen can depict, or tongue can describe."

In the final analysis, heaven can be seen partly as a state of nearness to God; hell is a state of remoteness from God. Each state follows as a natural consequence of individual efforts or the lack thereof, to develop spiritually. The key to spiritual progress is to follow the path outlined by the Manifestations of God.

Beyond this, the exact nature of the afterlife remains a mystery. "The nature of the soul after death can never be described," Baba'u'llah writes.

BAHA'IS AND BIBLICAL PROPHECY

The Baha'is claim that Baha'u'llah is the fulfillment of the biblical prophecies of the return of Christ.[1] Taken literally, of course, the biblical prophecies of Christ's return do not fit Bahau'llah. The Bible speaks of Jesus Himself returning in the skies before the entire world in a cataclysmic fashion to judge the living and the dead (e.g., Matt. 24). By contrast, Baha'is recognized as the "Christ" another person (Baha'u'llah) who came into the world in relative obscurity through natural means (i.e., conception and birth).[2]

How, then, can the Baha'is claim that Baha'u'llah fulfills the biblical prophecies of Christ's return? They can do this only by insisting that the literal meaning is to be ignored. According to

---

[1] See Abdu'l-Baha, 110-112

[2] Esslemont, 214

Baha'i doctrine, Jesus' description of His Second Coming in the Bible should be understood spiritually rather than literally. That is, the text of the Bible is said to have some symbolic meaning, which is contrary to the ordinary meaning of the words used.

BAHA'IS AND RELIGIOUS UNITY

The Baha'i argument against Christianity that Francis Beckworth address is the claim that Baha'ism must be God's true religion for the age because, unlike Christianity, lit has not suffered any schisms. One Baha'i writer takes this so far as to proclaim boldly that "there are not Baha'i sects. "There never can be."[3]

There are two problems with this argument: (1) It rests on a false premise -Baha'ism has in fact suffered divisions. (2) The conclusion does not follow — an undivided religion is not necessarily the true religion.

DIVISION IN BAHA'ISM

First, the fact is that Baha'ism has suffered several divisions, from its early days to the present. One group, known as the Free Baha'i has published a book denouncing Shoghi Effendl (who took over leadership of the Baha'is World Faith after Baba'u'llah's son Abdu'l-Baha died).[4] Another group, the Orthodox Baha'i Faith, was formed after Shoghl Effendi died, and recognizes Jason Remey as Effendi's successor.[5] Yet another group, Baha'i Under the Provision of the Covenant (BUPC), is

[3]Davis Hoffman, The Renewal of Civilization, Talishman Books (London: George Ronald, 1960),110

[4]Herman Zimmer, A Fraudulent Testament Devalues the Bahai Religion in the Bahai Religion into Political Shoghism, Trans. Jeannine Blackwell, rel. Karen Gasser and Gordon Campbell (Waliblinger/ Stuttgart: World Union For Universal Religion and Universal Peace-Free Bahais 1973).

[5]Vernon Elvin Johnson, An Historical Analysis of Critical Transformations in the Evolution of the Bahai World Faith (Ann Arbor, MI: University Microfilms, 1974), 362-80

led by Montana chiropractor Dr. Leland Jensen. Though it has "Baha'i" in its name, it is not endorsed or recognized by the main body "as a legitimate Baha'i organization."[6] As Vernon Elvin Johnson concludes, in his Baylor University dissertation, on the history of Baha'ism, obvious schism has occurred in the Baha'i religion, for various factions each claiming to belong to the Baha'i religion have existed in the course of the faith's history.[7]

Some Baha'is may be tempted to counter that anyone who breaks off from the Baha'i World Faith is automatically not a Baha'i and therefore no schism has really occurred. Such an argument is circular in nature and commits what Antony Flew calls the "no-true-Scotsman" fallacy ("No Scotsman would do such a thing. Well, no *true* Scotsman would."[8] Johnson points out, the Catholic and Mormon churches have used similar reasoning to defend their claim to be the one true church[9] (although the Catholic Church no longer tends to take such an exclusive stance).

DIVISION AND TRUTH

Second, it simply does not follow that a religion that is undivided must be the true religion, or that a religion that is divided cannot be the true religion. For the Baha'i argument to be persuasive it must be shown, and not simply assumed, that the true religion must be unified organizationally. This is not a biblical teaching: unity of the faith is presented in the Bible as a goal for the church to reach, not a *prerequisite* for the church to be Gods people (Eph. 4:11-16).

Since on independent grounds we know that Christianity is true, (for example, the evidence for the bodily resurrection of

---

[6]Joel Bjorling, "Leland Jensen: The Prophet Who Cried Wolf," Understanding Cults and Spiritual Movements 1,3 (1985):
[7]Johnson, 410
[8]Anthony Flew, Thinking Straight (Buffalo, NY: Promethens Books, 1975) 47
[9]Johnson, 412

Jesus[10], which Baha'is deny[11], we may justifiably conclude that organizational unity is not a requirement for a religion to be true. The argument can be stated more formally as follows:

1. Either the true religion is unified or it is not.
2. Christianity is the true religion and it is not unified.
3. Therefore, the true religion is not unified.

The truth of Christianity is independent of whether its adherents congregate under the same organizational banner. Its truth depends rather on the truth of the Bible's teachings concerning the person, life, death, and resurrection of Jesus Christ. This is not to deny that Christians have an obligation to exhibit unity and love as a testimony to the world of the truth of Jesus Christ (John 13:34-35; 17:21-23). To our shame we confess that although *Christianity* is true, *Christians* have not always been true to Christ. Nevertheless, this does not alter the fact that Jesus Christ is the only Savior from sin and God's last word to man prior to the consummation of history (John 14:6; Acts 4:12; Heb. 1: 1-3; 13:8). On this basis Christianity stands vindicated as true and Baha'ism stands condemned as a rejection of God's truth as revealed in Jesus Christ.

HOW BAHA'IS VIEW OTHER RELIGIONS

When Baha'is say that the various religions are one, they do not mean that the various religious creeds and organizations are the same. Rather, they believe that there is only one religion and all of the Messengers of God have progressively revealed its nature. Together, the world's great religions are expressions of a single unfolding Divine plan, "the changeless Faith of God, eternal in the past, eternal in the future."

---

[10]On the evidence for the resurrection, see especially William Lane Craig, Knowing the Truth About the Resurrection (Ann Arbor, MI: Servant Publications, 1981, and Gary Habermas, The Resurrection of Jesus: An Apologetic (Grand Rapids: Baker Book House, 1980).

[11]See Beckwith, Bahai, 14, 25-26

People from all of the major religious backgrounds have found that the promises and expectations of their own beliefs are fulfilled in the Baha'i Faith. Baha'i teachings fulfillment of prophetic visions.

For *Baha'is of Jewish background*, Baha'u'llah is the appearance of the promised "Lord of Hosts" come down "with ten thousands of saints." A descendent of Abraham and a "scion from the root of Jesse," Baha'u'llah has come to lead the way for nations to "beat their swords into plowshares." Many features of Baha'u'llah's involuntary exile to the Land of Israel, along with other historical events during Baha'u'llah's life and since are seen as fulfilling numerous prophecies in the Bible.

For *Baha'is of Buddhist background*, Baha'u'llah fulfills the prophecies for the coming of "a Buddha named Maitreye, the Buddha of universal fellowship" who will, according to Buddhist traditions, bring peace and enlightenment for all humanity. They see the fulfillment of numerous prophecies, such as the fact that the Buddha Maitreye is to come from "the West", noting the fact that Iran is west of India.

For *Baha'is of Hindu background*, Baha'u'llah comes as the new incarnation of Krishna, the "Tenth Avatar" and the "Most Great Spirit." He is "the birthless, the deathless" the One who, "when goodness grows weak," returns "in every age" to "establish righteousness" as promised in the Bhagavad-Gita.

For *Baha'is of Christian background*, Bahau'llah fulfills the paradoxical promises of Christ's return "in the Glory of the Father" and as a "thief in the night." That the Faith was founded in 1844 relates to numerous Christian prophecies. Baha'is note, for example, that central Africa was finally opened to Christianity in 1840's, and that event was widely seen as fulfilling the promise that Christ would return after "the Gospel had been preached "to all nations." In Baha'u'llah teachings Baha'is see fulfillment of Christ's promise to bring all people together so that "there shall be one fold, and one shepherd."

For *Baha'is of Muslim background*, Baha'u'llah fulfills the promise of the Qur'an for the "Day of God" and the "Great -Announcement," when "God" will come down "overshadowed with clouds." They see in the dramatic events of the Babi and

Baha'is a movement the fulfillment of many traditional statements of Muhammad, which has long been a puzzle.

Permission granted for: "Christian Research Journal," The Baha'is 1994: 17-19

AN APPRAISAL OF THE BAHA'I FAITH

DOCTRINAL EMPHASIS

1. The oneness of the world of humanity.
2. Independent investigation of the truth.
3. The foundation of all the religions is one.
4. Religion must be in accord with science and ream
5. Equality between men and women.
6. Prejudices of all kind must be forgotten.
7. Universal peace.
8. Universal education.
9. Solution of the education problem.
10. United States of the World

Many of these ideas are so general or so universally accepted that they scarcely require comment. One can believe in the Oneness of Humanity if one believes in Paul's words in Acts 17:26 that God "hath made of one blood all nations of men for to dwell on all the face of the earth." Of course, among all people this is easier to accept in theory than it is to put into practice. "The independent investigation of truth" can well be accepted by Christians as long as it does not imply there is no final revelation of truth. Christians are to "prove all things," but they also believe that only as we continue in Jesus' word are we His disciples in deed so that we can thus know the truth.

That *"the foundation of all religion is one"* is open to question. That there is one God only to whom all men inspire a nd by whom they are created is true. But that the foundation of Hinduism in it literature, the foundation of Islam in the Koran, or the foundation of Buddhism in the teaching of Gautama, are all "one" is difficult to believe. Future, as far as Christianity is concerned, the Apostle Paul testifies, "Other foundation can no man lay than that is laid, which is Jesus Christ" (I Corinthians 3: 11).

That *"religion must be the cause of unity"* is a statement, which fits in with the eclectic ideas of the Baha'i group. They want to make a synthesis of all the religions of the world. The directions of the founders of Baha'i are to be held as a kind of frosting to a cake of faith concocted from mixing all the different religions of the world. This is precisely where Christianity has always been different. The Roman Empire was the site of a great religious amalgamation .The religions of the entire world were accepted with broadminded acclaim, and Isis, Mithra, and Cybele were alike, worshipped along with the Roman Caesars. It was Christianity, which refused to be amalgamated.

From the days when Paul and Silas refused to be worshipped as Greek gods and when Christianity refused to become a reformed Judaism, this insistence on the uniqueness of Jesus as Christ and of His way as the one way to God has led to disunity among men where He has not been accepted. It is God's purpose to bring together all things *in Christ* and not to make Him only one in a religious melting pot.

That *"religion must be in accord with science and reason"* is a worthy ambition. But it would be better to say that true religion is in accord with true science and right reason. This idea that religion "must be in accord" with reason can lend it self to an adjustment of religion to whatever theories may be current among contemporary scientists and philosophers. This, indeed, is what Baha'i people do. "Where in the Holy Books they speak of raising the dead, the meaning is that the dead were blessed with eternal life; where it is said that the blind received sight, the signification is that he obtained the true perception."

"Equality between men and women" is an admirable ideal and is taught in the New Testament. That is, men and women have equal access to God and God loves men and women equally. All alike are the objects of the redemption of Christ and are alike admitted to His church on the same basis. But there are *differences* between men and women which give rise to the Biblical teaching of man's headship over her and of the necessity of feminine submission to masculine leadership in the church and in other areas of life. This does not mean men are better than women, but only that they have a different responsibility and function.

That *"Prejudice should be forgotten"* all could agree is an admirable aim. However, so deep-seated are some of these feelings that only the power of the redeeming Lord can effectively root them out of human lives, Here it is that conversion becomes necessary — a turning to God through Jesus. On the whole topic of sin and salvation, the Babai cause says very little. It aims at assimilation the taught, not at saving the lost.

The longing for universal peace and education is admirable and Christians are doing much through the spread of Christian truth, through missions, and through establishing schools in many dark areas of earth to overcome ignorance, Dr. Frank Laubauch, the "missionary to illiterates," has probably done more to life the blight of illiteracy from the world than all the Baha'i people put together. That the "economic problem" — whatever Abdul Baha had in mind by that vague statement — needs to be solved also is certainly true. The unity and good will that true faith in Christ brings men and help here.

The need for an auxiliary language and for some type of world government come under the heading of political and educational questions more than those that are religious do. Yet it is true that Christians find themselves speaking a universal language of love and devotion, whatever their nationality, when they cnter their thoughts upon Christ.

Permission granted for: "Christian Research Journal," The Baha'is 1994: 17-19

AFRICAN AMERICANS' ATTRACTION TO THE BAHA'I FAITH — AN INDEPENDENT RELIGION

AN APPRAISAL
BY JAMES G. VAN BUREN

The Baha'is emphasize certain great ideals such as world peace, world education, and world brotherhood. Their stress on the equality of men and women and of the various races contains much that is salutary. We may also agree that an attitude of conciliation or sympathy for those of divergent religious faiths ought to be cultivated more than it is. We can learn from others certain ways of looking at reality that will be valuable to us. In an age or rampant materialism those who stand up for the supremacy of spiritual values are, in part at least, fighting our battles for us.

On the other hand, the evangelical Christian cannot agree that Christianity is adequately represented because Jesus is given a place. In the New Testament view He must. be given first place. He is not just a Savior, but the Savior; not a "manifestation of God," but the only begotten of the Father. His is the only name given among men in which there is salvation. On this point Christians are firm, intolerant, unmoving. At the name of Jesus every knee shall bow and He alone has salvation, for there is none in any other.

The Baha'is say little about sin, because they do not exalt the worlds Savior from sin they do not exalt the Christian Scriptures for they testify of Him. They do not believe in the Christian ordinances and do not baptize people into Christ or remember Him in the Lord's Supper. It is, really, a variant of Persian Mohammedanism with a mixture of general religious and idealistic philosophy plastered over the outside. Several of the groups we have discussed are really variants or offshoots of authentic Christianity, but this is not true of the Baha'i cause. One of the observances of the Baha'is is the "Feast of Rizwan," a twelve-day festival which commemorates the twelve days

Baha-O-Llah spent in the Garden of Rizwan before his departure form Badgered in 1863. It celebrates the changing of the center of allegiance from The Bab to Baha-0-Llah and the shifting of the focus of the faith from a concentration on the reform of Islam to the idea of "World Reformation.[12]

We insist as Christians, on the primacy of Christ and must reject every effort to fuse His truth, in its unique testimony to Him, into a synthesis with other faiths. Yet we must not overlook the fact that many of His followers have not sufficiently carried out the implications and clear 'instructions of His Word in its relation to many human affairs and human institutions. We must know the mind of Christ and must also do all we can to let that mind be known in all the affairs of men. We must follow the apostle Paul in his effort at evangelism, "Casting down imaginations, and ever high thing that exalteth itself against the knowledge of God, and bringing into captivity every thought to the obedience of Christ" (2 Corinthians 10:5)

---

[12]Permission granted for reprint by The Standard Publishing Company, 8121 Hamilton Ave., Cincinnati, Ohio. 45204. CULTS CHALLENGE THE CHURCH, pg.99-100.By: James G. Van Buren

Why African American Youth Are Attracted To The Nation of Islam

Why African American Youth Are Attracted to the Nation of Islam

1. Their position against racism.

2. Group solidarity.

3. Their concern for the plight of Black Americans.

4. Failture of the Christian Church.

5. Redefinition of the roles of men and women.

6. Economic power.

7. Social programs: a) Jail and prison ministries. b) Offer to care for their own. c) Establishment of community owned businesses. d) Offers good security. e) Work together to clean up slums and ghettos. f) Great health care message. Demand strong discipline g) moral standards. h) Encourage strong family structure. i) Provide mentorship programs for African American youth, male and female. j) Emphasis on the building of self-esteem among African American youth.

"THE NATION OF ISLAM IN AMERICA" BY DR. JERRY L. BUCKNER

This article is about one of the most rapidly growing non-Christian black cults in America. It used to be known as Black Muslims, but today it is known as the Nation of Islam. The Nation of Islam is a serious threat to society, because they are challenging the church on every essential teaching in the Bible. We cannot, as the Body of Christ just sit back and let this go on as if they were a bad dream that would go away. There are black people, black Christians, and even black pastors who support the Nation of Islam, because they feel they are a voice in defense of their rights regarding racism. Also many of them feel Farrakhan has a way of boosting the morality in young black youths. If these people understood the Nation of Islam movement, they wouldn't feel this way.

Let me say something about the history of the movement — how it began, who the main leaders have been, and how it has grown. The Nation of Islam began in the ghettos of Detroit in 1930 with its founder Wallace Dodd Fard. He appealed to the illiterate, unskilled, and poor blacks that were struggling as new urbanites of Detroit. He masterfully appealed to them about proper living, civil rights, and racism. He sought to give them African identity. He urged them to give up their birth names, and to adopt African names, but Muslim names such as Mohammed.

Wallace D. Fard's mission was to educate people in the West to the truth about the white man and to prepare them for Armageddon. He went door-to-door with Watchtower literature tearing down his follower's faith in Jesus Christ. Then he used the Koran to get them away from the Bible. Then he spoke of Muhammad to get away from Jesus. Fard conditioned the poor blacks to not look for a Savior who would save them from their sins, but look for a black savior who would save them from their poverty here and now. Very little is known about Wallace Fard. All we know for sure from photos taken of him at the Detroit Police Department is that he was a white man who claimed to be of Turkish origins. A lot of people don't know this, even those caught in the web of deception don't know that the Orthodox Islam and the Black Islam were both started by a white man. It's equally interesting that the Nation of Islam today is following a man, whom like in the days of slavery, they call "Master Farad Muhammad". So when they say, "Christianity is the white man's religion", that's not true. Orthodox Islam and Black Islam are really the white man's religion, because the founders were both whites.

Wallace D. Fard mysteriously disappeared in 1934. After Fard's disappearance, Elijah Muhammad became the leader of the black cult and assumed the title "the Messenger of Allah" until his death on February 25, 1975 in Chicago. He was 77 years old. Wallace D. Fard influenced Elijah Muhammad, who influenced Malcolm X, who influenced Louis Farrakhan. And shortly after Malcolm X was murdered by some members of the Nation of Islam. Elijah Muhammad had appointed Louis Farrakhan as the national spokesman for the Black Muslims. After his death, Elijah Muhammad's son, Wallace D. Muhammad took over the movement and changed many of the Black Muslim doctrines. As a result, Farrakhan became disenchanted along with others and went out on his own to form the Nation of Islam group. He rebuilt it with old racist teachings that their original leader had laid down.

Why are there so many blacks attracted to the Nation of Islam, especially black males? No one can argue the fact that the members of the Nation of Islam are doing some good things in the community. They have always had good <u>social</u> programs, for example, in the jails and prison ministries. They offer the black community helps to build their own businesses. They emphasize to the black community to not wait on government to do everything, especially in the area of welfare. They offer to care for their own. They offer good security. They work together to clean up the slums and ghettoes.

The Black Muslims have a great <u>health care</u> message. They emphasize eating better, no smoking, no drinking, and no drugs. They offer a better lifestyle. They demand strong disciplined lives in terms of Moral standards. They demand that each man have a clean-cut look and image. You never hear about adultery, fornication or profanity within the Nation of Islam movement.

They emphasize strong family structure. They emphasize mentorship programs for black youths — male and female. They teach them the true meaning of being a man and a woman. They emphasize the building of self-esteem among black youths. They teach them knowledge of self.

There are other major reasons why so many black males are attracted to the Nation of Islam. When you look at the black church composition today, what is the percentage of black men in the black church today? It's a very low percentage. The black church is composed primarily of black women. The black pastors often have a very hard time relating to the younger generation. He is often far removed and not easily accessible to the black youth in the black community. So what do these black youths do? They end up in the Black Muslim mosque. What do they see when they go into the mosque? They see black males who are willing to be black mentors to young black youths, many of whom don't have fathers in the homes. These young black males need a black male image role model.

What are some of the Nation of Islam's beliefs regarding basic theological truths? They don't accept the Trinity, Deity of Christ, the virgin birth, the Atonement for our sins, or His bodily resurrection from the dead.

They believe that Master Fard Muhammad is Allah, or God manifested in the flesh. They believe that the black man is the original creation. They maintain that Allah or God did not create the white man. Instead a black scientist, an evil genius called "Yakub" created the white man and was expelled from paradise for it. The Nation of Islam believes in 24 black gods known as scientists who existed before Fard. They teach that their followers are black gods. They teach that the Allah the Black Muslims believe in is radically different from the Allah of Islam. The Nation of Islam believes like the Mormons that God is just a mere man of flesh and blood. Farrakhan teaches that Allah is no uncreated, immaterial or invisible in the sense of being a Spirit.

Wallace D. Fard, founder of the Nation of Islam, drew upon the Quran, the Bible, Free Masonry, Marcus Garveyism, Moorism, and literature of Jehovah's Witnesses to deceive people doctrinally towards their faith in the Bible. Elijah Muhammad taught his followers unknowingly to fight white racism with black racism.

What are some effective ways to communicate the gospel with those who are members of the Nation of Islam? The best way to communicate the gospel is by Scripture. What good is it to do all of these good external things and be internally lost? What good are all of these things, if you don't know the Jesus of historic Christianity? Ephesians 2:8-9 talks about no being "saved by works, but by grace through faith". Jesus said to the Pharisees in Matthew 23:28, "Even so ye also outwardly appear righteous unto men, but within ye are full of hypocrisy and iniquity". A lot of people are sincere, but sincerely wrong. The Nation of Islam regarding the issue of self-esteem or self-knowledge fools many. The Gnostics were more into a knowledge of self that a knowledge of God. Jesus taught us to deny self rather than elevate self. The Apostle Paul warned Timothy that some are "Ever learning and never able to come to the knowledge of the truth", 11 Timothy 3:7. The Black Muslims teach their followers that they are the first black race, black gods, descendants from the tribe of Shabbazz, and by nature righteous. But true self knowledge and true self esteem is personal freedom in Jesus Christ, and when He sets you free, you're free indeed. The basis of our true human dignity is not found in our kin color, but in the fact that we are all created equally in the image of God.

The Nation of Islam is not monotheistic, but polytheistic. The God of the Bible condemns polytheism. He warns us throughout the Bible about strange gods. Isaiah 43:10 says, "Ye are my witnesses, saith the Lord, and my servant whom I have chosen: that ye may know and believe me, and understand that I am he: before me there was no God formed, neither shall there be after me."

No one in the Nation of Islam will make it to Godhead. I Timothy 2:5 says, "For there is one God, and one mediator between God and men, the man Christ Jesus." This concept that you can become a god didn't start with the Nation of Islam. It all started in the Garden of Eden when Satan deceived our fore-parents into believing a lie that they could become a god by eating of the fruit from the forbidden tree. The Nation of Islam has fallen into the trap of self-righteousness that the Bible condemns. Roman 3:10 says "As it is written, There is none

116

righteous, no not one." Martin Luther, the Reformations father once said, "We aren't saved by works, but by a faith that works." Christianity is not doing religion; it's a done religion in Christ. Jesus said on the cross, "It's finished."

Now what can the black church do to counteract this black cult?

1. Have classes, workshops and seminars teaching the truth about what the Nation of Islam is all about.
2. Bring in the experts — the Church needs to remember that we have a greater power and authority that the Nation of Islam. Revival will happen if we are not only hearers of the Word, But doers of the Word also.

In terms of the white church, I have to address the white church, because the Nation of Islam focuses most of their attention on what the white man has done. One of the biggest reasons why the Nation of Islam has grown is because of white racism. It's crucial that the white church join hands with the black church to fight racism in the urban cities. The white church has been weak in this area. The Nation of Islam has been successful because they have addressed the issues of racism in our communities. Although their approach is not correct, it has helped them to gain new membership. The white church can't afford to just deal with theology, hermeneutics, missions — home and foreign, and baptism. The white church can't afford to just deal with the issues of homosexuality, abortion, abstinence before marriage, prayer in schools, and other various political issues of our day. White churches must balance these things out. They must address the issues of racism in the black community and nationwide. The white church must come over and learn from the black church about practical Christianity. The Church must come together — not the black church, white church, brown church or yellow church, but the Church of Jesus Christ must come together to not only work together in Christ, but to lead the way in evangelizing those in the Nation of Islam.

Permission granted for reprint by Dr. Jerry L. Buckner. Graduate of Golden Gate Baptist Theological Seminary. He is pastor of the Tiburon Christian Fellowship and is a lecturer, counselor and consultant.

117

AFRICAN AMERICAN ATTRACTION TO THE NATION OF ISLAM A NON-CHRISTIAN RELIGION

WHO IS THE NATION OF ISLAM?

The Black Muslims are an off brand sect of Islam which was founded by Elijah Muhammad. It was never an overwhelming popular sect until elevated to such a position by Malcolm, X who made the Muslims respectable in the black community. Since the death of its founder, Elijah Muhammad, and under the present leadership of Louis Farrakhan, the Black Muslims have undergone tremendous change.

Most simply, a Black Muslim is an African American who is a follower of Elijah Muhammad; "Spiritual Leader of the lost-found Nation 'in the West."

Black Muslims are distinguished from Orthodox Moslems not in the spelling of the word (strictly speaking, either form is correct) but in their belief that their leader, the Elijah Muhammad, is the messenger of Allah directly commissioned by Allah himself who came in person (under the name of Fard) to wake the sleeping Black Nation and rid them of the whites' age old domination.

Nation of Islam Leader Louis Farrakhan called for the Million-Man March to take place in Washington, D.C., on October 16, 1995, and black men across America responded.

The response was so enthusiastic that not even the march on Washington by the late Dr. Martin Luther King, Jr., surpassed the crowds that Farrakhan was able to bring together. Why was the Million-Man March so effective? Many saw it as a way the black community could stand together. Moreover, it encouraged black males to stand up and be men in their homes and communities.

The official membership of the nation of Islam has been estimated to be between 19,000 and 30,000. Others say they have 60,000 across America. Whatever the case, they have far more influence than their numbers would indicate, as the Million-Man March demonstrated.

The Nation of Islam represents a serious threat to the Christian community. The growing presence of the Nation of Islam and their attacks on essential Christian doctrines make it difficult to continue ignoring them. The black church must awake to the challenge. There have been two problems the black church has faced 'in rising to this challenge: (1) the lack of evangelism 'in fulfilling its role to the community and (2) the lack of biblical discipleship for church members.

Meanwhile, members of the Nation of Islam have proven themselves to be highly motivated and successful in their outreach efforts in the community. Not only are they encouraging young black males to join the Nation of Islam, but they are also recruiting them from our churches. In addition they have a strong presence in the jails and prisons. This was how Malcolm X and Mike Tyson were recruited. They are out in the community and on the streets training young black males in their peculiar version of Islam. Should we be afraid of the Islamic threat? No, but we should embrace this opportunity to sharpen our beliefs and strengthen our witness.

WITNESSING TO THE NATION OF ISLAM

The success of the Nation of Islam is not so much due to what the Nation of Islamic, doing but to what the church has failed to do. African American Christians and white Christians have different responsibilities in witnessing to the Nation of Islam. Much can be learned from the Nation of Islam itself. If the church can learn the things that attract people to the Nation of Islam, then they will be better able to witness to those in the group. The success of the Nation of Islam isn't so much due to what they are doing but to what the church has failed to do.

The Responsibility of Black Churches. The black church today has been passive and impotent addressing racism as a sin. The church must address racism in the black community; if this is not done, then black youths will be lost to the Nation of Islam. The reason why the Nation of Islam is extremely appealing to black men is because they address white racism and have a leader, Louis Farrakhan, who boldly defends black racism. The church must address these issues.

119

The church must develop a strong presence not only in the black community but also in the jails and prisons — especially ministering to young black men. Jesus warned, "I *was a stranger and you did not invite me in, I needed clothes and you did not clothe me, I was sick and in prison and you did not look after me" (Matt. 25:43, NIV).*

The church must develop economic empowerment programs for the community. The Nation of Islam has a strong economic base and is very good at providing for the have-nots in our society. They have designed a system of economic education and empowerment for the black community. The church can do more than the Nation of Islam in this area, if Christians all work together. The church can develop economic education programs that will have a dynamic effect on the black community.

The church needs to be involved in the communities and clean them up. The Nation of Islam emphasizes eating better, avoiding drugs, alcohol, and smoking. They work oil cleaning up the ghettos and slums by getting rid of drug pushers, prostitutes, and other negative elements in the community. The church can also do these things and more.

The Nation of Islam emphasizes a strong family structure — including fatherhood and black manhood. The church needs to provide mentorship and strong surrogate fatherhood to young black men who are without a good male role model. The church can have Christian black males work with young black males in the community in the areas of developing friendships, providing information, or obtaining jobs while helping them with horsing and assisting with their educational activities or endeavors. The church needs to have more youth activities. Much can be done to get youth in the community excited about Christian activities.

The Responsibility of White Churches. It is very difficult for white Christians to approach members of the Nation of Islam in an evangelistic way. This is true because of all of the racism that has taken place. As a reaction to white racism, black racism took form. The Nation of Islam emergence was a direct response to racism. Nevertheless, even though it is difficult to approach a member of the Nation of Islam, there are things white Christians can do.

White Christians need to take an aggressive stance against racism in America. They need to join hands with the black church to fight against any form of racism, because it is a sin. They need to strategically join together in an evangelistic reconciliation, a Christlike endeavor, in order to break down the barriers of racism. They need to worship together -a black church coming together with a white church, even exchanging pulpits. They can join hands as co-laborers to reach people in the inner cities. The white pastor can preach sermons from the pulpit against racism. Every person who come to the local church must be received with open arms, no matter what color he or she is.

The white church needs to work with the black church in developing partnerships around mentorship and surrogate fatherhood to black males in the urban cities. One pilot project in Houston serves as an example of successful mentorship. Several white suburban churches joined some urban black churches in an effort to do something about crime in the black community. Their ideas were indirect correlation to the fact that most crimes in the black community was committed by young black males who lacked a positive male role model in their lives. The churches provided substitute fathers for many of the fatherless black youths in the city. Results were astounding. Crimes committed by blacks, especially black youths, dropped dramatically. Having a father image made a significant impact upon these black youths. One thing is certain: We need to develop an agenda for reaching the black community.

Don'ts of Witnessing to the Nation of Islam. Don't try to convince them to get saved through your own strength. Trust the Holy Spirit to convince them to believe in Jesus. If God could save the apostle Paul, He can also save Louis Farrakhan and members of the Nation of Islam.

Don't become hostile with the members of the Nation of Islam. They are not enemies to be conquered. They are fellow human beings for whom Christ died on the cross.

Don't overwhelm them with Scripture. They will not listen if they are overwhelmed.

Don't use a King James Bible because, according to some Muslims, King James himself translated this version and corrupted it. I recommend using the New International Version of the New American Standard Version in witnessing to them. Don't use a Bible in which you have written notes or made marks. This indicates disrespect for the Word of God to members of the Nation of Islam.

Avoid all pictures of God, Jesus, or other biblical personalities as white with blue eyes and blond hair.

Don't use the word "Trinity" because this word often connotes the worship of three gods to the Nation of Islam. You can let them know from the Scriptures that God is indeed one Being, and this one Being exists eternally as Father, Son, and Holy Spirit — three persons.

In dealing with the members of the Nation of Islam, remove all offenses except the cross. They view Christian symbols as offensive.

Do's of Witnessing to the Nation of Islam. Remember your greatest weapon in witnessing is prayer. This is true when witnessing to any cultic group.

Learn to demonstrate love and patience when witnessing. "By this all men will know that you are my disciples, if you love one another." *(John 13:35, NIV).*

Know what you believe and why you believe it regarding the essentials of the historic Christian faith before you even begin witnessing. Know the original even before beginning to attempt to learn about the counterfeit.

All Muslim groups are different. Know which Black Muslim group you are witnessing to. Share the uniqueness of Jesus Christ as God manifested in the flesh with the Nation of Islam members. Jesus said, "I am the way, and the truth, and the life: No one comes to the Father except through me" *(John 14:6, NIV).* Remind those in the Nation of Islam that according to the Koran, "No true prophet of God can lie." If that's true, since they believe that Jesus is a prophet of God, then Jesus told the truth about being the only truth and way to God.

Left the Nation of Islam members know that true righteousness doesn't come through man's so-called righteousness, but through the righteousness of Christ's perfect life imputed as a free gift to those who believe.

Elijah Muhammad told his followers, "The greatest hindrance to the truth of our people [members of the Nation of Islam] is the preacher of Christianity.[1] My message to you is, keep on being a hindrance and telling them what is right. Be encouraged! There are many who have come out of the Nation of Islam to become strong Christians in the church.

Permission granted by Christian Research Institute International. P.O. Box 550, San Juan, Capistrano, CA. 92693. Article by: Dr. Jerry L. Buckner. He is a pastor, counselor, lecturer, and the host of Contending for the Faith radio broadcast on KFAX AM 1100 in the San Francisco Bay Area.

WITNESSING TO MUSLIMS

Because of the long history between Christians and Muslims, the Muslim views the Christian witness with great animosity. The roots of this tragedy go back to the Emperor Constantine who after allegedly having had a dream of the cross (313) wed the sword to the cross.

One of his successors, the Christian Emperor Herachus (reigned 610-641) was a contemporary of Muhammad (reigned 622-632). From Herachu's example, Muhammad learned well the concept of "Holy War" (jihad). Following Muhammad's death (632), Muslim armies swept the Christian Byzantines out of Syria, Palestine, and Egypt (636). Christians and Muslims have been at war with one another ever since.

Leaving aside the questions of Muslim atrocities against Christians of both the East and the West let me review the grievances of Muslims against the West, perceived as Christian. The Crusades (around 1050-1291) are painfully and permanently inscribed in Muslim memories. The Colonial Period (around 1450-1970), during which Western nations occupied about ninety percent of the Muslim world, has left the Muslim psyche with a deep sense of shame and humiliation that needs to be avenged.

---

[1] Muhammed, Message, 18.

But above all else, the loss of Jerusalem to the Jews in 1967, after more than thirteen hundred years of possession, rankles daily in Muslim minds. This, of course, is blamed on the "Christian" West because of the creation of the state of Israel in 1948 — perceived as the greatest sin ever committed against humanity.

We need to remember, when seeking to witness to Muslims, that we are working in an atmosphere poisoned by the memories of these and more recent (e.g., the U.S.'s two invasions of Lebanon) Muslim, casualties. It is only by the grace of God that we have as much opportunity as we do to working with Muslims. If we exhibit any form of cultural superiority, religious triumphalism, or selective amnesia concerns the sins of the West. perceived as Christian, we only make matters worse. More to the point, the denigration of Islam as a religion or slurs against its founder, Muhammad will not be tolerated. Working with Muslims calls for an especially sensitive approach. Thus, although I will address apologetic issues later in this series, it is first of all important for Christians to know something about how to approach Muslims.

In orthodox Islam, God has supposedly not spoken to a single human being since the year Muhammad died (632). For this reason, giving your own testimony of how you became a Christian — of how God revealed Himself to you — takes Muslims by surprise. This is a thoroughly biblical approach (I John 1:3). And there is no argument against a testimony.

Muslims are usually genuinely seeking to please God (as they understand him). They can be complimented, for example, on their practices of confessing God, praying five times daily, giving to the poor, keeping a month-long fast, perceiving themselves as pilgrims, and even striving (jihada) on the "way of God." Similar points of contact can be found in their belief system concerning God, prophets, holy books, angels and demons, the decree of God, and the Day of Judgment. Of course, on each subject there are points of variance between Islamic and Christian doctrine, but the point is to find a common starting place.

One will find that each subject can always be related to the teaching of the Lord Jesus and the apostles and other Scriptures. The Quran bears surprising witness to Jesus. It affirms His virgin birth, His ability to heal and raise the dead, that He is both a word from God and a spirit from God, that He is the Messiah, an all-righteous one (sinless), among those nearest to God, that He is alive in heaven now and win return to judge the earth (Quran 3:45, 49; 4:158; 82:22). Muslims often are convinced that Christ is greater than Muhammad from just reading the Quran. These above points are excellent starting places in leading Muslims to biblical truth about Jesus.

Indeed, in our effort to bring Muslims to study the Bible, we have an unexpected ally in Muhammad's book, the Quran. In a careful reading of Quranic references (3:84; 5:51, 7 1; 6:34; 10:37, 64, 94: 46:12) we find that Muhammad affirmed his belief in what was revealed to Moses and Jesus. He taught that God confirms and guards all previous scripture, that Christians are to stand fast on their own books of the Law and the Gospel, and that none could change the Word of God. Finally, the Muslim is told that if he has doubts he should ask the Jews and Christians, who were reading the Holy Books, before he was.

If and when a Muslim begins to study Scripture, he (or she) is going to be under suspicion by his family and friends. He will need strong support and encouragement from a Christian friend. This support is even more critical at the time of conversion, baptism and post-baptismal trauma. One must be ready to die with his or her disciple (John 15:13).

Even before all of the above begins, the Christian worker would do well to find a way to minister to human need in the environment of the disciple. This could take the form of personal help, medical service, teaching, relief in times of disaster, and development of programs of any kind to improve the quality of life (Matt. 25:31-46).

Finally, we must realize that this work is not simply an intellectual exercise; it involves the supernatural work of the Holy Spirit. In utter dependence on Him, we receive the insights and ideas that grip the mind and heart of our Muslim friend. And similarly, the Holy Spirit works in our friend to give understanding, insight, and receptivity to the good news of Jesus Christ. This trust in the work of the Holy Spirit is something to be cultivated in prayer and faith by the Christian worker.

Islam has as many branches and sects as Christianity. The two major ones are the Sunnis and the Shias. They split over the issue of apostolic succession. When Islam's founder Muhammad died unexpectedly in A.D. 632, he had left no arrangement for a successor. His followers divided into two camps. The Sunnis were those who thought the leader should be elected democratically from among his close followers, and the Shias were those who thought the leaders should be related to Muhammad.

Perhaps 85 to 90 percent of all Muslims would call themselves Sumus. The word Sunni comes from the Arabic Sunnah, which simply means "the trodden path," or "tradition." In the Islamic context, it means someone who follows the exemplary pattern of conduct established by Muhammad, believed to be the model for all humankind.

Since Muhammad was just one solitary man, confined to a slice of time in seventh century Atabia, he could not foresee the problems Islam would face in its rapid expansion into other lands. His followers — who were imbued with Muhammad's obsession with law -had to devise new laws based on their understanding of what Muhammad would have done, if he had remained among them. This process took almost two hundred years and resulted in the formation of Islamic or Shairah Law.

A Sunni, then, is a person who believes that the true way of life is to attempt to keep the laws of Islam (Shariah) derived form the Quran and the other collected sayings of Muhammad. For this person, paradise is the reward of those whose good deeds outweigh their bad on the Day of Judgment. With such a Muslim believer, there are two evangelistic approaches that can be used: to show the futility of the idea of salvation by law, and to show the inadequacy of Muhammand's life as a model for all humankind. Both approaches ultimately lead to the person and work of Jesus Christ.

Muhammad, in his obsession to discover and execute the will of God, set in motion a movement that resulted in a wild proliferation of laws attempting to cover every facet of life. By borrowing from the Egyptians the idea that God would weight our good deeds against our bad deeds in a balance scale on the Day of

Judgment, he betrayed a lack of understanding of the function of law. The law does not save; it condemns.

Christians can begin by Complimenting the Muslim on his or her zeal to keep the law of God as he or she understands it, but then we must go on to show that the law has the ultimate function of showing us where we failed. As Paul wrote, "the letter [law] kills, but the Spirit gives life" (I Cor. 3:6). Our Muslim friends also need to be disabused of the idea that 51 percent performance is good enough to obtain salvation. Show them what James wrote: "For whoever keeps the whole law and yet stumbles at just one point is guilty of breaking all of it" (James 2: 10). To this could be added Paul's words in Romans 3:20, "Therefore no one win be declared righteous in his sight by observing the law; rather through the law we become conscious of sin," and in Galatians 3:24, "The law was put in charge to lead us to Christ that we might be justified by faith" (Gal. 3:24). This then leads on to a discussion about Christ. And this discussion can be based on materials from both the Quran and the Scriptures.

In Quran 7:158, Muhammad asked people to follow him. Elsewhere in the Quran, Muhammad testified that Jesus was among those nearest to God, held 'in honor in this world and the hereafter (Quran 3:45). Muslims understand this to mean that Jesus was sinless and all righteous, something that the early Muslims never claimed for Muhammad. In fact, in several Quranic passages (16:6 1; 40:5 5; 42:5, 3 0; 47:19; 48:1-2) we read that Muhammad was exhorted to seek forgiveness for his faults, that not a single living creature would be left on earth if God punished everyone for their wrong doing, and that one of Muhammad's military victories served as an assurance of forgiveness of his sins, past and future. It is pointless for Muslims to argue for Muhammad's senselessness or to compare him to Jesus, whom Muslims consider to be both sinless and alive in heaven, near to God night now. The contrast could be more sharply drawn by pointing out that Muhammad's grave is in Medina today, whereas Christ is alive in heaven with God.

In the Quran (2:253; 3:45-49; 4:158, 171; 5:49; 19:33; 89:22) it is noted that Jesus was called the Messiah; He was born of a virgin; He was among the righteous ones — those nearest to God;

He received strength from the Holy Spirit; He could give sight to the blind, cure lepers, and raise the dead; He prophesied His own death and resurrection; He was called a Word from God and a Spirit from God; and finally, He is coming back with thousands of angels to judge the world. All these characterizations adds up to a powerful picture of a Christ who was more than a prophet, and — on Quarnic terms alone — superior to Muhammad.

From this point on, it is up to the Christian witness to lead the Muslim friend into a study of biblical material on the person and nature of Christ. One suggestion would be to start with John 1: 1-14, where Jesus is set forth as the eternal Word of God, an ideal Muslims implicitly accept. Then go on to show the purpose of God for Him in coming a man to carry out the will of God in accomplishing the salvation of lost humankind, who would not be saved by the law, either Islamic or Mosaic.

Permission granted for reprint by Christian Research Institute International. P.O. Box 500, San Juan Capistrano, CA. 92693-0500.
Article appeared in the spring 1993 CHRISTIAN RESEARCH JOURNAL. Article by Don McCurry.

METHODS OF RECRUITMENT — NATION OF ISLAM

(Newspapers, Leaflets, Prison)

Methods of recruitment are through the Muslims weekly paper, The Final Call and by the passing of some leaflets around shopping centers, as well as attending the Mosque and certain Muslim activities. The Muslims have established some elementary and secondary schools. They even have a University in Chicago, their mother city. They own a string of bakeries, dry cleaners and cafes which cater to Muslim clientele. There is other Muslim enterprises in the community. In the earlier period, a favorite method of recruitment was in prisons. Muslim ministers would minister to and convert prisoners. They would get them to persuade others in the prison by passing out Muslim literature. In fact, Malcolm X was recruited in this way.

During Malcolm' s career as minister, the Muslims sought to convert the lower classes in the black ghetto of large cities and the malcontent middle classes. It offered itself as an alternative to Christianity. It appealed to the militancy of the malcontent. It offered itself to Blacks as a Black mates religion. The Muslims grew by leaps and bounds in the Black community. Its doctrine for Blacks as purported to be a doctrine of freedom from the oppression of the blond hair-blue eyed devil X and various combinations of X's were taken by many as last names, signifying the shedding of a slave name. The Muslims grew by putting Christianity down as an oppressive religion and by ranting against whites. The Muslims demanded a separate society. It demanded that its women wear a modified type of Arab dress. Its young men dressed neatly and conservatively. They stayed away from the Afro natural, which they thought was hygienically unhealthy, unsightly, and ungodly. The Muslims committed its members not to get entangled with credit but rather to save and become economically secure. The Koran became their Holy Book.

YOUNG MUSLIMS INTERVIEWED

The young Muslims whom I interviewed all seemed to have come from a middle class background. What sold them on the Muslims was the belief that his was a Black man's natural religion, which enabled them to find themselves and their true God. They especially believed in the Muslim rendition of family structuring. A father's duties, a mother's duties, and a child's duties were all spelled out in the Koran. These young Muslims felt that they were persons of worth. Their dress and neatness reflected their worth that they were Godly. They even accepted Christians and Christ as the Koran taught them that "God made people different so that they may come to know each other; not despise or hate the other." Jesus, according to the Koran is a Prophet — the Prophet of love and peace.

The Black Muslims offer these young people the chance to find their "roots" so to speak; the deep African heritage which has been barred to them through the study of Africa and the Arabic language. It affords them a sense of self and self-worth that is not afforded in the larger community where beauty, intelligence, and worth are defined in terms related to whiteness.

While not shunning the poor of the Black ghetto, it appears that since the Black Muslims have become respectable, they are more interested in attracting the middle class youth and developing his intellectual capacity. The Muslims have become quiet in tone and have shed much of their former racist position. They do not scream blond haired, blue eyed devil to the top of their lungs. They do not agitate in belligerent voices for a separate nation. They recruit mainly through their papers, meetings and affairs.

The Muslims give the young Blacks a chance to shape their self-images as Black men by affording an avenue whereby young Blacks may explore their past in depth. They benefit young Blacks by instilling in them a sense of self and of dignity. Their dietary laws and strict observance of hygienic standards raise the level of living and adds to the longevity of life. Their insistence upon becoming self-supporting and independent helps young Blacks to become more economically secure. Their stress on family harmony, unity, and responsibilities has contributed to the solidarity of the black family, with father as head of the family. The family as such is more secure and more stable. The Mosque provides for the spiritual needs of the individual. A person relates to his God, Allah and to his fellow man during services. An offspring of Judaism and younger sibling of Christianity, the Muslim sect does not veer too far away from Jewish or Christian ethics. In fact, the Muslims appear more Christian than they do Moslem, its supposed parent. The one difference is the position of Jesus. People recruited into the Muslim sect from Christian bodies are at home with their newly found religious expression as the Koran is a reflection of The Old Testament, though from a different perspective.

The Muslims have offered to young Blacks itself as an alternative to Christianity while remaining religious. It has given young Blacks an avenue for expression and has lent stability, security and dignity to his life. In turn, young Blacks who are recruited into the Black Muslims give of their time, effort and donations to the continuing survival and glory of the Black

Muslim sect as an important religious edifice in the Black community.

WHO ARE THE BLACK MUSLIMS?

The Black Muslims are an off brand sect of Islam which was founded by Elijah Muhammad. It was never an overwhelming popular sect until elevated to such a position by Malcolm X who made the Muslims respectable in the black community. Since the death of it founder, Elijah Muhammad, and under the present leadership of Louis Farrakhan, the Black Muslims have undergone tremendous change.

Most simply a Black Muslim is an African American who is a follower of Elijah Muhammad, Spiritual Leader of the lost-found Nation in the West."

Black Muslims are distinguished from Orthodox Moslems not in the spelling of the word (strictly speaking, either form is correct) but in their belief that their leader, the Elijah Muhammad, is the messenger of Allah directly commissioned by Allah himself who came in person (under the name of Fard) to wake the sleeping Black Nation and rid them of the whites' age old domination.[1]

The Nation of Islam, once more commonly known as the "Black Muslims" represent the principal concuit linking the religion founder by the prophet Muhammad in the sixth century to the sudden "presence" of Islam in America. This is not an argument of creed or theological verification.[2]

The very first Muslim to come to America were undoubtedly of African origin, whether we speak of the Spanish invasions or the slaves brought from Africa by the English planters beginning in the first quarter of the seventeenth century. Whatever the point of beginning, by 1777 the colonial was titillate by news of the arrival of a ship load of Africans "who ate no pork and spoke

---

[1]*The Black Man In America* by C. Eric Lincoln, Third Edition, Copyright 1914, Wm. P. Eerrdmans Publishing Co. 225 Jefferson Ave. S.E. Grand Rapids, Michigan 49503 pg. 20

[2]Ibid, p. 256

Arabic" among themselves. Possibly this marked the beginning of an indefinite period during which new sources of slaves were opened and Africans confessing Islam were forced into the rapidly expanding slavery. In any case, the report of "Moors living in South Carolina" in the last decade of the eighteenth century would seem to suggest that the Muslims' presence was by then fairly substantial and no longer considered phenomena.[3]

The open practice of Islam, like the practice of all indigenous African religions was forbidden in the slaves, of course, in the interest of security and management, Nevertheless, clandestine religious practices were inevitable and no doubt persisted as long as the hazards of performance and transmission would allow. Hence, it is inaccurate to date the African American involvement in Islam from conversations beginning in the twentieth century. The African Americans were here with Islam before the founding of the republic. Although the first expressions of their religion was prohibited and suppressed during three centuries of servitude, the fire of the faith was never stuffed out. It survived in legends and tales, in memories and anti-dotes , in unexplained urgencies challenging the terrible aridity of consciousness bracketing the endless centuries of servitude.[4]

Elijah Muhammad was born Elijah Poole in Sanderville, Georgia, in 1897, the son of an itinerant Baptist preacher. He and his family were swept up in the great black exodus from the South that followed the trails of opportunities leading North during the era off the First World War. In Detroit Poole became a disciple of Wallace Farad, who, like Noble Drew Ali, had taken on the task of rescuing the Lost-Found Nation through the teachings of Islam.[5]

Farad's doctrines were somewhat at variance with those of Ali, who died in 1925 before Farad began his ministry in Detroit. Yet the core message was essentially the same. *African Americans were Asiatic people of noble heritage whose degraded condition*

---

[3]Ibid. p. 257
[4]Ibid, p. 267
[5]Ibid, p. 268

America could only be rectified by knowing and practicing their true and natural religion.

Islam! Elijah found Farad's logic and his message so compelling that he attached himself to "the perfect" and became his most loyal and ardent disciple. By the time Fard moved on in 1934 to the obligations elsewhere, Elijah had been rewarded with the name "Muhammad." As the designate "Messenger of Allah," he received the mantle of leadership and it fell from Fard's shoulder. For the next forty-one years, some of them excruciatingly difficult and fraught with controversy and frustration. Elijah wore the mantle of office with convictions and determination, leaving at his death in 1995 an enigmatic legacy of achievement in the name of Islam.

WHY YOUNG AFRICAN AMERICANS ARE DRAWN TO THE BLACK MUSLIMS

A. Group Solidarity

The fundamental attraction of the Black Muslims movement is its passion for group solidarity, its exaggerated sense of con-sciousness-of-kind. What matters above all is that individuals acknowledge themselves as black or white and that all blacks work together to accomplish their group aims. These aims have been summed up by a Muslim Minister as getting "The white man's foot off my neck, his hands out of my pocket and his carcass off my back. To sleep in my own bed without fear and to look straight into his cold blue eyes and call him a liar every time he parts his lips.[6]

The ultimate appeal of the movement, therefore is the chance to become identified with a power strong enough to overcome the dominion of whites — and perhaps even to subordinate them 'in turn.[7]

---

[6]From a series of interviews conducted by C. Eric Lincoln with Muslims leaders in Chicago and New York.

[7]C. Eric Lincoln, *The Black Muslim in America*, p. 26

In this context, although the Black Muslims call their movement a religion, religious values have a secondary importance. They are not part of the movement's basic appeal, except to the extent that they foster and strengthen the sense of group solidarity.[8]

In addition to other reasons why blacks are drawn to the Black Muslims, two key areas need to be examined in greater detail: the plight of the black man in America and the failure of the Christian Church.

The Muslims make no secret of the fact that they count themselves a part of the growing alliance of non-white people. Which they expect eventually to inundate the white race, washing away the hatred supremacy that the race has so long enjoyed. Years ago, Dr. Buell Gallaher warns about Orthodox Islam.[9] There are signs that the Pan-Isalamic movement may harden into a new political nationalism based on race, which replaces the Islam of an international and interracial brotherhood. This Pan-Islamic spirit which appears about to come to full fruition in a union of the Muslim world againt the rest of the globe is one of tomorrow's imponderables.[10]

B. The Plight of Blacks in America

Most white Americans have never experienced the depths of despair and hopelessness that black men, women and children in this country have endured. They have never been forced to live in ghettos or near-ghetto conditions surrounded by poverty and the violence and crime that poverty breeds. Forty-five percent of black children are born into poverty (as compared to only 15 percent of white children being born into poverty).[11]

Recent government statistics show that the economic/social plight of blacks in this country is not improving. Some of the more discouraging statistics show:

---

[8]Ibid.
[9]Ibid.
[10]Gallagher, *Color and Conscience* (New York: Harper, 1946) p. 191
[11]"More Children in Poverty", *The Final Call*, September 1986, p. 16

- Median Black family income in 1985 was about $1,000 less in dollars adjusted for inflation than in 1978.
- In 1985, the typical black family had about 58 cents to spend for every dollar a typical white family had to spend. That was the same as in 1980, and four cents less than in 1970.
- More than 31 percent of all black people were officially poor in 1985.
- Among black males 15 to 24 years old, homicide is the leading cause of death. A black man in America stands a 1-in-21 chance of being murdered in his lifetime.
- A black person was 37 percent more likely than a white person to be a victim of rape was robbery or assault in 1983 was.[12]

One thing is clear: there is millions of Americans black people who are suffering. Louis Lomax noted that members of the Nation of Islam aggressively proselytized "the abandoned black masses who live in a world of despair and futility.[13]

C. Failure of the Christian Church

One of Malcolm X's best tactics in recruiting members to the Nation of Islam was to describe graphically the horrors of the slave trade. How literally millions of blacks died on the trip over here, how the black women were raped and killed by the white "Christian" slave traders, etc. Labeling it the "so called Christian white man's crime." Malcolm stated that the dramatization of slavery never failed intensely to arouse Negroes hearing its horrors spelled out for the first time."[14]

Tragically, many black view all Christians as racists. What changed Malcolm. X's hatred of whites was the acceptance and brotherhood he saw among Muslims in Mecca. He wrote: "I have

---

[12]Ibid.

[13]Louis Lomas. *"A Phony Islam Unveiled Threat. True,"* December 1962, p. 16

[14]*The Autobiography of Malcolm X* (New York: Grove Press, 1964) p. 212

never before seen sincere and true brotherhood practiced by all colors together, irrespective of their color.[15]

For the most part the Christian church had not had the care and concern for the black man that it should have had. All to often it has shown little interest for his salvation for helping his economic/social plight. One of the greatest indictments against cultural Christianity is the racism that so-called Christians have shown, past and present. Members of the Nation of Islam have continuously capitalized on them.

During the heydays of the civil rights movement, the ministers of the Nation of Islam temples would point out that the most segregated institution in this country was the Christian church. During the Birmingham demonstrations one prominently displayed photo was a group of blacks, after being ejected from a white church, praying on the church steps with whites standing a few feet away threatening them with their fists balled up. More recently, a front-page headline in the Amsterdam News declared, "Pastor won't admit Blacks."[16]

But an increasingly number of African Americans is disillusioned by the continuation of racial segregation in the church and is coming to identify the church with social apathy and racial subordination. Malcolm X stated:

"Your Christian countries, if I am correct are Europe and North and South America. Predominantly, that is where you find Christianity, or at least people who represent themselves as Christians. Whether they practiced what Jesus taught is something we won't go into. The Christian world is what we usually called the Western world ... The colonization of the dark people in the rest of the world was done by Christian powers. The number one problem that most people face in the world today is how to get freedom from Christians. Wherever you find non-Christian people who represent themselves as

---

[15]Ibid, p. 340
[16]Simon Anekwa, *Pastor Won't Admit Blacks*, The Amsterdam News, December 7, 1985.

Christians, and if you ask these [subject] people their picture of a Christian, they will tell you a "white man a Slave-master." [17]

D. Redefinition of the Roles of Men and Women

A number of young people are <u>attracted by the Muslim's redefinition of the roles men and women should be</u> in the home and in the religious sect of life.[18]

Messenger Muhammad teaches The Women in Islam that Allah taught him that the Woman is the greatest pleasure that the man has. Nothing pleases man more than woman ... The Bible verifies this truth *(Genesis 2:18)* ... Black Man, the Original Man is the God, and after He made Himself, He was not satisfied alone and then He made Woman ... ALL PRAISES ARE DUE TO ALLAH!

Messenger Muhammad teaches ... that Man made Women for the purpose of his pleasure. He did not need the woman to put one star in the heavens. He wanted the woman for love and companionship. She is the field to produce a nation — ALL PRAISES ARE DUE TO ALLAH [for] this divine message.[19]

E. The Challenge of an Ascetic Idea

Another reason why blacks are drawn to the Black Muslims is the <u>challenge of an ascetic ideal, balanced by the absence of social barriers to affiliation and service</u>, which has brought thousands under the banner of Muhammad. Probably in no other religious organization are alcoholics, ex-convicts, pimps, prostitutes, and narcotic addicts welcomed so sincerely. The Christian church is, in most instances, careful to take none to its bosom until they are cleansed. The Muslims welcome the most

---

[17]Malcolm X, *"The Truth About the Black Muslim"* and address delivered at the Boston University School of Theology — May 24, 1960.

[18]Gallen, David, *"Malcolm X, As They Knew Him"* Carroll and Graf Publishers, Inc., 260 Fifth AVe., New York, NY 10001. Copyright 1992, p. 113

[19]Mary Hassain, *Muhammad Speaks*, October 29, 1971

unregenerate and then set about to rehabilitate them. They have stem rules of conduct, but none are condemned for what they were — only for what they refuse to be.[20]

They say a man should never be condemned or tried twice for the same crime once, he has paid the penalty. Yet when a man goes to prison and pays his debt to society, when he comes out he is still looked upon as a criminal ... Well, Mr. Muhammad has succeeded there where Western Christianity has failed. When a man becomes a Muslim, it doesn't make any difference what he was [doing] before as long as he has stopped doing this. He is looked upon with honor and respect, and is not judged for what he was doing yesterday. And this I think, explains why we have so many men who were in prison following Mr. Muhammad today.[21]

F. Outward Manifestation of Fraternal Responsibility ...

Another reason why they are drawn to the Black Muslims is: The movement's stress on — and the outward manifestation of — fraternal responsibility is a strong attraction for many blacks, whose social and civil insecurity is often extreme, African Americans have often been characterized as ready "joiners," and more often than not this characterization has been Justified. They are compelled to join in order to escape the isolation and sense of helplessness they experience as social outcasts. They join for recreation when public recreation is not available to them, and for security against sickness and want. They join for consolation and companionship — the attempt at fight of an earthbound black in a white dominated world.

All of these elements are present, to some degree, in the appeal of Muslim Membership. But the appeal goes deeper: all Muslims hold themselves ready to die for their brothers and sisters.[22]

[20]The Black Muslims in America, p. 28

[21]Malcom X at Boston University Human Relations Center, February 15, 1960.

[22]James Hicks, Editor of the New York Amsterdam News and a close observer of the movement, says, "They have high regard for their women and fight like hell for each other." (The Reporter, August 4, 1960, p.39)

G. The Membership is Young ...

The membership is young. Up to 80 percent of a typical congregation is between the ages of 17 and 35. This pattern has been noted again and again in temples across the country. In the newer temples, youth is even more pronounced; in some, fully three-quarters of the membership are under 30 years of age. About the same proportion of the ministers is under 35.

The reason for such a concentration of youth is clear. This is an activist movement, and the appeal is directed to youth. Large young families are eagerly sought, while least attention is paid to older people reared as Christians. Older people have a certain security in their familiar religious orientation, and they do not readily shift to a position so unfamiliar and radical as that preached by the Muslims.

The older people who do belong to the movement, especially in the Northern cities, are of the most part ex-Garveyites or ex-Moorish Science Moslems, or they have belonged to some of the more esoteric cults flourishing in Harlem, Detroit, or Chicago. Many of these older "nationalists" consider Muhammad a natural successor to both Garvey and Noble Drew Ali, and they have had little difficulty in making the transition. Muhammad himself professes "a very high opinion" of both Garvey and Nobel Drew Ali; he refers to them as fine"Muslims" and calls upon their sympathizers to "follow me and cooperate in our work because we are only trying to finish up what those before us started."[23]

H. The Membership is Predominantly Male

Unlike the typical Christian church, the Muslim temples attract many more men than women and men assume the full management of temple affairs. Women are honored, and they perform important functions within a defined role (they are not in any sense considered mere "property," as has sometimes been the case in classical Islam), but they do not constitute the

---

[23]*The Voodoo Cult Among Negro Migrants in Detroit,* American Journal of Sociology 43 (July 1937 – May 1938): 894-907, p. 898

organizational foundation through which the movement fictions, either in service or in finance. They work alongside the men in the various business enterprises owned by the temples, and they share in the affairs of the temples themselves, but almost always in roles not in conflict with the male assumption of primary responsibility.

The membership is essentially lower class. A generation ago Erdmann Beynon reported that "at the time of their first contact with the prophet practically all of the members of the cult were recipients of public welfare, unemployed and living in the most deteriorated areas of Negro settlement in Detroit.[24] That was in the early 1930s — the worst of the Depression years. However, in 1937 there were no known cases Beynon observed. At the present time, there are known cases of unemployment among these people. Practically all of them are working in the automobile and other factories. They live no longer in the slum section ... but rent homes in some of the best economic areas in which Negroes have settled. They tend to purchase more expensive furniture, automobiles and clothes than do their neighbors even in these areas of higher-class residence.[25]

The socioeconomic pattern today is a fusion of these two trends. Muslims are fully employed, yet many live and meet in the most deteriorated areas of the slums. But not exclusively: the "Protestant Ethic" is not abandoned in black Islam. The visible evidences of Muslim prosperity are increasingly noticeable in the best neighborhoods occupied by middle class African Americans.

Recruitment for the movement still takes place predominantly among low-income groups at the lower end of the educational scale. It has attracted a few intellectuals, an increasing number of college students, and a scattering of business executives and professionals, but a majority of the membership of any given temple is composed of domestic and factory workers, common laborers, and the like.[26] In an increasing number of the men, however, are skilled and semi-skilled craftsmen; the businesses

---

[24]Beynon, *"The Voodoo Cult Among Negro Migrants*, p. 9
[25]Ibid, p. 905
[26]Ibid, p. 905

owned by the group are usually housed in buildings renovated by the Muslims themselves — from the plumbing to the electric signs that mark the entrances.

I. The Membership is almost Wholly
American African American

The Garvey movement was built around a hard core of East Indians, who, sharing his nationality and cultural experiences, were most readily attracted to his program. American blacks gave Garvey little attention until he had already attracted a large following of West Indian immigrants.[27] But the Muslim leadership has not especially welcomed the West Indians in this country, possibly because the West Indian habit of making distinctions among themselves in terms of color could jeopardize the Muslim appeal for a united black front.

There may have been some Japanese "advisors" connected with the movement in its early days, when Major Takahashi was active in Detroit. The Muslims view all nonwhites as blacks, whatever their skin color, and it is worth noting that Muhammad was indicted for pro-Japanese sympathies in the first year of World War 11.[28] But no significant Oriental influence is apparent in the movement today.

WHAT DO THEY BELIEVE?

Their beliefs are as follows:

1. We believe in the one God Whose Proper name is Allah.
2. We believe in the Holy Quran and in the Scriptures of all the Prophets of God.
3. We believe "in the truth of the Bible," but we believe that it has been tampered with and must be reinterpreted so that mankind will not be snared by the falsehoods that have been added to it.

---

[27]E. Franklin Fraizer, Black Bourgeoisie, Flencoe, IL; Free Press, 1957, p. 120
[28]Chicago Sun, October 24, 1992

4. We believe in Allah's Prophets and the Scriptures they brought to the people.

5. We believe in the resurrection of the dead — not in physical resurrection but mental resurrection. We believe that the so-called Negroes are most in need of mental resurrection; therefore, they will be resurrected first.

   Furthermore, we believe we are the people of God's choice as it has been written that God would choose the rejected and the despised. We can find no other persons fitting this description in these last days more than the so-called Negroes in America. We believe in the resurrection of the righteous.

6. We further believe in the judgment. We believe this first judgment will take place, as God revealed, in America.

7. We believe this is the time in history for the separation of the so called Negroes and the so-called white Americans. We believe the black man should be freed in name as well as in fact. By this we mean that this should free him from names imposed upon him by his former slave-masters. Names which identified him as being the slave of a slave master. We believe that if we are free indeed, we should go in our own people's names — the black people of the earth.

8. We believe in justice for all whether in God or not. We believe as others that we are due equal justice as human beings. We believe in equality — as a nation — of equals. We do not believe that we are equal with our slave masters in the status of "Freed slaves."

   We recognize and respect American citizens as independent people, and we respect their laws, which govern this nation.

9. We believe that the offer of integration is hypocritical and is made by those who are lying to deceive the black peoples into believing that they're 400-year old open enemies of freedom, justice and equality are, all of a sudden, there "friends." Furthermore, we believe that such deception is intended to prevent black people from realizing that the time in history has arrived for the separation from the whites of this nation.

If the white people are truthful about their professed friendship toward the so-called Negro, they can prove it by dividing up America with their slaves. '

We do not believe that America will ever be able to furnish enough jobs for her own millions of unemployed in addition to jobs for the 20,000,000 black people.

10. *We believe that we who declared ourselves to be righteous Muslims should not participate in wars, which take the lives of humans. We do not believe this nation should force us to take part in such wars, for we have nothing to gain from it unless America agrees to give us the necessary territory wherein we may have something to fight for.*

11. *We believe our women should be respected and protected as the women of other nationalities are respected and protected.*

12. *We believe that Allah (God) appeared in the Person of Master W. Fard Muhammad, July 1930 — the long awaited "Messiah" of the Christians and the "Malidi" of the Muslims.*

We believe further and lastly that Allah is God and besides HIM there is no God and He will bring about a universal government of peace wherein we can live in peace together.[29]

WHAT DO THE MUSLIMS WANT?

This is the question asked most frequently by both the whites and the blacks. The answers to this question are as follows:

1. *We want freedom. We want a full and complete freedom..*

2. *We want justice. Equal justice under the law. We want justice applied equally to all regardless of creed, class or color.*

3. *We want equality of opportunity. We want equal membership in society with the best in civilized society.*

---

[29]Muhammad, Elijah, *Message to the Blackman in America,* Published by Muhammad Mosque of Islam No. 2, 5335 S. Greenwood Avenue, Chicago, IL, 1965 p. 163-64

grandparents were descendants from slaves to be allowed to establish a separate state or territory of their own — either on this continent or elsewhere. We believe that our former slave-masters are obligated to provide such land and that the area must be fertile and mineral rich. We believe that our former slave-masters are obligated to maintain and supply our needs in this separate territory for the next 20 or 25 years until we are able to produce and supply our own needs.

Since we cannot get along with them in peace and equality after giving them 400 years of our sweat and blood and receiving in return some of the worst treatment human beings have ever experienced, we believe our contributions to this land and the suffering forced upon us by white America justifies our demand for complete separation in a state or territory of our own.

5. *We want freedom for all Believers of Islam now held in federal prisons. We want freedom for all black men and women now under death sentence in innumerable prisons in the North as well as the South.*

We want every black man and woman to have the freedom to accept or reject being separated from the slave-masters' children and establish a land of their own.

We know that the above plan for the solution of the black and white conflict is the best and only answer to the problem between two people.

6. *We want an immediate end to the police brutality and mob attacks against the so-called Negro throughout the United States.*

We believe that the Federal government sh6uld intercede to see that black men and women tried in white courts receive justice in accordance with the laws of the land, or allow us to build a new nation for ourselves, dedicated to justice, freedom and liberty.

7 .*As long as we are not allowed to establish a state or territory of our own, we demand not only equal justice under the laws*

*of the United States by equal employment opportunities —
NOW!*

*We do not believe that after 400 years of free or nearly free
labor, sweat and blood, which has helped America become
rich and powerful, so many thousands of black people should
have to subsist on relief or charity or live in poor houses.*

8. *We want the government of the United States to exempt our
people from ALL taxation as long as we are deprived of equal
justice under the laws of the land.*

9. *We want equal education — but separate schools up to 16 for
boys and 18 for girls on the conditions that the girls be
sent to women's colleges and universities. We want all
black children educated, taught and trained by there own
teacher.*

*Under such school system we believe we will make a better
nation of people. The United States government should
provide free all necessary textbooks and equipment, schools
and college buildings. The Muslim teachers shall be left free
to teach and train their people in the way of righteousness,
decency and self-respect.*

10. *We believe that intermarriage or race mixing should be
prohibited. We want the religion of Islam taught without
hindrance or suppression. These are some of the things that
we, the Muslims, want for our people in North America.*[30]

A. A Program for Self-Development

We must remember that we just cannot depend on the white
race ever to do that which we can and should do for self The
American so-called Negroes are like the Bible story of Lazarus
and the rich man, the story that Jesus must have foreseen at the
time. This Bible beggar was chained by the wealth of the rich man
to whom he was a servant and he could not make up his mind to
go seek something for self.

---

[30]Ibid, pp. 162-163

This beggar was offered a home in Paradise but could not make up his mind to leave the gate of his master, the rich man, wishing for that which God had in stores for destruction along with its owner. The beggar's eyes could not turn from that perishable wealth. So it is with the American Negroes; they are charmed by the luxury of their slave-master, and cannot make up their minds to seek for self something of this good earth, though hatred and despised by the rich man and full of sores caused by the evil treatment of the rich man. On top of that he is chased by the rich man' s dogs and still remains a beggar at the gate, though the gates of Paradise were ever open to him and the gates of hell were open to receive his rich master.

The American Negroes have the same gates of Paradise open to them but are charmed by the wealth of America and cannot see the great opportunity that he has before them. They are suffering untold injustices at the hands of the rich; they have been and still are being lynched and burned they and their women and the rich slave-masters and their children beat children all over the country. The slaves houses and churches are bombed by the slave-masters; their girls are used as prostitutes and at times are raped in public. Yet the Negroes are on their knees begging the rich man to treat them as the rich man treats himself and his kind. The poor beggar kindly asks for the crumbs, a job and a house in the neighborhood of the rich man.

The Negro leaders are frightened to death and are afraid to ask for anything other than a job. The good things of this earth could be theirs if they would only unite and acquire wealth as the masters and the other independent nations have. The Negroes could have all of this if they could get up and go to work for self. The are far too lazy as a Nation — 100 years up from slavery and still looking to the master to care for them and give them a job, bread and a house to live in on the master's land. You should be ashamed of yourselves, surely the white race has been very good in the way of making jobs for their willing slaves, but his cannot go on forever; we are about at the end of it and must do something for self or else.

The slave-master have given you enough education to go and do for self, but this education is not being used for self, it is even offered back to the slave masters to help them to keep you a dependent people looking to them for support. Let us unite every good that is in us for the uplifting of the American so-called Negroes to the equal of the world's independent nations. Ask for a start for self and the American white people, I believe, are willing to help give us a start if they see you and I are willing to do for self It would remove from them no only the worry of tying to give jobs and schools to a lazy people but also would get them honor and sincere friendship all over the Asiatic world and God, Himself, would prolong their time on the earth.

We must stop relying upon the white man to care for us. We must become an independent people.

1. *Separate yourselves from the slave-master.*
2. *Pool your resources, education and qualifications for independence.*
3. *Stop forcing yourselves into places where you are not wanted.*
4. *Make your own neighborhood a decent place to live. Rid yourselves of the lust of wine and drink and learn to love self and your kind before loving others.*
5. *Unite to create a future for yourself.*
6. *Build your own homes, schools, hospitals, and factories.*
7. *Do not seek to mix your blood through racial integration.*
8. *Stop buying expensive cars, fine clothes and shoes before being able to live in a fine home.*
9. *Spend your money among yourselves,*
10. *Build an economic system among yourselves.*
11. *Protect your women.*

Stop allowing the white men to shake hands or speak to your women anytime or anywhere. This practice has ruined us. They wink their eye at your daughter after coming into your home — but you cannot go on the North side and do the same with his women.

No black man feels good — by nature — seeing a white man with a Negro woman. We have all colors in our race - red, yellow, brown and jet black -why should we need a white person?

Africans would not dare allow their women to be the targets that we allow ours to be.

If Allah (God) did not protect me, how would I be able to stand before this white man unafraid and speak as I do?

You educators, you Christian ministers should stop preaching integration. The most foolish thing an educator can do is to preach interracial marriage. It shows the white man you want to be white.

Educators should teach our people of the great history that was theirs before slave-masters brought them to America in shackles.

Our children should be trained in our own schools, not dropped into the schools of the enemy where they are taught that whites have been and forever will be world rulers.

I am the first man since the death of Yakub commissioned by God directly. I say no more than what Jesus said. He said that he came from God. I say that I am mission by God."[31]

The believers in truth, Islam, must stop looking up to the white race for justice and take the following steps to correct this problem.

Acknowledge and recognize that you are a member of the Creator's nation and act accordingly. This action, in the name of Allah, requires you, as a Muslim, to set an example for the lost-found, your brothers in the wilderness in North America. This requires action and deeds, not words and lip service. The following blueprint shows the way:

1. *Recognize the necessity for unity and group operations (activities).*
2. *Pool your resources, physically as well as financially.*
3. *Stop wanton criticisms of everything that is black-owned and black-operated.*
4. *Keep in mind — jealousy destroys from within.*

---

[31]Ibid, pp. 170-171

5. Observe the operations of the white man. He is successful. He makes no excuses for his failures. He works hard in a collective matter you do the same.[32]

If there are six or eight Muslims with knowledge and experience of the grocery business — pool your knowledge, open a grocery store — and you work collectively and harmoniously, Allah will bless you with success.

If there are those with knowledge of dressmaking, merchandising, trades, maintenance — pool such knowledge. Do not be ashamed to seek guidance and instructions from the brother or sister who has more experience, education and training than you have had, accept his or her assistance.

The white man spends his money with his own kind, which is natural. You, too, must do this. Help to make jobs for your own kind. Take a lesson from the Chinese and Japanese and go give employment and assistance to your own kind when they are in need. This is the first law of nature. Defend and support your own kind. True Muslims do this.

Because the so-called American Negro has been deceived and misled, he has become a victim of deception. He is today in the worst economic condition of North America. Unemployment is mounting, and he feels it most. He assisted in reducing himself to his present insecure economic condition.

---

[32]Ibid, p. 174

THE MUSLIMS OFFER ECONOMIC POWER

The Black Muslims are an intensely dedicated, tightly disciplined organization of African Americans, convinced that they have learned the ultimate truth and ready to make any sacrifice it may demand of them. Theirs is not a "Sunday religion". The Muslim temples hold frequent meetings, and every Muslim is required to attend two (and often more) meetings a week. Nor is it a religion that spares the billfold. The mass of Muslims are from the black lower class, with relatively low incomes, 'and they are encouraged to live respectably and provide for their families. The men are urged to hold steady jobs, and Muslims are forbidden to gamble, smoke, drink liquor, overeat, indulge in fripperies, or buy on credit. As a result most Muslims enjoy a health standard of living and still have enough cash left over to support the movement.[33]

All Muslims are expected to give a fixed percentage of their income to the movement each year. The figure is officially set at one-third of all earnings, but the amount collected is probably not always so high. In addition, the temples collect contribution for a variety of funds, many for local purposes, and at least six for the urge of the national headquarters at temple No. 2 in Chicago. Of the six known national funds, four are earmarked for real estate, public relations, official travel, and new cars: one is an annual collection on the anniversary of Fard's birthday, February 26, with no purpose designated; and one is a discretionary fund, the "No. 2 treasury and central Point Fund," for Muhammad to use as he sees fit.[34]

The Muslims power to influence the general American community is significant, not only because of their increasing financial resources, but also because they can be mobilized to act in unswerving unison on any matter designated by the leadership. Should they ever vote, for example, assuredly they will vote as their leadership tells them to vote and buy where they are told to buy. A Muslim block, therefore, even in a large city, could be the

---

[33]*The Black Muslim in America, p. 18*
[34]Ibid, p. 18

determining factor in the balance of political and economic power.[35]

It was once said in Harlem that Malcolm X, then minister of the large Temple 7 and Mohammed's chief lieutenant, could decide the election of U.S. Representative Adam Clayton Powell's successor.[36] This issue was mooted by Malcom's death, but the deference shown him — and his successor — by the political powers in Harlem is impressive. Even more impressive evidence of the Muslims' political weight is the fact that Fidel Castro, during his dramatic sojourn in Harlem in the autumn of 1960, invited Malcolm X to a private conference that lasted some two hours. Malcolm had earlier been invited, along with other important African Americans, to visit Castro in Cuba. That the invitation was not accepted or that acceptance was delayed — can be attributed in part to Muhammad's distaste for communism as a white ideology and in part to his doubt about whether Castro is a black man or a "blue-eyed devil" hiding behind a slogan and a sword.[37]

Muhammad has not yet seen fit to use the potential power of the Black Muslim vote as a lever to pry concessions from the white or the non-Muslim black community. From the start; Muslims have generally preferred not to vote at all. This has been due partly to their self-identification with Afro-Asia, partly to their beliefs that America is already corrupt and doomed, and partly to their sense of futility in electing any white to office. Malcolm X noted that "Roosevelt promised, Truman promised, Eisenhower promised. Blacks are still. knocking on the door begging for civil rights ... Do you mean to tell me that in a powerful country like this, a so-called *Christian* country, that a handful of men from the South cart prevent the North, the West, the Central States, and the East from giving Negroes the nights the Constitution says they already have? No! I don't believe that and neither do you. No white man really wants the Black Man to

---

[35]Ibid, p. 18
[36]Ibid, p. 18
[37]Ibid, p. 18

have his rights, or he'd have them. The United States does everything else it wants to do.[38]

The Muslims have also refrained from voting in an effort to keep their strength a secret. "If you don't vote, nobody knows what you can accomplish when you do," and so far there has been no issue worth a real display of strength. Muhammad admonishes those blacks that do vote to simply "go to the polls with your eyes and ears open, and remember that it is not necessary for you to go seeking justice for anyone but yourselves... The white people of America already have their freedom, justice and equal rights."[39]

The Black Muslims (political power) is ominous but, for the moment, latent. It is reckoned with seriously at the local and state level in many states, but Muhammad is not: seeking political alignments even there, and he is unlikely to attempt a national power play for some years to come. The Muslims economic power, on the other hand, is already being, felt in the black community. There is no organized boycott of white merchants, but all Muslims are expected to "buy black" — that is, to trade with their own kind in preference to "spending your money where you can't work and can't sit down." The Muslims were vocal in their contempt for the sit-in movement, in which blacks "went out of their way to force the white man to let them spend more money with him" rather than contributing to the establishment of businesses run by and for blacks.

The Muslims demand an entirely separate black economy, arguing that not until African Americans are economically independent will they be, in any real sense, free. The total annual income of the black community, they point out, is greater than the total income of Canada and greater than that of several European states. Such a purchasing power, if spent among black merchants and invested in black enterprises, would earn the respect of every nation in the world. The Muslims conceded that whites have, for the moment, an edge on technical and commercial expertise.

---

[38]Malcolm X *"The Truth About the Black Muslim"* Address at the Boston University School of Theology, May 24, 1960.

[39]*Muhammad*, New York Courier, August 6, 1960.

Blacks must learn whatever the whites can teach them and then outstrip the whites in productivity and trade.[40]

Economic growth for the Nation of Islam (NOI) comes via several channels (apart from donations and sales of their newspaper, *The Final Call*). The NOI owns 1,600 acres of Georgia farmland and plans to acquire 10,000 acres by the end of 1996, according to the *Christian Science Monitor.* The NOI has also started a commercial trucking industry with a handful of tractor-trailer rigs.

Beauty supplies stores, bookstores, and restaurants specializing in "bean pies" appears throughout the country. The Salaam Restaurant and Bakery, a fully paid for $5 million restaurant opened in Chicago in March 1995 with much fanfare and with menus for lower and upper-income patrons.

Amazingly, since 1991 the NOI's largest source of income has been the federal government, which has paid about $20 million to security services owned or controlled by the NOI. The U.S. Department of Housing and Urban Development has awarded contracts to public housing projects in Chicago, Los Angeles, Pittsburgh, Washington, and other cities to hire NOI-related security firms.

These businesses have brought safety to some housing projects. The *New York Times* reported praise for NOI Security in Baltimore, where tenants protested the cancellation of its contract. On the other hand, an investigative series by the *Chicago Tribune* in March 1995 published tenant complaints in Chicago and Washington of inadequate, absent or violent security guards. Meanwhile, Farrakhan refused 12 requests for an interview by the *Tribune.*[41]

---

[40]Ibid, p. 20
[41]Reprinted from the Christian Research Journal, Spring 1996, P.O. Box 500, San Juan Capistrano, CA 92693.

THE NATION OF ISLAM AND THE SOCIAL PROBLEMS

Blacks have suffered much because of racism. While many blacks have battled white racism in an exemplary manner, Black Muslims fight white racism with black racism. The Nation of Islam sees Christianity as the "white man's religion." These stems from the idea that the white man taught black slaves Christianity in order to continually oppress them. Slave owners used passages in the Bible that speak of slaves being obedient to their masters in order to keep the slaves in a docile, unquestioning attitude. In other words, Black Muslims teach that Christianity made slaves better slaves. Black Muslims also consider Christianity to be a passive religion — an "opiate" that permits injustice by urging the oppressed to "love their enemies." Christianity teaches the black man that all things will be resolved after death. There is therefore no need to get involved in any social concerns of this world. One of the major strengths of the Black Muslims, on the other hand, is their concern for social issues. They are involved with the most urgent needs of the black community. For instance, The Nation of Islam was one of the first organizations to respond to the LA riot crisis in late April 1992. Furthermore, Black Muslims claim that Christians are not as adequately involved in rehabilitating blacks. Black Muslims take pride in the fact that many of their converts were once in prison, or were once drug addicts, but The Nation of Islam transformed their lives.

Are the Black Muslim's criticisms of Christianity valid? Unfortunately, to some extent, they may be. First, Black Muslims may get the impression that Christianity is the "white man's religion" as long as there are white churches that are separated from black, Hispanic, or oriental churches. There should not be white churches, black churches, or any other type of church that separates races. Granted, it is necessary sometimes to have "minority churches" in America because many of the people in these congregations cannot adequately understand or speak English. But this is not always the case with oriental and Hispanic churches, and is seldom the case with black or white churches. Why then do these racial barriers exist in the American church?

Second, regarding social issues, Christian churches do need to amplify their efforts. Black Muslims should not be the only ones meeting the social needs of the black community. Our Christian testimony should be shared with others in both the spiritual and physical domains (Matt. 25:31-46). The Christians message of love should be among the first ideologies to help oppressed people.

Third, Christians have sometimes failed in the area of reaching out to the prisoners, drug addicts, gang members, and other outcasts of society. If the church does not fulfill its mission to preach the Gospel to everyone, then she leaves the door open for the cults to do so. The People's Temple, for example, consisted of many former drug addicts and street people. Reaching to desperate people was one of the primary objectives of Jesus Christ.

Nevertheless, it is not true that Christianity makes people apathetic toward social issues. Christ's command to "love your enemies" does not mean that we should turn a deaf ear to the cry of injustice. On the contrary, we should actualize Christian principles to meet social needs, as did Martin Luther King. Unfortunately, among certain evangelical circles there is such an emphasis on the teachings of end-time prophecy that some Christians can develop an indifferent attitude toward "worldly" affairs. After all, why bother meeting social needs if Christ is coming back in a few more years? This attitude must be stopped. If some Christians have not done a good job in demonstrating the Gospel to the oppressed, they have failed not because of the Bible, but in spite of it. *Genesis 1:26-27* teaches us that humans were created in the image of God. This shows us that all people should be respected and treated impartially, because they bear the image of God. We are all descendants of one man who was called Adam (Acts *17:26*). *As* God's creatures, we all have a calling to fulfill, and the right to do so. Depriving any person or group of their God given rights is a form of injustice.[42]

---

[42]Christian Research Institute, Statement No. 3. 136, P.O. Box 500, San Juan Capistrano, CA 92693-0500

WHO IS LOUIS FARRAKRAN?

Minister Louis Haleem Abdul Farrakhan was born Louis Eugene Walcott on May 11, 1933, in the Bronx, New York. He grew up in Boston as a devout Episcopalian and graduated from Boston Latin School with honors. He spent two years at Winston-Salem Teachers College in North Carolina. Walcott was recruited into the Nation of Islam by Malcolm X in the early 1950's and was eventually appointed minister of Muhammad's Temple No.11 in Boston. When Malcolm left the Nation following his suspension in 1964, Farrakhan succeeded him a minister of the prestigious Mosque No. 7 in Harlem, and as national spokesman for the Nation as well.[43]

Like his famous mentor Malcolm X, Minister Farrakhan is a person of extraordinary charisma and charm, but, armed with a rapier-like wit, he is well practiced in polemical skills. He roclaims a fervid belief in the doctrines and the vision of Elijah Muhammad, and, in the characteristic fashion of the true believer, he denounced Malcolm X for his break with Elijah instantly, acrimoniously, and relentlessly, In a cosmocentric society there can be but one loyalty, and it must be to one leader. There must be no room for doubt. Perhaps some such precognition shadowed the mind of Irmam. Warith Muhammad when he recalled Farrakhan from his Harlem outpost and reassigned him to duties on the West Side of Chicago.[44]

At first Farrakhan accepted his reassignment to invisibility in the hinterlands, but gradually he came to believe that the Wallace reformation was aimed at cloaking the entire vision of Elijah and dismantling the structure that made it live as he, Farrakhan, had understood that vision. To be so near the scene of the destruction and yet so far from the power required to stop it eventually required a decision on Farrakhan's part that neither he nor Wallace wanted to face, for neither could be true to himself and live comfortably with. the "truth" of the other. Something had to give, and it did. In 1977 after some thirty months, of the Wallace

---

[43]*The Black Muslims in America*, p. 268.
[44]Ibid, p. 268.

reformation, Farrakhan left Imam Warith Muhammad's World Community of Islam in the West to rebuild Elijah Muhammads Lost-Found Nation of Islam in the Wilderness of North America. The parting was peaceful, much to the surprise of outside observers, and relationships among all of the various factions have remained so. One factor of significance could be the fact that some of Farrakhan's eleven children had intermarried with some of the grandchildren of Messenger Muhammad. Perhaps this genealogical interfusion set the tone in establishing a climate for the coexistence of a whole spectrum of variously focused Muslim groups competing for identity in the midst of a vaunted Judeo-Christian culture. In any case, reports of internecine Muslim conflict are quite rare. In 1990 Farrakhan was permitted to address the Continental Muslim Council. In the course of his address he affirmed his commitment to the Shahadah (the basic confession of Islamic belief), and on the strength of overt support from Imam Wallace Muhammad, among others, Farrakhan was accepted for membership on "profession of faith."

Oddly enough, the respect and acceptance shown Minister Farrakhan by the Continental Council could only have derived from his extraordinary accomplishment in. rebuilding the Nation of Islam over the previous thirteen years. He began by rebuilding the infrastructure of his "new" Nation solidly and unequivocally on the foundations laid by the founding fathers. The teachings about the nature of Allah, Yacub, the white man, Armageddon, and the like were reiterated without change. The ancient declaration of "What the Muslims Believe" and "What the Muslims Want" remained intact. The house organ *Muhammad Speaks* (changed by Wallace to the Bilalian *News)* was resurrected as *The Final Call,* which Elijah had founded in 1934. Muslim entrepreneurship was once again made an important aspect of the faith. In the face of escalating unemployment, the Nation sought to take care of its own as Elijah had taught it to do.[45]

---

[45]Ibid, p. 269.

THE BEGINNING OF HIS MINISTRY

Louis first went to Boston as a captain in the Fruit of Islam, since Elijah Muhammad decided to delay making him a minister until he had proved how well he could perform under the authority of others. In a few months, when Louis was finally promoted to minister, he decided that there would be no temples in apartments for him. He wanted a *real* temple in *a real* building. After scouting around Roxbury, a NOI member found the right site: an Orthodox rabbinic seminary on Intervale Avenue that was for sale. He told the owners he was searching for a place for a church: "If we said it was for a mosque, they probably wouldn't have sold it to us." A Nation member put up his mortgage as collateral, and the deal went through. To mark the occasion, Louis visited the Reverend Nathan Wright, the minister who had married him at St. Cyprian's Church about four years before, to say he had followed him "into the ministry."[46]

Louis may have been a Muslim, but he had not forgotten his Christian roots. If anything, his visit to Wright made it clear that Louis did not think he had abandoned the faith of his youth by joining the NOI. Rather, he was spearheading a parallel church, a "protest" church, and a reform movement that would purge Christianity of its hypocrisy and spiritual sterility. Wright, who within a few years would be active in the Black Power movement, was not unsympathetic to Louis' mission. He gave him fifty chairs that St. Cyprian was throwing out to use in the unfurnished new temple.

Wright also gave Low's a list of young men he had recently compiled that he knew the church could not reach: "The first twenty of his first twenty-five members I gave him. I knew they would never get the caring they needed in my church."[47]

Helped by Malcolm X's occasional trips up from New York to speak at the temple, Louis X began to put Temple No. 11 on the map. By November 1957 — six months after Louis took over the

---

[46]Khallaq interview, June 1, 1995; (Nathan Wright) interviewed, May 26, 1995 — on Farrakhan's arrival in Boston as an FOI captain, Philadelphia Civic Center, January 20, 1992.

[47]Nathan Wright interview, May 26, 1995.

temple — Malcolm said that under the new minister, the Nation was; "making amazing strides forward" in Boston. At meetings on Mondays, Wednesdays, Friday and Saturday evenings, and Sunday afternoon, Louis or an assistant minister lectured about current events, discipline, honesty, monogamy, faithfulness, sobriety — and, of course, about the sly ways of the white "devils..." In the lecture hall, once the Jewish seminary's main study hall, was a large photo of a lynching down south: a black body dangling from a tree above a crowd of pleased and smiling whites, a few of whom were not just "white" but what one visitor called "shoe-polish white." Temple No.11 and its new minister knew how to draw the color lines to make them distinct and inviolable — and how to invoke more anger in those who listened than they had when they walked in.[48]

People came, more than before. But even Malcolm worried about Minister Louis fairly quick success in Boston. Maybe, he mused, the Nation was running into a trap, since "many had left beautiful churches to come to learn about Islam at the Boston Temple and [then] described it as a shack." But maybe, he reasoned, it was "better to go into a shack where there are wise people than [to] go into a palace with fools."[49]

The proportion of members with bachelor's degrees or better did not sit well, however, with the former song-and-dance man Louis X, who realized quickly that being a NOI minister was not about putting on a Jive-talking, sweet-talking, make-your-audience-smile, tap-their-toes, move-their-hips, hum-along calypso show. This was the Big Time. Salvation. Deliverance. God's Own Blueprint for Liberation. The Showdown before the Final Battle. Apocalypse Almost Now. And Louis began to get the willies: "I was not able to relate to many of the educated persons who joined the Boston Temple as they were much more intelligent than I. And because I couldn't understand their ideas, I thought they were enemies of Islam and "— borrowing a phrase more often used about a rebel who evicted money changers from

---

[48] *"Malcom X in Boston,"* New York Amsterdam News, also, *"The Black Muslims are a Fraud,"* Saturday Evening Post, February 27, 1963, p. 25.
[49] FBI memo, April 30, 1958.

159

a certain temple in Jerusalem two millennia before I drove them out of the temple." Louis X asked Elijah Muhammad to relieve him of his post and to let him bear the responsibility for "any sins" committed by the ex-members while they were banned from the temple. Impressed by this "display of compassion," Elijah let the dismissed members return to the temple — and kept Louis as their minister.[50]

Gradually, Louis gained confidence. Within five years, he almost tripled the Boston temple's membership and an aura of invincibility began to surround him and the "Moos-lims" as they were called. They were exotic, disciplined, uncompromising, and tough. They took care of their own — and took no guff from whites or from their own. From Chicago, Elijah Muhammad ran the tightest ship in the black community, achieving, said *Sepia* magazine, an "outstanding goal in Negro leadership that has eluded other leaders in the past. He has instilled in his followers an "unto the death" obedience and discipline that amazes outsiders." "Even [Marcus] Garvey," said one New York black politician, "couldn't control his followers, at least not on the level where Mr. Muhammad operates. His followers believe his teachings more strongly than the 'angels' [members of the Peace Mission Movement] believed in Father Divine."[51]

NATION OF ISLAM: DOCTRINAL DISTINCTIVES

"The Nation of Islam, under the leadership of Louis Farrakhan, teaches that Blacks are Gods chosen race who were the "Original Man" created during the Big Bang which occurred over 66 trillion years ago. (Such a notion is entirely unscientific.) The first men on earth were blacks, but one mad black scientist called "Yakub" began to breed lighter skinned blacks until he created other non-white races. Finally, he created the white "beast," the only human with no black gene in him. The white man was permitted to reign for 6,000 years until 1914. Black

---

[50]Sterling X Hobbs, *"Miracle Man of The Muslims,"* Sepia (May 1975); p. 29.
[51]According to Bruce Perry, The Boston Temple's membership was around *250 in 1964*; Malcolm (Barrytown, NY: Station Hill Press, 1992) p. 289.

Muslims believe that the time has not come for blacks to regain their superior position here on Earth. They teach that blacks need to keep segregated from whites because the two races cannot get along. However, The Nation of Islam believes that the Federal government owes the blacks a separate state or territory as a recompense for 400 years of slavery and injustice.

There are many inconsistencies and false teachings in Black Islam. First of all, orthodox Muslims do not even regard The Nation of Islam as a genuine part of the Islamic faith. Black Muslims believe that God is a man — more specifically, Wallace Fard, the founder of their movement, is God. Not only is Fard God, but all blacks are gods. Both Islam and Christianity despise these notions.

Second, similar to orthodox Islam, the Black Muslims claim that the Bible has been distorted. Former leader Elijah Muhammad even said the Bible was a "poisoned book" of slavery. Ironically, the Koran promotes slavery, and the Arabs have also oppressed the blacks. If Black Muslims were consistent, they would also have to say the Koran is a "poisoned book."

Third, Black Muslims teach that Christ was black, and only a prophet. Christ has actually returned in the person of Elijah Muhammad who is "The Savior." Yet Elijah Muhammads life and teachings did not reflect those of Jesus Christ. Christ's message was one of love — Elijah Muhammad's message was one of hate. Christ was sinless, as even the Koran affirms, but Elijah Muhammad was involved in several adulterous affairs. He had five wives and four illegitimate children. Additionally, Elijah Muhammad was a false prophet. He predicted that the whites would be destroyed in 1970. The Black Muslim called 1970 their "D-Day."

Fourth, if a black scientist by the name of Yakub was responsible for creating the "evil" white men, then ultimately, a black man was the author of evil! Thus, Black Muslims really cannot blame whites for oppressing them. Rather, they should blame a black for all the sorrow and misery that has come to the world. Actually, there is no historical evidence for their claim. Black Muslims cannot verify the historicity of their view of Yakub any more than Walt Disney can verify the historicity of Snow White.

In the final analysis, The Nation of Islam is an inconsistent religion begotten of racism and hate. The Black Muslim's solution to racism simply prolongs it, for The Nation of Islam itself is a racist religion that should be denounced just as much as the white supremacists."[52]

THE PLEDGE

The Black Muslims pledge is as follows:

I pledge that from this day forward I will strive to love my brother as I love myself, from this day forward, improve myself spiritually, morally, mentally, socially, politically, and economically for the benefit of myself, my family, and my people. I pledge that I will strive to build businesses, build houses, build hospitals, build factories, and enter into international trade for the good of my family my people and myself.

I pledge that from this day forward I will never raise my hand with a knife or a gun to beat, cut, and shoot any member of my family of any human being except in self-defense. I pledge from this day forward I will never abuse my wife by striking her, - disrespecting her, for she is the mother of my children and the producer of my future. I pledge that from this day forward I will never engage in the abuse of children, little boys or little girls, for sexual gratification. For I will let them grow in peace to be strong men and women for the future of our people. I will never again use the B-word to describe any female — but particularly my own Black sister.

I pledge from this day forward that I will not poison my body with drugs or that, which is destructive to my health and my well being. I pledge from this day forward I will support Black newspapers, Black radio, and Black television. I will support Black artists who clean up their act to show respect for their people and respect for the heirs of the human family.

I will do all of this, so help me God.[53]

---

[52]Reprinted from the Christian Research Institute International, Statement No. 3.135.

[53]Michael H. Cottman, *"The Million Man March"* Copyright 1995, p. 79. Published by Crown Trade Paperbacks, 201 E. 50th St., New York, NY 10022.

THE FUTURE

"Long live the spirit of the Million Man March!" the Black men chanted with pride, their clenched fists raised in the air. "Long live the spirit of the Million Man March!"The invigorating refrain followed a solemn pledge uttered in unison by more than one million African American men who stood shoulder to shoulder on the Mall in Washington, DC., an oath for self-rehabilitation and self-respect. But after the euphoria wears off, after the speeches, poems, and prayers, after the Mall returns to an empty silence, there are hard questions that echo across America: What now? Where do African American men go from here? How do Black men keep the spirit of the March alive? How do Black men cement the instinctive alliance that was forged during one fifteen-hour day? Will we work to rebuild our communities, provide unity within our families, join a church, and nurture young Black men who have lost their way? Perhaps the answers to these questions can be found inside each one of us.

"We're already beginning to see evidence of Black men returning home, atoning and establishing a solid foundation for their families," said Conrad Muhammad. "I spoke with a sister who had not talked to her husband in two years. He had not made one single alimony payment, but after the March, she received a check for three thousand dollars. This is an example of the kind of goodwill that is taking place as a result of the Million Man March. There is more courtesy on the streets. This is the Lord's doings. Some of us have lost our way, we have not been involved in social movements after the sixties, drugs took up our time — but today there is a movement-taking place; we'll see murder go down, we'll see robberies go down, and we'll begin to focus on each other. Minister Farrakhan asked us to go back to our towns and join a church or some religious organizations, and we're already seeing a larger number of people joining these institutions. At our mosque, we had to put chairs outside the past weeks to handle the numbers. The Minister said that we don't have to reinvent the wheel, but to join organizations that already exist."

"We're getting reports that young Black men have gone back to their communities and have taken their pledge of working in their communities to heart, said the Reverend Benjamin Chavis. "They're joining organizations; they're talking about reducing Black-on-Black crime; they're setting up voter registration drives. The March was a transforming event, which is going to impact in a positive way on the lives of millions of African American men who are carrying the spirit of the March with them."

"The first thing we do is remain bonded. We must join some group or church or mosque or organization whose teachings are in synch with our principles," said the Reverend Al Sharpton. "We must remain active and committed to bringing other Black men into the circle of commitment to voter registration, adopt children, and put aside time to volunteer to work in the community. We must make helping each other part of our existence, part of our lifestyle. I see this demonstration going way beyond the leaders who organized it — I see Black people organizing themselves."

Herb Boys said the increased voter registration and, in turn, political power in the African American community is likely to emerge as a result of the March. "The increased voter rolls, many pundits contend, could have an impact on state, city, and county legislative bodies," Boyd said. "Two days after the March, Minister Farrakhan intimated the possibility of forming an alternative force. He said, rather than establishing a third political power that will draw from the Democrats, the Republicans, and the Independents, we would work together. Should these plans cohere, it will mark the first time the Nation of Islam — which during the last decade dropped its disavowal of elector-at politics - has joined in a united front effort or hinted at coalition politics. This political force driven by the Nation of Islam could alter the political landscape in the country."

"We must not let the message of the Million Man March be mangled by the discordant commentary that has surrounded it," The Reverend Jesse Jackson wrote in *The Los Angles Times.* "Hundreds of thousands of African American men gathered together in a historic witness that confounded cynics. Their spirit was purposeful, not hostile. They found joy in unity, not division... As a minority against terrible odds, African-Americans have always known that political action grows out of personal responsibility, that pain must be turned to power."

Bob Law, nationally syndicated radio talk show host and March coordinator said, "It has created a new mindset that makes the rest of what has to be done possible. The principle on which the March was based is from the Bible ... work on the renewal of your mind and all of you shall be redeemed."

"On a practical level, the self-examination and self-rehabilitation is something that must be taken seriously," said Michael Eric Dyson. "We must put into action a concrete application for higher ideals and responsible action. One can get involved in a local boys club, work with the needy, there are many ways to become involved in the community, but the point is to translate that pledge of spirit to spiritual renewal." We have to translate that pledge into policing our communities, getting rid of crack houses, helping Black men who are displaced and who have slipped between the cracks, and helping them find gainful employment. We have to translate that euphoria and good feeling into something ongoing.

"Many of these men don't have the resources to behave decently. They have to endure! financial assault and economic misery. They don't have the inspiration or the material or political means to be counted as worthwhile in our culture. So, unless the laws of the land are reshaped to bolster political and public policy to attend to those economic and social practices that harm Black men, the inspiration to act better may evaporate under the thick pressure of political resistance," Dyson said."[54]

CURRENT TRENDS

The Million Man March

In a moving display of pride and mutual support, hundreds of thousand of black men stood shoulder to shoulder in a crowd that stretched from the Capitol to the Washington Monument and

---

[54]Ibid, pp 83-85.

beyond Monday as speakers at the "Million Man March" urged them to dedicate their lives to curing the ills afflicting black America.

Basking in the racial solidarity of attending the largest gathering of African Americans in the nation's history, participants embraced each other and the march's theme of "atonement" to create an event significantly different from civil rights protests of the past.

As many of the speakers and numerous participants made clear, Monday's assemblage was sharply focused on what black men should do for them, not what others should do for them. Unlike past Washington demonstrations -such as the historic 1963 March on Washington, where 250,000 people heard Dr. Martin Luther King Jr.'s passionate "I have a dream" speech — few of Monday's speakers appealed to government for help.

"Today, we ask nothing of the government," Baltimore Mayor Kurt Schmoke declared before a crowd officially estimated at 400,000, but "we ask everything of ourselves."

The march's primary organizer, Nation of Islam leader Louis Farrakhan, delivered a searing demands for self-discipline in a more-than two-hour speech at the end of the day.

"We cannot continue the destruction of our lives and the destruction of our communities, "Farrakhan said to cheers and nods of agreement. Black men must stop the "death of the babies by the senseless slaughter" in black neighborhoods, he said, calling on members of the crowd to pledge never again to commit violence, use drugs, abuse women or children or otherwise degrade themselves or their community.

Rosa Parks, whose refusal to give up her seat on the bus in Montgomery, Alabama in 1955 marked a turning point in the civil rights struggle and who was one of several women to address the march, urged black men "to make changes in their lives for the better". While such messages of blame and demands for improvement often quieted the crowd, they did not stifle its remarkable sense of warmth and community.

"I don't see no strangers here," declared George Grover, a mechanic from Virginia Beach, Virginia, who passed through the crowd offering handshakes to everyone he met. "These are my brothers. We might have been strangers, but I've been telling everyone: "Hey, man! I'm your brother, George."

Although the march had become ensnared in a controversy that divided both blacks and whites, primarily because of Farrakhan, the day's events were marked by messages of peace, reverence, celebration and optimism.

Even Farrakhan suggested the time might have come for him to sit down with leaders of the Jewish community, whom he has denounced as "bloodsuckers" and who has denounced him as anti-Semitic.

Farrakhan brushed aside criticism of his role in the, saying he had divine guidance. "Whether you like it or not, God brought the idea through me, and he did bring it through me because my heart was dark with hatred and anti-Semitism," he said. "If my heart was that dark, how is the message so bright?"

He urged the men to go home and join black organizations — even those that refused to endorse his rally — to take hold of political power, unite against racism and cleanse black communities of crime, drugs and violence.

Away from the Mall, critics continued to denounce Farrakhan, and some prominent blacks remained ambivalent about the event.

Clinton Speech

President Clinton, in a speech in Austin, Texas, that focused on race relations, referred obliquely to Farrakhan, saying: "One million men do not make right one man's message of malice and division. No good house was ever built on a bad foundation."

Clinton later flew to Los Angeles to speak at a celebrity-filled benefit concert at the Pantages Theater in Hollywood slated to raise money for the fight against substance abuse. He was to return to Texas today.

House Speaker Newt Gingrich (R-Ga.), commenting during a trip to his home state, called Farrakhan "an unrepentant bigot" and predicted he would draw strength and legitimacy from the march.

Retired Gen. Colin L. Powell, a possible presidential candidate, expressed the ambivalence many black leaders have felt about the event because of Farrakhan's role: "If I was there, I would be tom between the opportunity to present a message of family and reconciliation to the group," Powell said in New York. "But at the same time ... I would be a little reluctant to lend too much credibility to his [Farrakhan's] leadership of the event.

"Let's not prejudge what might be accomplished," Powell added. "Let's let the people who are at the march make that judgment. We can trust them to separate out what is wisdom in the message from Minister Farrakhan and what is not wisdom, what are anti-Semitic, racist statements. They can sort that out."

That was just what George Raging, a plumber from Landover, MD seemed to do as he surveyed the scene from a grassy knoll next to the gleaming dome of the Capitol. The sight of black men stretching out before him to the west in wave after wave overcame him as far as he could see.

"We're all together here today, and hopefully we'll stay together," he said. "I hope this march is the beginning of wonderful things."

Measure of Anxiety

The prospect of so many black men massing together had spread a measure of anxiety throughout the Washington metropolitan area — concern about snarled traffic and more.

Indeed, so many people stayed away from the downtown area that normally busy streets and expressways were all but deserted.

Yet as a testament to the good feelings that permeated the rally, law enforcement officials spent much of the day with little police work to do. By mid-afternoon, D.C. Metropolitan Police and U.S. Park Police said they had made three arrests for unlicensed vending. In addition, the metropolitan police said they received a telephone bomb threat, which was traced to a pay telephone and a suspect was arrested.

The Associated Press reported that one elderly man in the crowd suffered a heart attack and died, and some two dozen participants were treated in area hospitals for minor injuries.

The idea for the "Million Man March" surfaced last year, shortly after co-organizer Benjamin F. Chavis Jr. was ousted as executive director of the National Association for the Advancement of Colored People. Farrakhan and Chavis said then they would attempt to lead one million black men in a march on Washington during a "holy day of atonement" for the sins that black men have committed against themselves and their communities.

Almost from the beginning, the idea provoked division. Some dismissed it as impossible or racially divisive because two controversial black activists were leading it. Farrakhan, who has been rebuked repeatedly for making anti-Semitic comments, has drawn the ire of Jewish leaders and organizations, many of them traditional allies for civil rights organizations. Chavis' firing by the NAACP because of a money and sex scandal seemed to make him an unlikely leader for a ceremony of atonement.

Nevertheless, Farrakhan and Chavis pressed ahead with the idea without encouragement from most traditional black organizations and with no financial support from white groups. Word of the "Million Man March" was passed along among grass-roots activists in black communities and was heavily promoted on black-oriented radio shows.

Even as the march moved toward becoming a reality, controversy followed as groups of black women and others protested the all-male and racially exclusive nature of the assembly. Farrakhan had asked that women not attend the rally but instead support the march by staying home with their children and sending the men to Washington.

In the end, women joined in the march. Some, such as Parks and National Council of Negro Women President Dorothy Height, addressed the crowd from the podium at the foot of the west front of the Capitol.

Poet Maya Angelou, in a reprise of her appearance at the inauguration of Clinton, read a poem written for the day:

"Draw near to one another,
Save your race.
You have been paid for in a distant place.
The old ones remind us that slavery's chains
Have paid for our freedom again and again."

The Rev. Jesse Jackson praised the crowd for its resolve to change the fate of black America. "The idea of a million men has touched a nerve deep in the hearts of people yearning to breathe free,"he said. "Big meetings were never allowed on the plantation. We've always yearned for a big meeting. Today we've left the plantation. This is a big meeting."

Jackson noted that the 1963 march was a historic step in the civil rights struggle and he suggested that the "Million Man March" might be remembered in the same light. "America will benefit and ultimately be grateful for this day," he said. "When the rising tide for racial Justice and gender equality and family stability lifts the boats stuck at the bottom, all boats benefit."

Grass Roots Resolve

Although Jackson and Farrakhan were among some familiar faces, most of the speakers were not well known personalities, even to the black population. Many represented Farrakhan's highly secretive Nation of Islam; others were activists little known outside their own communities.

Together, they offered a full-throated exhibition of grass-roots frustration and resolve to improve the plight of black men.

One of the most stirring speeches of the day came from 10-year old Tiffany Maytr, of Waldorf, Md., who called on the men to stand up for young girls. "I need the protection of every black man."

She said in a clear, melodious voice, "I'm a girl. Won't you look after me? I am not yet a woman, even if I pretend to be. Save me from abusers. I am not the cause of pain in your life, I am not the stand-in for your girlfriend or your wife."

Ron Sailor, who represented a contingent of young NAACP activists from Atlanta, led the crowd in a chant: "Praise God for young black males!"

He then admonished the audience to work on the public perception of black men. "I'm so tired of America treating young black males like we are prodigal children," he said, encouraging black men to go home and get involved in turning around their neighborhoods and holding political leaders accountable to black people.

"It's time to go home, "he said. But before they left, nearly everyone — those in the crowd before him and those watching on television — wanted to hear what Farrakhan would say.

Dressed in a blue, double-breasted suit with his traditional bow tie, Farrakhan spoke for more than two hours — from the warm glow of a perfect autumn afternoon until the shadows of a cold evening had stretched across the Mall. Instead of the fiery speeches that are his trademark, he struck a conciliatory tone by paying tribute to all other religions.

Urging his listeners to become involved in community life when they return to their homes, Farrakhan told them to attend "church, synagogue, temple or mosque." Quoting more from the Old and New Testaments of the Bible than from the Koran, the holy book of Islam, he talked extensively of Jesus Christ's teachings.

Acknowledging and responding to the concerns of some critics of the march, as well as many of its participants, Farrakhan said the march was not a political platform for his own views. "I don't want to take credit for a day like this, "he said. "It's bigger than all of us."

Farrakhan also called for a dialogue with the Jewish community, saying reducing tensions between blacks and Jews would be positive for the nation.

"I don't like this squabble with the members of the Jewish community," he said. "Perhaps in the light of what we see today, it's time to sit down and talk, not with any preconditions."

Jewish groups, however, responded with skepticism and demanded the man who once labeled their religion "dirty" repudiate his past rhetoric. "Minister Farrakhan wants dialogue but has done nothing to demonstrate that dialogue would be meaningful," said David Friedman, executive director of the AntiDefamation League's Washington office.[55]

---

[55]Permission granted by the *Los Angeles Times*, Copyright 1995, and The Times Mirror Company. Tuesday, october 17, 1995, part A, pp. 1-3.

The "Million Man March" organized by Nation of Islam leader Louis Farrakhan drew an estimated 400,000 African American men to the nation's capital October 16, where they heard a variety of messages from black leaders.

The rally was billed as a "day of atonement and reconciliation" for America's black men. Many speakers urged those present to recommit themselves to their wives, their children and their communities — making the rally sound more like a Promise Keepers convention than a civil rights event. But the politically charged rhetoric of some speakers combined with Farrakhan's controversial views cast a shadow on one of the largest events ever held in Washington, D.C.

The rally day began with 7 a.m. prayers, where thousands of people sang gospel hymns and prayed for the day to come. That was followed by an 11-hour rally featuring speeches from a wide variety of black leaders — including a two-and-a-half hour speech by Farrakhan himself.

Many speakers stuck to the day's themes of self-reliance and atonement. Baltimore Mayor Kurt Schmoke called on black men to be self-reliant saying; "Today we asked nothing of the government. Today we ask everything of ourselves." He added, "Let our choices be for life, for protecting our women, our children, keeping our brothers free of drugs, free of crime."

The Rev. Jesse Jackson urged the crowd to join him in praying, "In the spirit of atonement, we pray to God to forgive us for our sins and the foolishness of our ways as we seek to do better and never to become bitter, and let nothing, nobody stand between us and the love of God."

Other speakers took a more political tone, Former Chicago congressman Gus Savage, who lost a reelection bid after making anti-Semitic and racially offensive remarks, used his address to the crowd to condemn white America, saying blacks are not angry enough. "Many, if not most of us, are proud to be black and prefer not to talk, act, and think like whites, " Savage said. "White dreams have crippled many black children and white values have maimed many black families."

The Rev. Al Sharpton said that Republicans had been elected "in 1994 by the angry white man" vote, and warned the nation to "get ready for the story of 1996, when the angry black man brings in new Congress."

Much of Farrakhan's address to the Million-Man March centered on the need of black men to take responsibility for themselves, their families, and their communities. "We must accept the responsibility that God has put upon us not only to be good husbands and fathers and builders of our community, but God is now calling up the despised and the rejected to become the cornerstone and the builders of a new world, "he said.

Farrakhan pointed to racial inequality in America. "There's still two Americas, one black, one white, separate and unequal," he said. "The real evil in America is the idea that undergirds the setup of the Western world, and that idea is called white supremacy."

Farrakhan said black men must take a renewed sense of purpose back with them to bring healing to their families and communities. He urged his listeners to avoid foul language, immoral music, and other vices. "Demonstrate your gift, not your breast," he said. "Demonstrate your gift, not what is between your legs, clean up, black man, and the world will respect and honor you. But you have fallen down like the prodigal son and your Hussein corn and feeding swine."

Farrakhan added, "Moral and spiritual renewal is a necessity. Every one of you must go back home and join some church, synagogue, temple or mosque that is teaching spiritual and oral uplift... The men are in the streets, and we got to get back to the houses of God."

Farrakhan brushed off the comments of critics who said that while the march was a good idea, Farrakhan's extremist views made him the wrong man to lead it. He said, "Whether you like it or not God brought the idea through me, and He didn't bring it through me because my heart was dark with hatred and anti-Semitism. If my heart was that dark, how is the message so bright?"

He also rejected those who sought to separate the message of the march from its organizer. "You can't separate Newton from the law that Newton discovered, nor can you separate Einstein from the theory of relativity. It would be silly to try to separate

173

Moses from the Torah or Jesus from the Gospel or Muhammad from the Koran," he said.

Farrakhan's frequent offensive remarks led many mainstream black organizations — such as the National Association for the Advancement of Colored People (NAACP), National Urban League, National Baptist Convention USA, and Progressive National Baptist Convention — to distance themselves from the event.

Bishop George McKinney from St. Stephens Church of God in Christ in San Diego said that the issues Farrakhan addressed should be separated from his agenda. "The response in Washington indicates the importance of some of the issues being addressed, and should be separated from the agenda Mr. Farrakhan has," said McKinney. "He preaches an agenda of hate mongering and divisiveness, and he seeks to build a platform to strengthen his organization, Crime, drugs, promiscuity, abandonment of babies and families — those are the issues I preach."

E.V. Hill, pastor of Mount Zion Church in Los Angeles, helped plan the 1963 march with Martin Luther King, Jr. and has spoken at several Promise Keepers events on "Raising the Standard in Our Personal Life." On the Million Man March, Hill stated that he is amazed at how many claim to have never heard before what Farrakhan has been saying about unity and personal responsibility.

"His message is not unique," said Hill. "It is insulting to the pulpits of the land to suggest we haven't been saying that. Small storefront churches have been saying this for years."

Hill stated that the difference between Promise Keepers and Farrakhan's march is that "Promise Keepers is Christo-centric. It invites every man, no matter his color or creed to come."

Pastor Guy A. Williams of Parker Memorial Baptist in Takoma Park urged his men to stay away from the event because it was organized by non-Christians. "How are you going to march on D.C. with somebody who doesn't believe in your God?" Williams asked from the pulpit the day before the march. "Power doesn't come on tomorrow. Power comes from the Holy Ghost."

The Congressional Black Caucus endorsed the event, as did the Reverend Joseph Lowery, head of the influential Southern Christian Leadership Conference. Lowery participated dispirit his reservations about Farrakhan. "We need to go back to our communities with a new sense of Godness," he told congregants at Union Temple Baptist Church in Anacostia. "As we leave this place, God will show us the way"[56]

[56]Permission granted for repirnt, Southern California Christian Times, Volume 13, No. 11, November 1998, pp 1, 10.

Why African American
Youth Are Attracted
To
The Jehovah Witnesses

Why African American Youth Are Attracted To The Jehovah Witnesses

1. Family togetherness.

2. Social outlets.

3. Work provisions.

4. Possession of internal peace.

5. Hope of salvation.

6. Sincerity and intensity of Jehovah Witness and their willingness of members to witness to community residence with fervor and to hold to the convictions even at the cost of public disapproval and imprisonment as opposed to apathy of their regular church member.

INTRODUCTION TO
THE JEHOVAH'S WITNESSES

The Jehovah's Witnesses have called almost everyone, at one time or another. Many people, believers and unbelievers, know that their teaching is wrong, but not usually in what respects. It is not sufficient to not answer the door or tell the to go away when they call as they will come back again and again. To quote the Bible, John 8:32 says, "You shall know the truth, and the truth shall set you free." They do not have the truth, although they think they have. To be able to minister to them effectively when they come knocking on your door, it is important to know exactly what their beliefs are, where they get them from, and the real Scriptures and reasons to show them that their beliefs are wrong. They will quote scriptures to support their beliefs, although these are almost exclusively from their own Bible translation and are usually taken out of context by ignoring surrounding scriptures to make up the full picture of God's word. These scriptures often bear little resemblance to the same scripture in other Bibles, the translators of the Witnesses unique Bible having mistranslated it from the original Greek or Hebrew texts by breaking the rules of Greek grammar, and changing or adding words to passages to make it fit their beliefs — examples of this you will find throughout this document. Some of their teaching has been taken directly from other cults or sects, such as the annihilation of the wicked idea which has been pinched directly from Adventism; although they will deny these links. They will refer to themselves as "Christians," but when examining this claim, it is clear that they are not. They also claim to be the "only true religion", as do many other cults, but this too can be shown to be false.

It is important to let them know where you and they stand if you wish to discuss their beliefs and the truth that the Bible shows with them. You need to be very aware of your beliefs and how to support this, as they give a convincing and difficult to break argument that they have the truth and you do not. Their usual method of "recruitment" is to suggest that they come round for a Bible study (using their own translation, of course), then after several such meetings suggest that you "may like" to come along to one of their meetings, which leads to more meeting invitations, then eventually when the time comes that you have "'entered into the kingdom" fully, only then do you find out the whole of their beliefs, as until then they seem very reluctant to disclose the all.

The more people that they come across with the true Christian message and the truth that comes with it, eventually seeds of doubt will be sown in their minds, and they will begin to question whether what they actually have found is true, which in turn may turn them away from their deceit and into the glorious Truth which can be found in Christ Jesus. Although it is unlikely that you will be able to break through to them to "save" them there and then, if they have called on people that day and have been given the Christian message a dozen or so times, their faith may just be rocky enough for you to make them see the light! At all times, we should show our love towards them, although the are believing deceit, as Jesus said in Matthew 5:43-44 "You have heard that it was said, love your friends, hate your enemies. But now I tell you: love your enemies and pray for those who persecute you. Be gentle but firm with them, remember, as what they believe is as valuable to them as our faith is to us, and to destroy it without offering the only true alternative is dangerous."

They call mainly during the day, I believe, as normally many vulnerable people are at home, often alone, such as the unemployed (who will often be depressed, bored, lonely or all three), young or single mothers, and elderly; and not during the evening when the whole family might be around for an objective discussion. By selecting lonely people, the "friendship" they offer is subtly used as a fear against leaving later — if they leave, they will find themselves totally cut off from everyone they have met through the Jehovah's Witnesses (which by now us probably the only people that they know and will talk to them), and this fear of being lonely again often forces people to keep going. By demonstrating Christian love to these people, it can sometimes be enough to break this fear. The fact that Jesus loves them, and the friendly invitation we can give them, rather than slamming the door in their faces, also helps our case. By convincingly portraying that they have found the answer, many of these vulnerable people — who often don't know any kind of answer except "um, never thought about it much" — find themselves unable to withstand their argument and are convincingly led into their deceit. If you have an answer, they will often point to things in the original Greek Hebrew texts (which, they of course will have translated to suit their arguments) to try and prove you wrong, thus taking advantage of most peoples lack of knowledge of Greek and Hebrew language. However, having several Bible translations handy to show that none of your translations have their message is a useful defense.

They call on you in pairs (apart from the fact that Jesus sent his disciples out in pairs) because if one of them does not know the answer to your question the other usually does, and it is difficult top break through their patter. On initial visits, one is usually an experienced Witness and the other a "trainee", and you will soon find out which is which — if you direct your questions at the trainee, the trainee will soon get confused and they will soon both leave. After a few visits, if they feel that you are more of a challenge that they can cope with, they will send the "heavy mob" around — usually one or two of the "elders", or someone who has been a Witness a long time, to try and out argue you. If you find yourself getting stuck into an argument which you do not sufficiently know the answer to or scripture for it, there is no shame in telling them that you do not know the complete answer immediately and need to look it up, and perhaps even to ask them to come back later, as we cannot be expected to know everything. Remember that they "learn" a subject each week and they then have to go and spread that message over the following weeks, so it is totally fresh in their minds, and they will rarely willingly stray off that subject.

They do not learn the Bible freely as we are able to and need to, but in their weekly "Bible studies" they are essentially told what to read, how it is to be interpreted and why it is "true". From this they get what can be likened to "trigger responses" to questions and answers you may have (like a pushy door-to-door salesman) which can be quite hard to break through — although they seem to know everything off the top of their heads, they "remember" scriptures like a theatrical script to be repeated rather than understood, interpreted and applied to your life. Each week's learning is then to be "spread" over the next weeks, so a good start is to try and steer them away from the original subject of conversation onto something of your choosing. They will be able to detect when they are losing the conversation, and will make their excuses and leave, if you can begin to convince them that your faith is strong and they are in deceit.

They will leave colorful, glossy brochures or their magazines such as Awake! Or Watchtower, with some nice, general interest Reader Digest-type articles thrown in to mask the teaching enclosed, but good quality printing and pretty pictures cannot hide lies. One brochure, "Why is life so full of problems?" on the outside cover has a beautiful full-color scene of trees, blue sky, smiling faces, and people cuddling wild animals, whereas on the inside we have bland and white pictures of a starving child, an old lady being mugged, industrial pollution and the 1995 massacre in Rwanda, with the cheerful message "Serious problems grow worse. Why? The world's religions have failed". I usually accept their brochures as a matter of courtesy (it also helps to find out more about them), but in return makes them take a Christian tract in exchange. However, they are taught that someone accepting a tract means that they have to call on you again, although it may not be the same people that call, and is worth remembering if you are or are not happy to talk further with them.

Two good points to begin with when talking to them are firstly your testimony of how you came to Jesus (although they will argue scriptures, they cannot easily disprove personal experiences, however "coincidental" they may seem) and ask them how and why they became Jehovah's Witnesses: and secondly tell them of Jesus' love for all of us including them and what He has done for you in your life, as it is clear that they do not have a personal relationship with Jesus Christ, although not surprising considering their teaching about Him. Do pray with/for them if you are able to, although this will often encourage them to leave (useful if you would like them to leave!)

They have an obvious "hierarchy" system, which you will eventually work your way through if you keep asking them back and discussing the errors of their beliefs in depth. This starts at the bottom with trainees and "new converts" who basically will only drop leaflets and are told not enter into deep discussion with you. Next are two or three levels of "middle members" who generally are ranked depending on how long they have been a Witness, beginning at the lowest who will only talk with you about the week's learned subject, up to the top level who will try to tackle you on most subjects. Each level, if they are tackled on a subject they are insufficiently taught on, will make their excuses and leave, then upon return to the Kingdom Hall simply seek the answers from the next "level" and arrange for one of the next level members, who doesn't "know the answer'" to come round. If, however, you can out-argue them, then the Elders will start coming round in pairs to you. That is usually the top level that they will take you on at give up (blacklist) you, and you will be classed as "wicked and ungodly" as you do not accept their message. Above that, there are a team of "Regional Overseeing Ministers" who are responsible for the "well being" of a particular region, who may be brought to see you if you are a really stubborn challenge and they think that they can still win you for their "kingdom". After each visit, they will make notes about you to pass back to the "senior members'" to try and find a weakness in your faith, which they will then tackle you on next time, and by appearing to have all the answers they think that they can win you.

In this document I have outlined some of the main Jehovah's Witnesses teaching, where they get this from, and some scriptures that disprove their beliefs; undoubtedly you will be able to add many more. Although most of the scriptures I quote are reproduced simply to support the arguments and to enable the document to be read independently, you are encouraged to "check them out" and find the translations in your own Bibles while reading through to make everything clear in your own mind and with your translation's wording ready for you to tackle them. However strong your arguments seem to be, remember that the

Holy Spirit is the one that will ultimately lead to the truth, and be sensitive to Him yourself for any "pointers" while talking to them.

Permission granted by Tom Biggs, University of Tulsa, Tulsa, Oklahoma.

JEHOVAH'S WITNESSES

Among the conspicuous religious expressions which are typically American in origin and development, the Jehovah's witnesses have attracted much attention in recent years.[1] My interest in the Movement has been awakened primarily because of certain doctrinal interpretations and emphases, and because of its present phenomenal growth.

Many observers of the Jehovah's Witnesses have concluded that it is a "Christian deviation"[2] in that its system of doctrine imitates, and at the same time distorts, the essential Christian beliefs. The Jehovah's Witnesses are typical in many ways of the religious groups which emphasize millennialism as a major doctrine. Although millenarianism is not new in the history of the Christian church, a new interpretation of the Old Testament foundations for the beliefs, especially in the book of Daniel, is given by this Movement with an appeal to a philosophy of history to support this particular interpretation. In the tradition of millenarianism, the Jehovah's Witnesses regard the prophetic and apocalyptic books as storehouse of hidden information (being revealed only, to those who are Witnesses of Jehovah), which may enable the Bible student to predict the future in detail.[3]

At a time when church membership in the United States is on the increase, this Movement, which was almost obscure a half century ago, is drawing into its fold a major share of the

---

[1]Herbert H. Storup, *The Jehovah's Witnesses* (New York: Columbia University Press, 1945), p. I.

[2]Horton Davis, Christian Deviations (New York: The Philosophical Library, 1954). (This book is an apology for historic Christianity and contains valuable criticisms and evaluation of the Jehovah's Witnesses.)

[3]Ibid, pp. 10, 11.

religious converts. At the same time, it is attracting large numbers of proselytes from Christian denominations.[4] Not only has unprecedented growth been achieved in the United States, but also the missionary appeal in foreign lands has met with astounding success.

Reverend Charles P. Greco, Bishop of the Roman Catholic Church in Alexandria has observed: "In 1940 they (the Jehovah's Witnesses) had a world membership of 44,000. By 1946 they had skyrocketed to the incredible total of 500,000 — an increase of more than 1, 100 percent in six years! This is the most sensational increase achieved by an religious organization in modem times."[5] Morley Cole in his book, *Jehovah's Witnesses*, agrees with the above statement that the Movement is growing faster than any religious group today. "During the decade 1942-52 the number of Jehovah's Witnesses doubled in North America, multiplied five times in Asia, more than six times in the Pacific Islands, about seven times in Europe and Africa, more than twelve times in the Atlantic Islands, and nearly fifteen times in South America."[6]

A large number of Witnesses contacted during this study consisted of proselytes from Christian denominations.

Historically speaking, the Jehovah's Witnesses claim to be the oldest line of "true" worshipers of God. For Jehovah God has had Witnesses on earth for about sixty centuries.[7] The line is traced back to Abel, the second son of Adam and Eve, who "offered unto God a more excellent sacrifice than Cain [his brother], by which he obtained witness that he was righteous *(Hebrews 11:4)*. His brother, Cain, thus becoming the first martyr for religious freedom, murdered Abel. Outstanding among the witnesses down through the ages have been saints and seers, namely, Enoch, Noah, Abraham, Moses, Jeremiah, John the Baptist, Jesus Christ, who is pre-eminent among them, and

---

[4]A large number of Witnesses contacted during this study consisted of proselytes from Christian denominations.

[5]*Our Sunday Visitor*, Volume XLIV, pp. 15, 23.

[6]Morley Cole, *Jehovah's Witnesses* (New York: Vantage Press, 1955), p. 25.

[7]According to the Jehovah's Witnesses' calculation of time, this is approximately the number of years having passed since the creation of Adam in the fall of 4025 B.C.: see *New Heavens and a New Earth*, pp. 36, 53.

Charles T. Russell, who is regarded as the most significant religious reformer since New Testament times.[8] Only in 1872 (A.D.) in America did the Witnesses begin to draw together for worldwide work after many centuries of being unorganized and scattered over the face of the earth. The prophet and leader who gave fresh impetus to the "age old" movement in modem times was Charles Taze Russell of Allegheny, Pennsylvania.[9]

Since the Society considers itself to be the only remnant of true worshipers, it alone is the custodian of the Divine Plan. The Witnesses, therefore, are those who have made a covenant with Jehovah God to carry out His plan.[10]

Jehovah's Witnesses constitute a body or group of persons consecrated to do the will of Almighty God, under the leadership of His Son, Christ Jesus. They have drawn together of the purpose of declaring that he whose name alone is Jehovah is the Universal Sovereign, and that He is the Author and Creator of Earth's permanent heavenly government of righteousness for which Christ Jesus taught his disciples to pray to Almighty God. To everyone they point out the only way to that kingdom, which shall Almighty permanently take the place of all earth's present governments that shall be destroyed soon in Jehovah's battle at Armageddon.[11]

Although Charles Taze Russell is regarded by observers as the founder of the Jehovah's witnesses organization, the Witnesses prefer to regard him as the Millennium's foremost prophet and organizer of the legal corporation known as the Watch Tower Bible & Tract Society, in 1884. As for founding the spiritual society of Jehovah's Witnesses, the Witnesses categorically deny that it was the work of any man. They affirm that the movement was one of the fruits of the kingdom itself. It was the result of "returning to pure Bible teaching." They hold

---

[8]Royston Pike, *The Jehovah's Witnesses* (New York: Philosophical Library, 1954) p. 8.

[9]*Let God Be True*, pp. 210, 211.

[10]Herbert H. Stroup, *The Jehovah's Witnesses* (New York: Columbia University Press; 1945) p. 23; also see Marcus Bach, *These Have Found a Faith* (New York: The Bobbs Merrill Co.,1946), p. 51.

[11]*Let God Be True*, pp. 210, 211.

that "when hundreds and thousands of minds and hearts were drawn together by the pure lingual of the Scriptures, the power that produced the Bible necessarily produced the society of modem Bible adherents."

There is no doubt, then, that the spiritual society is produced by Jehovah's spirit. Nevertheless, a consideration of the three important leaders of the Society since 1884 may enlighten the historical perspective.

ITS ORIGIN AND DEVELOPMENT

In 1879 a Bible study leader named Charles Taze Russell was looking for a way to expound his somewhat peculiar teachings. He had departed from orthodoxy by denying the existence of hell, the Trinity, and the deity of Christ, and felt compelled to reach a larger audience. He co-published the *Herald of the Morning* magazine with its founder, N.H. Barbour, and it is here that we find the first records of Russell's movement. By 1884 Russell controlled the publication, renamed it the *watchtower Announcing Jehovah's Kingdom*, and founded Zion's watchtower Tract Society (now known as the Watch Tower Bible and Tract Society). The first edition of the *watchtower* magazine was only 6,000 copies each month. Today the Witnesses' publishing complex in Brooklyn, New York, churns out 100,000 books and 800,000 copies of its two magazines daily!

Russell's theology established the foundation of the Witnesses militant opposition to all other church organizations. Until his death in 1916, aboard a train in Texas, Russell insisted that the Bible could be understood only according to his interpretation. At the heart of his system as a prophetic chronology that predicted the Gentile era would end in 1914. (Russell had already concluded that Christ had returned in 1874, but as a "presence in the upper air," not a visible manifestation.) The end of the sealing of the 144,000 saints who would be "Kings and priest in heaven" was also designated to occur in 1914. Those saved after that would belong to a servant class, "the great company," who would rule on earth under the tutelage of the 144,000.

After the death of Russell, a Missouri lawyer named Joseph Franklin Rutherford took over the presidency of the WatchTower Society. At a Columbus, Ohio convention in 1931, he cited Isaiah 43: 10 as the pretext for changing the name of the organization to "Jehovah's Witnesses." Thus, the stigma of Russell's questionable scholarship (he had only a seventh grade education) and morals was resolved. Rutherford assumed total charge of the organization, and from then on his prolific writings were the source of divine mandate. This consolidation of power enabled him to discard some of Russell's less desirable teachings about the gathering of the Jews and the great pyramid theory.

After Rutherford's death, Nathan Knorr took over. In the same way that Rutherford had sought to supplant Russell's influence, Knorr ignored the works of Rutherford. Today, the Society is led by Frederick William franz, a widower in his eighties, who wields papal power over the lives of 4.1 million Witnesses all over the world.

The pronouncements that issue forth from the Brooklyn headquarters (known to members as "Bethel") are binding, and no deviation is tolerated. Strict theological control ensures a consistency of doctrine. Witnesses avoid contact with outsiders, and the rare chance to meet one usually occurs when they knock on the door. Never identifying who they are, these friendly but persistent zealots deserve high marks for perseverance. Society statistics indicate that 740 house calls are required to recruit each of the nearly 200,000 new members who join every year.

TECHNIQUES FOR RECRUITMENT

A. Personal Contact

The Jehovah Witnesses have become a large body since their founding. They have recruited many Black youths into their membership rank. They are particularly strong evangelists and their missionary endeavors are very strong in the black ghettos of many American cities throughout the USA the Witnesses' method of recruiting is personal contact and through the media of their pamphlet and book: *The Watchtower*. Witnesses encourage and train their members to become evangelizes and ministers.

B. through the Media of Pamphlets & Books

The Witnesses usually are in front of stores peddling their Watchtower literature. They are usually in groups of two's or three's. It is not an unusual sight to see small children holding out *The Watchtower*. It also is not unusual to see Chicano and Black Members at these gathering spots. It is very common for several members to make a canvass of various neighborhoods on Saturdays to peddle their literature.

C. Invitations to Kingdom Hall & D. Home Visits

The technique for recruiting members is to see the prospective members on their brand of Christianity via personal persuasion based upon witness of transformation of their lives upon induction into the Jehovah Witnesses. Usually at storefronts or knocking on doors, a prospective convert is engaged in conversation, the basis of which first is to sell the magazine. The Witness points out to his prospective convert what the Witness takes to be an especially important article about something that is happening currently and then points to a passage in the Bible which the Witness argues forewarns of the event which is presently transpiring. For the Witness all truth is grounded only in the Bible. The Witness then invests the prospective member with leaflets and invitations to visit Kingdom Hall. If the perspective member shows signs of intense interest, then a home meeting or visit is immediately scheduled. About three or four members will come on this visit. They then endeavor to persuade the prospective member through argument and accounts of personal witness that the Jehovah Witness is the only truly Christian religious group that there is. All other groups, according to them, have been tainted with ungodliness by straying away from the Word and the Law of God. These other religious groups, including the orthodox groups have taken on paganism by observing holidays, such as Christmas and Easter. These religious groups have also been led astray by science, technology, and by a very materialistic and wanton generation. They have instituted blood transfusions, which are against the rule of God, and the salute to the flag is a sign of a wanton generation that put other things before God.

REFUSING BLOOD TRANSFUSIONS

Refusing to accept blood transfusions is just one of several distinctive beliefs associated with Jehovah's Witnesses. They do not donate vital organs nor receive transplants. Until 1952, they were forbidden smallpox vaccinations. They also refuse to vote, salute the flag, sign "The Star Spangled Banner" (or any nationalistic anthem), and will not serve in the Armed Forces. Witnesses who depart from such injunctions are dis-fellowshiped. From then on, Kingdom Hall worshipers (even family members) consider them as dead. The excommunicated "apostate" is told he will not rise from the grave on Judgment Day.

YOUNGSTERS INTERVIEWED

Most of the Black youngsters that were interviewed by me who were members of the Witnesses indicated that their membership was the result of the parents being recruited into the organization. Their young also were inducted and inculcated in the faith. These youth seemed secure and very self-assured that they were doing the right thing. In fact, some felt that they were superior or in that they were "saved." They were God loving and God fearing. The group promoted *family togetherness*. Children worked and walked with their mothers and fathers in their evangelical quests. They attended the same functions that their parents attended. Young people attended Bible study groups at their homes and at the homes of others. They attended affairs and events as well as worship services at their assemblies and halls. They were invited to and did attend various other assemblies, halls and conventions within the *Witnesses* connection. The Witnesses provided a *social outlet* and entertainment for their members. They also *provide work* which is rewarding for members. The Witnesses gives to its membership a sense of worth and integrity. Members are in the Legion of Jehovah fighting against the Prince of Darkness, who presently holds the world firmly in his palm, by tying to wring away from his grip the souls of as many people over to entry into Jehovah's Kingdom when the end does come.

There were some young Blacks to whom I talked who were recruited from the street or in their homes by Witnesses. They expressed that before joining the Witnesses that their lives were very insecure and drab. They now are happy and at *peace internally* as members of the Witnesses. They loved their work with the Witnesses and they feel great satisfaction in "opening the eyes" of others, as their own eyes had been open by those before them. They are firmly committed to Jehovah, who is their only Judge and Guide. They scorn in particular medical science, saying that it is a tool in the hand of the prince of evil. These young people placed no trust any confidence in government since it is a man-made and man-run institution. They are very comfortable being with their own group. They indicated that they felt that judgment was near at hand. These young minority people expressed confidence in the fact that they were ready to face judgment but expressed some sorrow that not everyone would be saved. Their aim in life seemed to be saving the presently unsavable by opening up their eyes to God's Kingdom.

From individual accounts, it appears that the Jehovah Witnesses offer their members the *hope of* salvation when the time of judgment arrives, which is rapidly approaching from their point of reference. They shall, at that time, take their rightful places in Jehovah's Kingdom. The Witnesses also offer to their member's social and recreational outlets within the framework of Witness rationale. These members become friends and co-workers in God's mission on earth. Their lives are regulated within the Witnesses moral and ethical framework. They do not aimlessly spend money on Christmas gifts, feasts for Easter or Christmas or clothes for these occasions. They also do not spend money on tobacco nor spirited drinks, which is a "no-no" for them. Thus, even if depressed wage earners, they tend to save and become more economically independent and secure than other ghetto dwellers. They are family oriented and feel a sense of worth and integrity about their person. They have great personal satisfaction in their soul "saving" enterprise.

BENEFITS TO MEMBERS

The Witnesses have thus benefited its members by giving them an opportunity to cope with their economic and social problems as well as resolve psychological problems. They have developed a personal relationship to God via prayer. They are more economically secure and independent; being free of reckless Christmas and Easter spending as well as the expense of cigarettes and alcohol. Psychologically, they feel a sense of pride and dignity about their person. The group provides them with friends, companions and mates, who all strive to better their lives and to bring that life in balance with the Will and Rule of God. In. turn, these members serve the Witnesses well by bringing into the fold more members through their evangelical endeavors.

Jehovah's Witnesses Limit Shunning

Reprint from the Los Angeles Times

Jehovah's Witnesses leaders have eased their policy of "shunning" erring followers, limiting the silent treatment only to baptized members.

An article in the authoritative Watchtower magazine dated November 15 informs its members that unbaptized people who become "publishers" — that is, witness door-to-door or on street corners — and then drop out or violate church rules should no longer be shunned.

"The Bible does not require that Witnesses avoid speaking with (them)," the magazine said. "Previously, unbaptized ones who unrepentingly sinned were completely avoided." Nevertheless, the magazine cautioned that I Corinthians 15:33 ("Bad company ruins good morals") should be observed.

At the Witnesses' Brooklyn headquarters a spokesman said there are nearly 3.4 million publishers worldwide and about 797,000 in the United States. While confirming that the Nov. 15 issue notes the new policy, the spokesman did not comment on what effect the change might have.

191

But ex-member David T. Brown of Phoenix, an active critic of the organization, said the greatest impact should be on the children of active Witnesses who had joined their parents in neighborhood canvassing but were shunned after breaking church rules. "Tens of thousand once viewed as dead have suddenly been restored to their families," Brown said.[12]

Jehovah's s Witnesses Still Opening Doors

Reprint from the Los Angeles Times

It is Saturday morning and you are sitting at home when the doorbell rings. You hurry to the door, expecting a delivery perhaps, and find two earnest looking people holding Bibles and newsprint pamphlets.

Chances are they are Jehovah's Witnesses, members of a fundamentalist religious organization founded in Pittsburgh 110 years ago by Charles Taze Russell, a men's clothing retailer, Russell, who started with a six-member Bible study group, created a religion that had thousands of adherents in the United States by the time he died in 1916.

Like other fundamentalist religions that have attracted members disenchanted with what they consider an increasingly immoral world, the Jehovah's Witnesses are growing rapidly.

They now claim more than 4 million members worldwide, double their membership only 15 years ago.

Though the sect's insistent door-to-door ministry has been the subject of many popular jokes, Witnesses adhere to an austere belief system. They say they try to live as closely as possible according to their interpretation of the Bible.

"Everything we need in dealing with life is containedd in the Scriptures," said Rodney Griffiths, a Witness from Johnstown, PA "We look at the Bible ... as a book of daily living, for guidance, for direction."

One result of that belief is those door-to-door visits.

---

[12]Permission granted for repirnt, *Los Angeles Times*, Metro, Part 2, Page 7. Copyright 1988 The Times Mirror Company.

Jehovah's Witnesses are required to act as missionaries because the Apostles and other Biblical figures did so.

Also as a result of their literal interpretation of the Old and New Testaments, Witnesses decline to pledge allegiance to any national flag or serve in any nation's army.

"He who lives by the sword, dies by the sword, "Griffiths said.

Members were jailed in the United States during World War II for refusing to fight and many died in concentration camps in Germany because they did not support the Nazi regime.

Witnesses also refuse blood transfusions, citing a passage in the book of Leviticus: "Whatsoever man ... eats any manner of blood, I will cut him off from among his people."

Spokesmen for the Witnesses, who have headquarters in Brooklyn, NY, deny that this practice has led to many fatalities, but medical authorities disagree.

"People do die," said Gary Gruen, an orthopedic surgeon at Presbyterian University Hospital in Pittsburgh, who has treated members of the sect.

Without blood transfusions after serious accidents or during surgery, he said, if sometimes their heart has to work so fast that it puts them in jeopardy for heart attacks and decreased blood flow to the brain.

Recently, 14-year-old Kevin Rattenbury died at a suburban Detroit hospital during surgery to repair injuries from a motorbike accident. His parents, Jehovah's Witnesses, had refused to allow a blood transfusion.

A spokesman for the hospital said it had obtained a court order to allow the transfusion but it came too late.

Witnesses also believe, based on the Book of Revelation and other biblical passages, that the world as we know it will end by early next century and be replaced by a blessed community consisting mostly of Jehovah's Witnesses.

In the meantime, do not expect the door-to-door visits to stop. They apparently work.[13]

"Mary works as a medical assistant at a hospital. One requirement she has to abide by in her work is confidentiality. She must keep documents and information pertaining to her work from going to unauthorized persons. Law codes in her state also regulate the disclosure of confidential information on patients..."

So begins a September 1, 1987, *Watchtower* magazine article that goes on to instruct Jehovah's Witnesses (J.W.'s) to "breach the requirements of confidentiality because of the superior demands of divine law." In spite of solemn oaths and laws to the contrary, the four-page article instructs JW.'s to "bring a matter to the attention of the elders" in the Witness congregation, even if they learned of the matter in a context of professional confidence.

"Mary" in the article is a hypothetical case, but the newly enunciated policy is already making itself felt in concrete terms in the lives of Watchtower followers around the world. And it has stirred considerable controversy in the press over public concern that confidentiality will be shattered in hospitals, law offices, tax accounting firms, and other sensitive fields where Jehovah's Witnesses are employed. The *Los Angeles Times* (August 27, 1987) devoted 28 column-inches to the subject, including quotes from a telephone interview with Watchtower headquarters spokesman William Van De Wall. According to the *Times*, Van De Wall said those individuals "who seek out an attorney or doctor would know if they were of the same religion. If a witness wanted to avoid telling him something, he would seek someone else." This fails to take into consideration, though, the possibility that a JW. secretary, typist, or clerk working for a non-Witness professional might also be in a position to leak confidential information to sect leaders.

For example, one disgruntled Witness known to *Christian Research Journal*, who had been secretly purchasing Christian literature from an ex-JW ministry, now finds that checks he had written are being offered as evidence against him as he is called

---

[13]Permission granted for reprint by the *Los Angeles Times*, Calendar, part F, p. 15, Copright 1991 The Times Mirror Company, Saturday, October 5, 1991.

194

to stand trial before an Internal Watchtower "Judicial committee." Did a JW working at his local bank turns the records over the sect? Or had the Watchtower sent a loyal follower to work at the bank where the ex-J.W. ministry's funds are kept to keep track of who might be contributing? The victim of this breach of bank secrecy doesn't know who informed on him, but he does know that continued contact with life-long friends and family — and even his marriage — could be terminated depending on the outcome of the closed door "trial" where the checks are presented as evidence.

"The objective would not be to spy on anther's freedom but to help erring ones and to keep the Christian congregation clean," the Watchtower article insists. These "erring ones," though, could include not only Witnesses receiving medical treatment for venereal disease, AIDS or pregnancy out of wedlock, but also individuals subscribing to forbidden publications (such as *Christian Research Journal*), donating blood, or receiving a transfusion — all of which actions would be viewed as errors threatening the "cleanness" of the JW congregation.

Other information on Witness patients/clients likely to be reported by fellow Witnesses having access to records include:

- Donating sperm or an ovum to a fertility bank
- Artificial insemination (which the Witnesses view as adultery)
- Use of tobacco
- Contributing to the campaign fund of a political candidate
- Receiving income from a military or religious organization
- Receiving income from gambling
- Giving birthday or Christmas gifts
- Receiving a speeding ticket or other fine
- Divorce proceedings on grounds other than adultery

Since the official policy of breaking professional confidentiality was promulgated only a few months ago, it is yet too soon to see lawsuits form the victims of such invasion of privacy. But some newspaper articles appearing on the subject see this as inevitable fallout, with employers reaping potential problems from violations by their Jehovah's Witness employees. Long viewed by many as exemplary workers, the Witnesses may gain a different reputation in the work place a they begin to obey their organizations new instructions to break oaths and laws protecting client/patient confidentiality.[14]

AN EVALUATION

The sincerity and intensity of Jehovah's Witnesses must be appreciated. When one considers the apathy of many members of the "regular" churches, the door-to-door calling and aggressive efforts to the Witnesses is even more remarkable. The willingness of the members of this group to hold their convictions, even at the cost of public disapproval and imprisonment, is also commendable. Their fervor and organizing skill have become evident, in recent years, in the huge public gatherings or assemblies they have conducted. In 1950 their Assembly at Yankee Stadium in New York City was attended by 127,707; in 1953 by 165,829; and in 958 (when the Polo Grounds was also used) there were 253,922.

The sect is, however, very limited in its outlook and concentrated in its program. It is not interested in doing the works of God in helping, healing, or uplifting men. It wants to just "witness to Jehovah." The Seventh Day Adventists, for instance, teach, heal, and minister to human needs in many ways, but not so Jehovah's Witnesses. Further, they certainly are in fundamental error in their presentation of God in which a "Jehovah" of power and justice is much more evident thant "the Father in heaven." They are fatally in error in their view of Jesus Christ as a creature of God and an angel. Their view of the Holy Spirit does not at all agree with the teaching of the New Testament.

They have several other peculiar views, which have not been dealt with so far. One of these is the idea that because Leviticus 17:14 says the Hebrews shall "eat the blood of no manner of

---

[14]*Christian Research Journal*, Fall 1987, Christian Research Institute International, P.O. Box 500, San Juan Capistrano, CA 92693-0500, USA.

flesh" that blood transfusions are forbidden, because this is an "eating of blood"! They also present Acts 15:28, 29 in support of this view. Because Jeremiah 10:3, 4 speaks of the cutting down of a tree (really, to make an idol of it) and to decking it "with silver and with gold," they say Christmas trees are forbidden. They also teach that a flag is a graven image and therefore refuse to pledge allegiance to it or salute it. This holds true for every country in the world and has led to the persecution of many Witnesses. They refuse to vote, to bear arms, or to hold any political office, although they do pay taxes.

We should pray for the many earnest persons who are deluded by the literature and personal teaching of Jehovah's Witnesses.

Studies and
Non-Religious Holidays

Why African American Youth Are Attracted To The Hebrew Israelites

INTRODUCTION

Shalam Brothers and Sisters,

Thank you for attending the Hebrew Israelite Ministries (H.I.M.) Institute of Study, for the benefit of you gaining the knowledge of your true nationality. We are one of many organized brothers and sisters that have awakened to our true nationality according to the Holy Bible. We have acknowledged the fact that we are the *true, original* and authentic Israelites whom the Bible constantly speaks of.

The Hebrew Israelites are not, I repeat, "are not" a group; sect; cult; religion; or some organization you can just join. We are a Nation of People. A Holy and True nation (Deut. 7:6). No! Everyone can not be an Israelite, just as everyone cannot be Caucasian, Japanese, Arab, etc.... You must be a true descendant of the Biblical Israelites (1 Chr. 9:1, "So all Israel were reckoned by genealogies;") and *yes* the true Israelites are still here today in the flesh.

The lie has been told, that the Israelites (Jews) are no longer in existence is exactly what it is, A LIE! How can the Lord's Holy and True people no longer be in existence? **(Read Rom. 11:1 and also Jer. 31:35-37)** (If the rumor has it that the Israelites (Jews) are no longer in existence, then who are those so called Jews in Palestine trying to be?)

You see, that's where we the true Israelites come in. To teach the Truth of God and His Word because there are so many stories and lies in the world, and for this reason God is angry (Hos. 4:1). So now, in these days God has awakened us to teach the *WHOLE TRUTH* and nothing but the TRUTH (Jer. 3:15; Hab. 2:2-3; 1 Cor. 4:9), for the edification of our *people*, the **"TWELVE LOST TRIBES OF THE NATION OF ISRAEL"** TO RECLAIM OUR TRUE HERITAGE AND SPIRITUAL POSITION WITH God (Deut. 28:1, Deut. 7:6, 1 Chr. 17:21-24).

THE BIBLE

The Bible we use is the King James 1611 Edition. Reason being, it is the closet version to the original Hebrew. Let's get another lie straight, King James DID NOT write the Bible, he only authorized its translation and protection for the corrupt popes and bishops who corrupted previous translations of the scriptures for their own personal and religious gain, during the times of Henry VIII, Edward VI, and the Infamous Rodrigo Borgia, the Father of Caesar Borgia, the Caucasian who the entire world perceives as Jesus Christ. This is the biggest and most blasphemous lie ever told, that Christ was a white man, when the Bible clearly states he had the skin complexion of burned brass and had woolly hair (Rev. 1:1315). But as it was stated earlier, there are so many lies in the world, mainly about The Bible. So to repeat, King James *DID NOT* write the Bible. He was actually fulfilling prophecy by translating the Bible into English so we (Israelites) would not be without the Word of God: Isa. 28:9-11. Verse I reads,

"For with stammering lips and another tongue will he speak to this people."

Now "THIS PEOPLE" is referring to the Israelites (us) and "ANOTHER TONGUE" is English.

NATION OF ISRAEL

Who are the true Israelites? We are the Nation that God chose to give his covenant, laws, and promises to (Rom. 9:4-5). God chose the Nation of Israel to "BE US SPECIAL PEOPLE ABOVE ALL OTHER PEOPLE ON THE FACE OF THE EARTH..." (Deut .7:6) and to carry out his will of righteousness and judgment (Ps .78:5-8).

The key to knowing who the true Israelites (Jews) are today, you must first know and understand, that the Bible was written for the Nation of Israel only! And we only can decipher the hidden messages and prophecies contained in the Bible, Ps. 147:19-20 reads:

"He sheweth his word unto Jacob, his statutes and his judgments unto Israel."

Meaning God reveals the messages of the Bible to the Israelites. ("Jacob" and "Israel" are one in the same. Read: Isa 48: 1) but, Psalm 147, verse 20 makes it even clearer.

"He hath not dealt so with any nation; and as for his judgments, they have not known them. Praise ye the Lord. "

This passage alone clearly explains why everyone can't and will not understand the Bible, and so they count it as "contradictory" or "made up", when the truth is, the Bible doesn't pertain to them."HE HATH NOT DEALT SO WITH ANY NATION."

So now that the word having been shown to *us* the TRUE Israelites (Jews), we can begin to understand whom the Nation of Israel truly is. Through Bible prophecy, history archeology and anthropology we can see what people make up the "TWELVE LOST TRIBES OF THE NATION OF ISRAEL."

12 LOST TRIBES OF ISRAEL

Biblical Name	Name known by today
Judah	Negroes
Benjamin	West Indians
Levi	Haitians
Simeon	Dominicans
Reuben	Seminole Indians
Gad	North American Indians
Manasseh	Cubans
Ephraim	Puerto Ricans
Zebulun	Guatamala – Panama
Asher	Brazilians
Issachar	Mexicans
Naplitall	Aruentina – Chile

202

How do these people make up the 12 lost tribes of Israel? (For specific details of each tribe, come to the classes for that information, it is too extensive for this pamphlet). I will touch a few points on them.

Now if we go back into the book of Exodus Chapter 24 and verse 7, the Israelites agree here to follow all the Laws of God which are contained in the Bible. Now, the *deal (covenant) that God made* with his people was, if the Israelites (Jews) continued to *follow the Laws, he would bless them* (Deut. 28:1-14), but if they did not keep the Laws he would curse them (Deut. 28:15-68). When you later read, the Israelites broke the Laws of God (Ps.106:33-43) thus bringing the punishment (curses) upon them and their children as we see it today (Lam. 5:7).

Let's look at the prophecy of the Nation of Israel being called by other names other than which they truly are. Isa. 65:15

"And ye shall leave your name for a curse unto my chosen: for the Lord God shall slay thee and call his servants by another name."

The Nation of Israel left their Holy, True and most Royal name God gave them, when they broke the laws (covenant), "AND YE SHALL LEAVE YOUR NAME FOR A CURSE UNTO my CHOSEN" and the names we have now were put on us by our slave masters. However they were put on us against our will, this is the reason why we have last names; it is a token of ownership. Many Israelites accepted the new names such as Negro (which is Latin for "Black"), Indian (which comes from the word "indigenous" or "indignant" which means "wild" or untamed"), Haitian ("hell") Puerto Rican ("rich port"). All are derogatory names. However the Israelites that would not accept the "slave names" were severely punished or killed.

"FOR THE LORD GOD SHALL SLAY THEE." Just as the movie "Roots" showed how Kunta Kinte would not accept the name of "Toby", so he was beaten till he did. This happened constantly until their true names (Israel) were forgotten (Read Ps. 83a).

"...AND CALL HIS SERVANTS BY ANOTHER NAME:" God's true servants are Israelites (Lev. 25:55). The other names are what we go by today; Black, Indian, Mexican, Haitian etc....

Review the list of the "Twelve Tribes of Israel" and their "slave names" and ask yourself "what other nations in the world have been labeled with "slave names" against their will which would determine their nationality? (Don't take too long!) Let's take the name "Black" (Negroes) for example. How can color determine one's nationality? If this is true, why does the name "Black" only apply to the so-called Negroes, when in fact, many nations (Gentiles) have a darker skin complexion than the Negroes. Such as the Arabs, East Indians (India, Persia, etc....), Aborigines, and Egyptians. Speaking of Egypt, Africans are not even considered "Black", inasmuch as they even get offended when they are called "Black." So in a nutshell the name "Black" pertains to the Negroes in North America.

Another issue that's well known but constantly avoided is "slavery." Slavery is another punishment (curse) that came upon the Nation of Israel for breaking God's Laws. The Bible records us (Israel) being taken on ships and sold as slaves. (Many so-called Negro preachers have never even read this scripture.) Deut. 28:68.

*"And the Lord shall bring thee into Egypt again with ships, by the way whereof I spake unto thee: thou shall see it no more again: and there ye shall be **sold unto** your enemies for bondmen and bondsmen and no Man shall buy you."*

Here Moses is giving the Nation of Israel warning of a prophecy that was to happen over two thousand years later, in which the Nation of Israel would be taken into bondage or slavery (Egypt is a Greek word meaning bondage or slavery, Mizraim is the true name in the Hebrew.), by way of ships. (Cargo slave ships remember those?) The Nation of Israel has not seen their true land "Israel" because we are still in our bondage at this present time.

"THOU SHALT SEE IT NO MORE AGAIN..." The Tribes of Judah, Benjamin, and a portion of the Tribe of Levi were taken from the Gold Coast of Africa. (Israelites are not of *African descent*. Neither are we from Africa. Israelites are of Shemetic descent. Africans are of Hametic descent; there's a huge difference. All dark skinned people are not the same people! *Israelites were in Africa* at that time having fled from the Romans into Africa (when Jerusalem was destroyed in 70 AD) on ships and brought to America to be sold and purchased as slaves. The other 9-1/2 tribes of Israel (refer to previous list) scattered throughout North, South and Central America, were taken on ships to Spain and additional Spanish colonies to be slaves then brought back to the Americas to be slaves on their own land, What is really interesting about this prophecy is, all the tribes of Israel have the same "enemy" in common.

"AND YE SHALL BE SOLD UNTO YOUR ENEMIES FOR BONDMEN AND BONDWOMEN..." Judah (Negroes), Levi (Haitians), and Benjamin (West Indians) were brought to America by Caucasians, sold by Caucasians (Whites) and purchased by Caucasians. GAD (North American Indians) were slaughtered by the white (Caucasians) troops and calvaries, thrown on reservations to live as animals (by the way what are they being reserved for?). The other tribes in South and Central America were slaughtered by the Spaniards and Conquistadors (whites), taken to Spanish colonies as slaves and brought back to suffer bondage here in the Americas.

Let me say this, we know slavery has often occurred throughout history, but never was an entire nation of people taken to suffer slavery by ways of ships, scattered, and still served bondage simultaneously in different parts of the world except "The Nation of Israel."

One more point to examine, is the fact that the results of Israel's slavery are still present today. Study the previous page that lists the "Nation of Israel" and who they are today. What do all the tribes have in common? All of them suffer from slavery and slave conditions such as: *all* are still under bondage by their present and previous slave owner, the White man (Acts 7:6). All of them have the same enemy, the White man (Deut.28:68). All of them are in their enemies' (the white man) land and not in their own. (Read Jer. 5:19 by the way, where is the land "Black" or the land "Indians"") All of them speak their enemy's language:

English, Spanish, French, Portuguese, and Latin. All which *belongs* to the White man (Duet .28:49). Is this a coincidence? No! It was prophesied in the Bible long ago. Read Deut. 28:15-68.

Note: For more information in detail consults the classes we offer daily.

WHO ARE THE TRUE JEWS?

According to the *KING JAMES, 1611* version of the bible, the JEWS (Israelites) are the so-called Negroes and Latinos located throughout North, South and Central America. *The 12 Lost Tribes of the Nation of Israel:*

1. Judah	Negroes
2. Benjamin	West Indians
3. Levi	Haitians
4. Simeon	Dominicans
5. Zebulon	Guatemala to Panama
6. Ephraim	Puerto Ricans
7. Manesseh	Cubans
8. Gad	N. Americans Indians
9. Reuben	Seminole Indians
10. Napthali	Argentina & Chile
11. Asher	Columbia to Uruguay
12. Issachar	Mexicans

Deut. 28:68 — Tells how the Jews would be brought to America by ships and sold. An event that never happened to the Caucasian Jews.

Job 30:30, Jer. 14:2, Lam. 5:10, Song of Solomon 1:5 — Proves the Jews (Israelites) are people of color (dark skinned).

Isa. 29:22 — Says the Israelites (Jews) would never turn white (pale).

Rev. 1:13-15 — Jesus Christ King of the Jews is also dark skinned (burned brass).

Isa. 1:7 — Proves the true Israelites are not in their land Israel.

Q: If the true Jews are not in their land, then who is occupying Palestine (Israel) today?

A: IMPOSTORS! Read: **Rev. 2:9 and 3:9** also **Ez. 35:10-12**.

Q: How did they become Jews?

A: European Jewry began approx. in the 7th and 8th century A.D. in Europe in a region called Khazaria. Taught by true Israelites, the Caucasians there were taught to be civil and cleansed from their savage ways. The Caucasians later altered the teachings of the Israelites, and began what is known today as "Judaism", later spreading to America.

Q: What about the Hitler Holocaust?

A: The Jewish men and women slain by the Nazis were labeled as "sellouts". Hitler, trying to establish a white superior race could not have a sect of his people (Caucasians) pretending to be Jews which are black people. Therefore many of them were exterminated.

Q: What's the bottom line?

A: The Caucasians calling themselves Jews or Jewish are "Liars"

For more information, visit the SONS OF JACOB located at 3742 Martin Luther King Blvd., Santa Barbara Plaza, Ste. 164, on Mon., Tues., Wed, & Fri. from 7-10:00 P.M. (323) 290-1745. ALL CLASSES ARE FREE.

WHAT DO YOU MEAN JOHN 3:16?

"For God so loved the WORLD, that he gave his only begotten Son that whosoever believeth in him should perish, but have everlasting life."

The word *"WORLD"* as defined in the Webster's dictionary reads, "WORLD" (1) the planet earth (2) *A realm domain or particular society* (3) *having like customs, common interest and all people or things that pertain to it.*

Heb. 1:2 proves God has created many different **WORLDS**. Example: the animal world, the Greco-Roman world, the vegetable world, the insect world etc. So then what WORLD is JOHN 3:16 referring to?

John 17:9 reads *"I pray for them (Israelites not for the WORLD, but for them, which thou hast given me; for they are thine."*

Christ expresses that he prays not for the **WORLD**. The Bible is not by any means contradicting (religion and man's philosophies are). So who is the "thine" (which is simply a passive pronoun showing ownership) being referred to in the Scripture?

Isaiah 43:1, 1 Chr. 17:21,22, Joel 2:27 proves that ISRAEL is the nation God possesses unto himself, and has chosen "them" to be his special people forever. The fact is, Christ came and died to deliver ISRAEL from their sins and give them Salvation. (Acts 5:31, Matt. 15:24, Matt. 10:5,6).

Isaiah 45:17 reads *"But Israel shall be saved in the Lord with an everlasting salvation: ye shall not be ashamed nor confounded WORLD without end." So the Nation of Israel is the WORLD God loves in JOHN 3:16.*

Ask yourself, why would God love the WORLD he is going to destroy for its wickedness and constant breaking of his laws? (I John 2:15,16; 2 Peter 3:7). JAMES 4:4 reads *"Ye adulterers and adulteresses, know ye not the friendship of the WORLD is enmity with God? Whosoever therefore will be a friend of the WORLD is the enemy of God.*

God never wanted the Nation of Israel to become associated or integrated among the other nations of people (Gentiles). (Psalms 106:34-39, Jer.10: 2)

Point: The other nations were not given the law or the promises of salvation, only the *Israelites!* (Ps 105:9,10; Rom. 9:4;; Ps. 147:19,20) Therefore the other nations (Gentiles) cannot have redemption for something that does not pertain to them. *So the WORLD not prayed for in John 17:9 are the other nations* — (A WORLD OF WICKEDNESS).

The truth begins when knowledge, wisdom, and understanding is applied to studying the bible, which eliminates all lies, contradictions, religion and ultimate confusion. **John 8:32** *"And ye shall know the truth and the truth shall make you free."*

NATIVE AMERICANS WAKE UP — AND LEARN THE TRUTH!

We are the Lord's chosen people, the 12 Lost Tribes of Israel. (Read Deut. 7:6 & Deut. 14:2)

Judah – Negroes and the true Israelites of the Bible
Benjamin — W. Indians
It's important to know that we Levi-Haitians belong to the Nation of Israel
Simeon – Dominicians

Defined by our race not religion

Zebulun– Guatemala to Panama
Ephraim – Puerto Ricans
Naphtali – Argentina to Chile
Asher – Colombia to Uruguay
Issachar – Mexicans

So-called Native Americans, Latinos and Negroes are a conquered and oppressed people due to their forsaken of the Holy Laws of Their Heavenly Father.

The tribe of Reuben is identified in Gen. 49:3 as the **EXCELLENCY OF DIGNITY** And The Excellency of Power. The **Reubenities** were known as excellent dressers, often weaning mitre (priestly Israelite headwrap) and royal garments displaying this nobility of character. Also they were the only tribe to NEVER sign a peace treaty with the so called white man and were regarded as the most fearsome and relentless enemies they encountered.

Prophesy states: "TROOP SHALL OVERCOME Him: BUT HE SHALL OVERCOME IN THE END" Gen. 49:19

209

This troop, as the U.S. Calvary which slaughtered and destroyed over 77 million Native Americans, from 1620 to 1890 in the bloody Conquest of this land. (Read Deut .28:48-50)

The tribe of Gad are men of valor. (Read 1 Chr. 12: 8, Deut. 3:20-21, Num. 15:3 7-40 and WAKE UP AND LEARN! (1 Chr. 5:18)

For more information, call or write to:

PO Box 61457
Los Angeles, CA 90061-0457
(213) 960-5577
(213) 290-1745

Class Schedule
Mon – Bible study
Friday – Sabbath Service
Saturday – Leimert Park
All classes are free of charge

MASTER SWORDSMAN

Is the level we all want to achieve as teachers of the Word of the Most High. The Bible is a sword, the ultimate means of defense (Heb. 4:12), if used righteously (I Tim. 1:8). Just as any martial art or warfare training, one must apply the same diligence, discipline, desire and zeal to properly wheel the spiritual sword.

2 Tim. 2:15, 1 Pet. 3:15, Prov. 15:28, 23:23 and Is. 33:6). The sword (Bible) is a weapon used to destroy the evil spiritual beings that walk the spiritual realm of the earth. They posses and devour weak and helpless souls by methods such as deceit, lies, seduction, pride, vanity and everything else contrary to the Word of the Most High, leaving their victims caught in a whirlpool of iniquity which results in death (1 Pet. 5:8). The earth is infested with billions of these invisible demons as we speak. However those skilled and able to wheel the spiritual sword can destroy these powerful spirits protecting themselves and their nation (James 1:21, 4:7, 5:20; 2 Pet.1:5-10).

On the other hand those that don't take the warfare seriously (Eph. 6:12) by not arming themselves, will be destroyed and left naked by the demons previously mentioned (Prov. 12:24, 14:14-15, 19:15; 2 Pet. 2:17, 2:2.1-2 3:16).

"The hand of the diligent shall bear rule: but the slothful shall be under tribute." Proverbs 12:24

Here are a **list of a few commonly** asked questions and scriptures to prove each point to aid you in your studies.

Statement: Christ died for the whole world according to Jn. 3:16.

Answer: No! The world God loves is the Nation of Israel (Isa. 45:17). How can God love the world he is going to destroy? Christ died for the Nation of Israel, not the world. (Acts 5:30-31, 13:22-24; Matt. 1:21, 15:24; Jn. 4:22, Rom. 10: 1, Lk 1:77-80, Isa. 14:1, 46:13)

Statement: The Israelites of the Bible were Caucasians.

Answer: No! They were dark skinned people, color of Christ (Rev .1: 13-15) Color of other Israelites (Job 30:30; Song of Solomon 1:5, Lam. 5:10) Color of Apostles

(Acts 13:1 "Niger" is Latin for black) Color of Moses (Ex. 4:6-7 his land could not turn white if he was white to begin with)

Statement: God only does peaceful and loving things.

Answer: No! (Deut. 32:39, Isa. 45:7, Prov.16:4)

Statement: We are not obligated to follow the laws anymore.

Answer: This is the biggest lie! (Matt. 5:17, Rom. 3:31, 6:23, 7:1, 7:12; 1 Jn. 2:34, Rev. 22:14, Ps. 111:7, 1 Tim. 1:9-10, Jn. 14:15, 15:9-10).

Statement: God doesn't hate!

Answer: He sure does. (Ro,. 9:13-15)

Statement: I'm saved, are you?

Answer: No one is saved, yet (Jer. 8:20, Matt. 24:13)

Statement: God cast away the Israelites for us Gentiles.

Answer: Never! (Rom. 11:1-2, Isa. 48:9-11)

Statement: **What about the Gentiles?**

Answer: They will be taught the gospel in truth after Israel receives it (Matt. 15:26, Mk. 7:27, Micah 4:1-3) the only reason why they think they have salvation is to provoke Israel to jealousy (Rom. 11:11, Deut.32: 21). After the Gentiles are taught the gospel, they will be our servants in the New Kingdom of the Most High. (Isa. 14:1-3, Zech. 8:21-23, Isa. 60:12)

Statement: I'm going to the church to be baptized.

Answer: For what? Water *won't do anything* for you. Water is just symbolic of the true *baptism* THE WORD (Eph. 4:5, 5:26; Jn. 15:13, 17:17).

Statement: But John the Baptist baptized with water.

Answer: John knew the water was symbolic, he truly baptized repentance to Israel (Acts 19:4).

Statement: It's not important for me to know my nationality or my history.

Answer: It most definitely is (Job 8:8, 9:21; Isa. 46:10) The Most High declares a fate to all nations. If you don't know who you are, what is your fate?

Statement: Should I believe my preacher?

Answer: Hell no! (Jer. 17:5, Isa. 8:20, 1 Pet 4:11, 2 Pet 2:1-3, 1 Tim. 6:3-5, Eph .5:6) Believe no mail that does not follow the laws of the Most High, and be careful of those that do. Believe in the Lord! (Jer. 17:5, Acts 5:29).

Statement: Should I believe Israelites that are more knowledgeable than myself?

Answer: Be careful of everyone! (1 Jn. 4:1) especially those with superlative knowledge of the Bible (Tit. 1:10-11). Even with the truth, the evil, deceitful, and seducing spirits that lurk about do not discriminate. They prey on the prideful, egotistical and self willed, which brings spiritual warfare to a higher level.

Our goal is to enlighten people to the Nation THE 12 LOST Tribes of Israel the ethnic group which is the central figure of the spiritual and historical message JUDAH = African Americans Of the HOLY BIBLE. This knowledge necessary Because it will help one to BENJAMIN = W. Indians understand the present social, economical, LEVI Haitians political, and spiritual status of the Hebrew SIMEON = Dominicans Israelites. All descendants of the 12 tribes REUBEN = Seminole of Israel have a place in society and a divine Gad = N. American Indians mission to perform, for the betterment of NAPTHAL = Argentina & Chile humanity. (1 Peter 2:9-10, Matt. 5:14-16).

We, the Hebrew Israelites are teaching true Nationality according to the Holy Bible King James version 1611. All dark-skinned people are not the same nationality or race. We, the so-called Blacks, W. Indians, and Haitians, There are those that try to deceive trying to be the real Jews of Israel. Read: Rev. 2:9, Rev. 3:9 & Isa. 29:22

DEUT. 28:68 — AND THE LORD SHALL BRING THEE INTO EGYPT (EGPYT is a Greek word meaning bondage or slavery) AGAIN WITH SHIPS... The cargo slave ships were used in the triangular slave trade from the 1520's to the 1770's. We, as a people, are the only nation to go into captivity in its entirety on ships. AND THERE YE SHALL BE SOLD In Jamestown, VA, St. Augustine, Fl, JAMAICA, Brazil, Hispanola, etc. (Joel 3:6) UNTO YOUR ENEMIES The English, Dutch,

French, Spaniards all so-called white men (Job 16:11) FOR BONDMEN and BONDWOMEN Slave men and women.

Color of Christ

Revelation 1:1, 14-15

Daniel 10:5-6 Gen. 49:8 — JUDAH, THOU WHOM THY RETHEREN SHALL PRAISE. All twelve tribes look to the so-called Black Man to start the trends in fashion, music, etc., most importantly leadership. **THY HANDS** SHALL BE IN THE **NECK OF THY ENEMIES.** Of all the tribes of Israel, Judah has been the most aggressive against the establishment and the status quo. For example, Nat Turner, Black Panthers, Civil Rights Movement. Hebrew Israelites. **THY FATHER'S CHILDREN WILL BOW DOWN BEFORE THEE.**

THE SONS OF JACOB
P.O. Box 61457
Los Angeles, CA. 90061-0457
Class Schedule: Mon/Tues. – Bible Study
(323) 290-1745 Friday – Sabbath Service
Saturday Leimert Park are free and
(323) 960-5577 begins at 7:30 P.M.

I AM NOT SENT BUT UNTO THE LOST SHEEP OF THE HOUSE OF ISRAEL.

JUDAH – NEGROES
BENJAMIN – WEST INDIANS
LEVI – HAITIAN
SIMEON – DOMINICIANS
ZEBULUN – GUATEMALA TO PANAMA
EPHRAIM – PUERTO RICANS
MANASSEH – CUBANS
GAD – NORTH AMERICAN INDIANS
REUBEN – SEMINOLE INDIANS
NAPTHALI – COLUMBIA TO URUGUAY
ISSACHAR – MEXICANS

THE TRUTH

Jn. 8:32 — *"and ye shalt know the truth and the truth shall make you free."* In this verse, Christ, (a so-called Blackman) was referring to the Bible. When you find out that the Bible truly pertains to you (an Israelite), and begin to understand and know the prophecies of the Bible and follow God's Laws, then you will be truly FREE from the prison of ignorance that is upon our people the "NATION OF ISRAEL."

Another reason why people cannot accept the entire Bible or would rather count it as "contradictory" or "made up" is the fact that it is 100% pure, untainted, unfiltered, solid TRUTH.

Num. 23:19 — *"God is not a man that he should lie...."* There is separatism, hate, racism, violence, and discrimination in the Bible, which people cannot grasp the concept of. Whether you accept the concept or not, God's Word shall stand.

Rom. 3:3 — *"For what if some did not believe will their unbelief make the faith of God without effect? God forbid; yea let God be true and every man a liar ...."* So it's not about what anyone thinks, it's about what **GOD SAYS!**

Acts 5:29 — *"Then Peter and the other Apostles answered and said, we ought to obey God rather than men."* This is so true. If we would just listen and *do* what God says, it would cut out a whole lot of confusion.

Here are some lies in the world today. However if we study our Bible they can all be proven false:

Q. When did God ordain religion?

A. He didn't. Moses did not come from Mt. Sinai with the ten world religions, he came with Laws, which were to be given to the Israelites (Ps. 78:5-8) there is *no passage* in the entire Bible where God ordained religion. Religion is a man made tool used to relax or pacify the minds of people. It's also man's own opinion of how the word of God "should be" rather than how it is. True. (Isa. 29:13; Rom. 10:33; Prov. 16:25; Matt. 15:9, Mk. 7:7)

Q. Is God all peaceful and all loving?

A. *Ex 15:3* — *"Lord is a man of war."* In the book of Joshua Chapter I verse 18, God commands all people who don't follow his Laws, to be put to death. The Israelites themselves should really be able to testify to this seeing that we suffer from the punishment of God. Deut. 32:39 *"I kill, and I make alive: I wound, and I heal...."* That doesn't sound too "all loving" to me. Our Father is very merciful and loving but not at all some "love junky" or "peace fanatic" as religion portrays him to be. (Remember this scripture always: Heb. 10:31)

Q. Does God discriminate?

A. Yes. As we read earlier Ps. 147:19-20, God gave the Bible only to the Israelites. Joel 2:27 *"and ye shall know that I am in the midst of Israel and that I am the Lord your God and none else: and my people shall never be ashamed."* Here God says he is a God to Israel and none else. (Is that a discriminative statement?) Deut. 7:6 *"For thou art an holy people unto the Lord **thy** God: the Lord **thy** God hath chosen thee to be a special people unto himself, above **all people** that are upon the face of the earth."* This passage alone says it all. First notice the word "THY" in this verse. "THY' means

"YOUR!" a possessive pronoun shows ownership. "THE LORD THY GOD" He is the Lord "YOUR" God, the Nation of Israel's God! (Also read Ex. 29:45-46; and 1 Chr. 17:21-22 and verse 24.) This passage also tells us that *all* men ARE NOT created equal, the Nation of Israel is *above* every other nation of people on the entire earth: "GOD HAS CHOSEN THEE TO BE A SPECIAL PEOPLE UNTO HIMSELF, ABOVE ALL PEOPLE THAT ARE UPON THE FACE OF THE EARTH."

Look at the list of the true Israelites again...

Judah	Negroes
Benjamin	West Indians
LevI	Haitians
Simeon	Dominicans
Reuben	Seminole Indians
GAD	North American Indians
Manasseh	Cubans
Ephraim	Puerto Ricans
Zebulun	Guatamala – Panama
Asher	Brazilians
Issachar	Mexicans
Naphtali	Argentina – Chile

Compare the true Israelites to the other nations (Gentiles) in the world. *We* are above them. We excel the nations (Gentiles) in everything such as sports, music, spirituality, common sense, and inventions (by the way *everything* came from the Israelites. Jer. 10:16) Medicine, architecture, style, and war you name it. Whatever it is out there, best believe Israel has "been there and done that."

One more scripture to prove God discriminates, is the "New Covenant" he is *going* to make with the Israelites and not the world.

Heb. 8:10 — *For this is the covenant that I will make with the House of **Israel** after those days, saith the Lord:*

Q. Did Christ die for the world?

A. No! Christ our Lord and savior, an Israelite from the tribe of Judah (Heb. 7:14) Died for His people THE ISRAELITES! Read Matt. 1:21; Acts 5:30-31; Acts 13:23-24, Matt.15:24; Is. 46:13; Isa. 48:9; Jn. 4:22; Matt.10:5-7. Christ, the sacrificial Lamb, gave his life to cleanse Israel of their sins. Now if sin is the breaking of God's Laws, why would Christ die for everyone? They weren't given the Law, the Israelites were (Ps. 105:9-10). Therefore the other nations (Gentiles) cannot have redemption for something that does not pertain to them.

Q. If the Negroes, North American Indians, Mexicans etc. *are the true* Jews, then Who are the people in Palestine (Israel) today?

A. They are fake Jews or rather impostors. Christ condemns them as fake (Read Rev. 2:9 and Rev. 3:9) also Isaiah 1:7 lets you *know strangers (Gentiles) occupy our land.* Also Ps.79:1 explains why they claim our culture.

Q. Will the Nation of Israel ever be delivered from their bondage and curse condition?

A. Yes. Those of us that turn from our sin and follow the Laws of God to attain righteousness will be delivered. The others that won't follow God will perish (and you think we have it bad now?) Zech. 13:8-9, Isa. 3733 1-32; Isa. 46:13), Isa. 49:13, Isa. 51:11, Isa. 54:7-8, Isa.14:1-3, Ps. 14:7.

EPILOGUE

We hope this pamphlet will aid you in your quest for the Truth. We sincerely pray that you continue to study, for your edification and also to edify our people, the "TWELVE LOST TRIBES OF ISRAEL." This is the reason why we have a place of study. For once our people can study the Truth with brothers and sisters who LIVE the Truth. We encourage our people to come to the class and ask your very important questions and we assure you they will be answered by the "WORD OF GOD" in truth. If there is anything discussed in this pamphlet which you don't agree with, we oblige you to come also and contest your point. However we will "PROVE ALL THINGS ...." (1 Thes. .5:21) and establish the TRUTH. shalam

RA-IM
Nation of Israel

For class schedules and additional information call (323) 960-5577.

So who wrote the Bible? Who do you think? GOD! (2 Tim.3:16, 2 Pet. 1:20-21) by the hand of Israelites. Now what about the other LIES such as "the Bible has been tampered with" or "there's over 5,000 contradictions in the Bible? It's truly amazing how many people agree with these statements and cannot prove either one. But what's truly amazing is, many people make these comments and haven't even read the Bible but will agree with the hype. Col. 2:8 says:

"Beware lest any man spoil you through philosophy and vain deceit, after the tradition of men, after the rudiments of the world, and not after Christ."

Also read Jer.17:5. The people, who make these comments and have read the Bible, it's because they don't understand, and not willing to admit that they don't understand, they become frustrated and blame the bible as "contradictory" or "tampered with." Isa. 29: 10 says:

"For the Lord hath poured out upon you the spirit of deep sleep, and hath closed your eyes."

So now the truth is, God hath shut down or has closed their minds from understanding the Bible, and because they don't understand, they draw their own conclusions (Rom. 10:3), which has an awful conclusion in itself (2 Pet. 3:16).

So *we* see that the Bible is not contradictory. God does not contradict himself (1 Cor.14:33)). Neither has it been tampered with. On the other hand the minds of the people have been tampered with by the lies out there (Eph. 4:14).

The lies about the Bible will continue until the Israelites teach the world the Truth (Micah 4:1-2). But first the Israelites themselves must be awakened (1 Pet. 4:17, Mk.7:27). This is the importance of the Bible and our mission to awaken the "TWELVE LOST TRIBES OF THE NATION OF ISRAEL."

ADDITIONAL NOTE

If the Bible is so contradictory, or rather "made up" then why do scholars use it and historians of every nation, as the focal point of their historical or prophetic research? Why do they make you swear on it in a court of law? THINK ABOUT IT!

So with this: Study, Study, Meditate, and Live according to the truth. Above all apply righteous faith in the Most High (not man!) and prevail with the Sword of Righteousness.

Ecclesiastics 4:28 (Apocrypha)

"Strive for the truth unto death, and the Lord shall fight for thee."

Note: Just knowing this information and additional information from classes and your own studies does not qualify you as an expert swordsman. To become an expert you must learn the Art of properly utilizing the precepts and applying them in every day life (Heb.5:13-14, 1 Tim. 3:16)

Experience is The Ultimate Tool of Learning

Why African American Youth Are Attracted To Amon RAH

Amon-RAH Believes in the following:

WE MUST FREE OUR MINDS
WA ARE A SPIRITUAL PEOPLE
WE ARE AN AFRICAN PEOPLE
"There is No Greater Knowledge
than the Knowledge of Self..."
For to know Thy Self is to Know God
KNOW THY SELF

6825 South Crenshaw Blvd.
Los Angeles, CA. 90043

Why African Americans Are Attracted To Are Attracted To The Study And Practice Of Kwanzaa

KWANZAA
A CELEBRATION OF FAMILY,
COMMUNITY AND CULTURE

Kwanzaa is an African American holiday celebrated from 26 December through 1 January. It is based on the agriculture celebration of Africa called "the first fruits" celebration which were times of harvest, ingathering, reverence, commemoration, recommitment, and celebration. Therefore, Kwanzaa is a time for ingathering of African Americans for celebration of their heritage and their achievements reverence for the creator and creation, commemoration of the past, recommitment to cultural ideas and celebration of the good. To achieve this Kwanzaa focuses on fundamental collective values rooted in African culture and reflected in the best practices of African American people.

Kwanzaa was created in 1966 by Dr. Maulana Karenga, professor and chair, Department of Black Studies, California State University, Long Beach; chair of the Organization US and the National Association of Kwaida Organization (NAKO); author and scholaractivist who stresses the indispensable need to preserve, continually revitalize and promote African culture.

Finally, it is important to note Kwanzaa is a cultural holiday, not a religious one, therefore it is available to and practiced by Africans of all religious faiths.

THE NGUZO SABA (THE SEVEN PRINCIPLES)

Kwanzaa was created to introduce and reinforce seven basic values of African culture which contribute to building and reinforcing community among African American people as well as Africans throughout the world African community. These values are called the Nguzo Saba which in Swahili means the seven principles. Developed by Dr. Karenga, the Nguzo Saba stand at the heart of the origin and meaning of Kwanzaa, for it is these values which are not only the building blocks for community but serves also as its social glue.

Umoja (Unity) — To strive for and maintain unity in the family, community, nation and race.

Kujuchagulia (Self Determination) — To define ourselves, name ourselves, create for us and speak for ourselves.

UJIMA (Collective Work and Responsibility) — To build and maintain our community together and make our brother's and sister's problems our problems and to solve them together.

Ujamaa (Cooperative Economics) — To build and maintain our own stores, shops and other businesses and to profit from them together.

NIA (Purpose) — To make our collective vocation the building and developing of our communities in order to restore our people to their traditional greatness.

KUUMBA (Creativity) — To do always as much as we can, in the way we can, in order to leave our community more beautiful and beneficial than we inherited it.

Imani (Faith) — To believe with all our heart in our people, our parents, our teachers, our leaders and the righteousness and victory of our struggle.

THE SYMBOLS OF KWANZAA

Kwanzaa has seven basic symbols and two supplemental ones. Each represents values and concepts reflective of African culture and contributes to community building and reinforcement.

Mazoa (The Crops) — Symbolic of African harvest celebrations and of the rewards of productive and collective labor.

Mkeka (The Mat) — Symbolic of our tradition and history and therefore the foundation on which we build.

Kinara (The candle Holder) — Symbolic of our roots, our parent people — continental Africans.

Muhindi (The Corn) — Symbolic of our children and our future which they embody.

Mishaumaa Saba (The Seven Candles) — Symbolic of the Nguzo, Saba, the seven principles, the matrix and minimum set of values which Black people are urged to live by in order to rescue and reconstruct their lives in their own image and according to their own needs.

Kikombe cha Umoja (The Unity Cup) — Symbolic of the foundational principle and practice of unity which make all else possible.

Zawadi (the Gifts) — Symbolic of the labor and love of parents and the commitments made and kept by the children.

The two supplemental symbols are:

Bendera (Flag) — The colors of the Kwanzaa bendera are black, red, and green. Black for the people, red for their struggle and green for the future and hope that comes from their struggle. It is based on the colors given by the Hon. Marcus Garvey as National colors for African people.

Nguzo Saba (Seven Principles) Poster Greetings — The greetings during Kwanzaa are in Swahili. Swahili is a Pan-African language and is chosen to reflect African Americans' commitment to the whole of Africa and African culture rather than to a specific ethnic or national group or culture. The greetings are to reinforce awareness of and commitment to the Seven Principles. It is: "Habari gani?" and the answer is each of the principles for each of the days of Kwanzaa. I.e., "Umoja", on December 26 the first day, "Kujuchagulia". on December 27 the second day, etc.

Gifts

Gifts are given mainly to children, but must always include a book and a heritage symbol. The book is to emphasize the African value and tradition of learning stressed since ancient Egypt, and the heritage symbol to reaffirm and reinforce the African commitment to tradition and history.

Colors and Decoration

The colors of Kwanzaa are black, red and green as noted above and can be utilized in decorations for Kwanzaa. Also decorations should include traditional African items, i.e., African baskets, cloth, pattern, art objects, harvest symbols, etc.

Summarized from Chance: A Celebration of Family, Community and Culture, Maulana Karenga, 1998. Los Angeles: University of SanKore Press, (323) 295-9799.

SHOULD CHRISTIANS CELEBRATE KWANZAA?

Kwanzaa — a spiritual alternative to Christmas? Christianity — a myth in which Jesus Christ never existed and a white man's religion? These are a few of the disturbing words that I have either read or heard through books and seminars for the creator of Kwanzaa, DR Maulana Karenga.

Kwanzaa is a colorful new holiday that many African-American families are celebrating after, or as an alternative to Christmas. Kwanzaa means "first fruits," and is centered upon seven principles for living called the Nguzo Saba. It lasts f rom December 26 to January 1 as each day of Kwanzaa is observed by discussing one of these principles, with the seventh day culminating in gift giving.

Dr. Karenga, who created Kwanzaa in 1966, is the leader of the Black Nationalist cultural group US, the chairman of Black Studies at CSU Long Beach, and the author of several books as well as gifted speaker and active community leader in Los

Angeles and San Diego.

With Kwanzaa gaining in popularity, so is the need to discover the true meaning of this new African-American holiday.

In many of our schools, Kwanzaa is celebrated alongside Christmas, and organizations are spreading, such as the Nia-Umoja club for African-American boys. You can even find the Nguzo Saba combined with lessons on Christian living in the Sunday school books of many of our Black churches. Chance greeting cards, posters, books, clothing, and other like items are also growing in number in stores from coast to coast.

Chance outwardly appears to be just a colorful African celebration; but, *The African American Holiday of Kwanzaa* and *The Kawaida Theory*, and attending some of his community seminars, I have learned that Kwanzaa is more that a cultural festival. It is very religious in nature as his own writings will show.

I first learned of Dr. Karenga and his teachings during the early 1980's while in Los Angeles, when one of my relatives — who was later married by Dr. Karenga in an African-style wedding — invited me to come with her to hear him speak. I was shocked from the discussions that followed.

Dr. Karenga called Christianity a white man's religion — with the white man, as our oppressor — and said that Christ never existed.

I went to another meeting, this time bringing a Christian friend along with me. On this day, Dr. Karenga had invited a Christian leader to speak on the resurrection of Christ. I sat dumbfounded as this man explained that Christ never arose from the grave! Many people then chanted, "Teach! Teach!" with each word, said against Christianity.

Why is it important for us to know what Dr. Karenga teaches about Christianity? According to both of his books, he founded Kwanzaa so that African Americans could have a spiritual alternative to the commercialism of Christmas. Is it only the commercialism that he is rejecting and substituting, or is it the Christianity doctrine altogether?

The Nguzo Saba, also created by Dr. Karenga, is the center-piece and the principles by which Kwanzaa is built upon. The seven principles are as follows:

Umoja — unity;
Kujuchagulia — self-determination;
Ujima — collective work and responsibility;
Ujamaa — cooperative economics;
Nia — purpose;
Kuumba — creativity; and
Imani — faith.

The Nguzo Saba, according to Dr. Karenga, are the minimum set of values that African Americans need to rebuild their lives and community and to maintain an Afrocentric family.

In his book, *The African American Holiday of Kwanzaa*, he gives several purposes of these principals, with one of these being ".... To serve as a contribution to a core system of communitarian ethical values for the moral guidance and instruction of the community, especially for children."

Evidently, a purpose of establishing the Nguzo Saba is so that African-Americans could have their own moral and ethical principles. Although insisting that Kwanzaa is not religious, Dr. Karenga contradicts himself in his book, *The Kawaida Theory*, by listing the Nguzo Saba among religions such as Buddhism, Christianity, Judaism, and ancient African religions.

It is in this book that he criticizes the religious who pray to "spooks," and claims that Christianity is a myth. Some examples of "myths" that he gives are the Biblical accounts of creation and the doctrines of the resurrection, sin, heaven, and hell.

Although faith in a creator is not in Dr. Karenga's earlier versions of the Nguzo Saba, he does now include it in his seventh principle, Imani (faith), and he describes it as follows: "To believe with all our heart in our Creator, our people, our parents, our teachers, our leaders, and the righteousness and victory if our cause."

From *The African American Holiday of Kwanzaa*, he adds: "For in all African spiritual traditions, from Egypt on, it is taught that we are in the image of the Creator and thus capable of ultimate righteousness and creativity through self-mastery ... Therefore, faith in ourselves is key here. faith in our capacity to live righteously..."

Faith in man is stressed more than faith in God, and self-righteousness through self-mastery is the objective. Quite the contrary to the Christian who is taught in the Bible that "righteous" living is impossible without Christ (Romans 3:10,23 and 2 Cor. 5:2 1).

Dr. Karenga is teaching a way of life, not just ethics. He is teaching faith, spirituality, righteousness, and even a minimal mention of a "creator." As Christians, we should not celebrate Kwanzaa because of its false spirituality.

To celebrate Kwanzaa is to celebrate living without our Lord, righteousness without Christ, and faith in man instead of God. If Kwanzaa was simply a colorful cultural celebration, then yes, we could celebrate our rich African heritage.

Sadly true, Christmas has become quite commercialized, but its meaning remains the same. It is the celebration of the birth of our Savior, Jesus Christ. Let's not compromise our faith, but remember the reason for the holiday is that God came in flesh of man, Jesus Christ our Lord!

Comments and questions about Kwanzaa can be sent to Carlotta Morrow, P.O. Box 740605, San Diego, California 92174-0605.

Why African American Youth Are Attracted To The Cults!

Why African American Youth Are Attracted To Cults

1. Their protest against social injustice

2. Their agenda to improve the world.

3. Provisions and a place to live.

4. Their encouragement of personal development of members.

5. Their agenda to provide a finer, purer, physical and moral   environment.

6. Their agenda to lessen cultural differences.

7. The agenda to provide an alternative to employment and dead-end jobs.

WHY SHOULD WE STUDY THE CULTS?

Why if one is healthy does he think about the signs of cancer, for instance? The reason is, of course, that he may take steps in time to prevent the fatal spread of the disease. We need to know the general nature of these groups and something about their special characteristics in order to be kept from being led astray by them. And, of course, we should not only be concerned about ourselves. It may be that an understanding of these teachings and positions may enable us to rescue our neighbors or friends or fellow church members from an involvement with a group whose false teachings will take the away from the true faith they should have in Christ. Familiarity with cultic printing companies, colleges, magazines, and general emphases will enable us to uncover the real promoters of special Christians movies, religious dramas, or other efforts that seem at first laudable or "interdenominational."

Perhaps everything said so far has sounded negative and depreciating. It is, of course, true that warnings against dangers — whether from poisons, approaching trains, or treacherous shoals — have a negative and peremptory tone. *However, while the perils and pitfalls of cults should not be minimized, their good points and their genuine achievements in many areas do not need to be hidden or overlooked.* There are colleges, hospitals, orphanages, newspapers, and other practical expressions of the life of these groups, which bring benefits to men. We should appreciate these and every legitimate credit should be given for them. If *there is any virtue or anything we can praise, we should not hesitate to notice or to speak of it.*[1]

It should be recognized that we are not presenting a fully developed discussion of any cult in these pages. Our space and our intentions do not permit this.[2]

---

[1]Cults-Challenge the Church by James G. Van Vuren. Copyright 1963 by Standard Publishing Co., Cincinnati, OH.
[2]Ibid 13

DISPELLING THE MYTHS

The Psychological Consequences of Cultic Involvement

Myth One

Ex-cult members do not have psychological problems. Their problems are wholly spiritual.

Although often believed by both Christians and ex-cultists, myth #1 has no basis in reality. As a result of extensive research with some 3,000 ex-cultists, Dr. Margaret Singer observed significant instances of depression, loneliness, anxiety, low self-esteem, over dependence, confusion, inability to concentrate, somatic complaints, and, at times, psychosis. In addition to Singer's authoritative research, there are many articles and books that describe the psychological distress of excultist. (Many of these findings will be referred to in the body of this article.)

My own experience verifies the findings of Dr. Singer. Lori (a girl I treated after she left an aberration church group) presents a typical example of the *over dependence and insecurity* of a former cultist. She asked me: "Is it okay to have cold cereal for breakfast? "Can I listen to the radio?" It was as though Lori was a little child needing approval and guidance for her every move.

Mental health professionals also propagate the first part of myth #1. While not endorsing cult membership, Dr. Saul Levine, department head for psychiatry at Sunnybrook Medical Center in Toronto, asserts that the experience can be "therapeutic" and that "a reassuring majority have not been damaged."

Though I do not totally doubt the accuracy of Levine's findings, I am troubled that he wrote his material *after (and in spite of* the horrors of Jonestown. He makes no reference to the countless tales of woe related by thousands of former cult members.

A large part of the difference between Levine's findings and those of researchers who recognize problems among ex-cultists could be due to the populations sampled. Levine studied people who were generally in cultic groups for short periods and who volunteered to be interviewed. As opposed to this, it is doubtful whether some members of "utopian" or separatist cults would volunteer to talk to a psychiatrist if they were having real doubts about the group. The members' fear and guilt — as well as distrust of the psychiatric profession — would perhaps be too great an obstacle. Additionally, Levine admitted that evens his sample of cultist experience "sever emotional upheaval in the first few months" after returning home.[1]

Researchers who report problems usually have dealt with people who have left on their own, were counseled to leave, or have been deprogrammed, and want help. In such cases the problems were real and the hurt very apparent. Researchers, however, have not settled the issue of what percentage of people in these groups suffer psychological harm. Nor have they shown what personality types will be detrimentally affected by cultic involvement.

Concerning the spiritual problems experienced by cultist, it is true that these are often present in addition to the emotional distress. These spiritual problems, however, generally originate with the group's unbiblical teachings rather than having their source in the individual's own relationship with God. It has been my experience that almost all former members of religious cults or extremist sects (including those, which claim to be evangelical) are confused about such things as the grace of God, the nature of God, submission to authority, and self-denial. It is noteworthy that groups with widely varying doctrinal stances — from the Hare Krishna's to Jehovah's Witnesses — uniformly distort God's grace and character.

Myth Two

Ex-cult members do have psychological disorders. But these people have come from clearly, non-Christian cults.

Myth #2 is really assuming one of two things. First it may assume that genuine Christians never have psychological problems. However, many well-known Christian theologians and

---

[1] Saul V. Levine, "Radical Departures," Psychology Today, August 1984, 27.

psychologists are on record as stating that true Christian's do suffer psychologically. The late Dr. Francis A Schaeffer, for example, wrote:

> All men since the fall have had some psychological problems. It is utter nonsense, a romanticism that has nothing to do with biblical Christian, to say that a Christian never has psychological problems. All men have psychological problems. They differ in degree and they differ in kind, but since the fall all men have more or less a problem psychologically. And dealing with this, too, is part of the present aspect of the gospel and of the finished work of Christ on Calvary's cross.[2]

Second, Myth #2 may presume that there are only non-Christian cults. And yet my personal experience (which has been verified by the considerable research of others) has been that some Christian groups are cultic in practice. This being the case, abusive Christian groups can and frequently do exacerbate previously existing psychological disorders relating to the individual's personality, family, occupation, etc., and can even produce such disorders where they were not already present.[3]

A number of recent studies have shown that members in both Bible-based (and even doctrinally orthodox) groups and non-Bible-based groups experience psychological distresses. In fact, the psychological problems are similar. Flavil R. Yeakley, Jr., reports that a certain type of group-induced personality distortion has contributed to guilt, low self-esteem, frustration, depression, serious emotional problems, overdependence, and irrational behaviors in a number of well-known religious organizations.[4] Of the groups he studied, the following indicated

---

[2]Ibid, 27.

[3]Francis A. Schaeffer, True Spirituality (Wheaton, IL: Tyndale House Publishers, 1971), 132. See all of chapter 10, "Substantial Healing of Psychological Problems."

[4]Ronald M. Enroth "The Power Abuser", Eternity, October 1979: Enroth, The Lure of Cults and New Religions (Downers Grove, IL: 1987): Enroth: "Churches on the Fringe", Eternity, October 1986.

objectively measured signs of personal distortion: the Boston Church of Christ, the Church of Scientology, the Hare Krishnas, Maranatha Campus Ministries, the Children of God (now called the Family of Love), the Unification Church, and The Way International.

Now, Maranatha and the Boston Church of Christ are seemingly Bible-based ministries. Maranatha is a fundamental, charismatic sect (advocating "dominion" or "kingdom theology") that has been criticized at times for authoritarian excesses, among other things. Likewise, the Boston Church of Christ and its many sister campus churches all over the U.S. have been roundly criticized at times for authoritarianism and coercive persuasion techniques. Both of these groups would contain "born-again" members.

What is alarming about these findings is that groups which are at least marginally Christian are producing psychological harm quite similar to that produced by non-Bible based cults. All of these groups were found to be molding their members into a composite personality that included judging (i.e., relating to the world in terms of value judgments) and extroversion. But not all people are by nature extroverts or judge-type personalities. Some people are by nature introverts and receiver-types (i.e., those who view the world in a descriptive manner without needing to draw conclusions based on their observations). To attempt an alteration of personality types is to invite disaster in the form of neurosis and other emotional difficulties.

Yeakley also tested members of the main-line churches of Christ denomination (not associated with the shepherding/disciplining movement, as is the Boston church), as well as members of the Catholic, Baptist, Lutheran, Methodist, and Presbyterian churches.[5] In these groups, he did not find any evidence of group induced personality distortion that would lead to psychological distress.

Unfortunately, orthodoxy per se is no guarantee that harms will occur. My own research (with several hundred ex-cultists and

---

[5]Flavil R. Yeakley, Jr., *The Discipling Dilemma* (Nashville: The Gospel Advocate Co., 1987) 23-28.

about 50 on an intensive basis totaling about 2,000 hours) indicates that the severity of problems suffered by those in the extremist evangelical sects may be equal to or greater that that experienced by members of the better-known cults such as ISKCON, the Church of Scientology, the "Moomes", The Divine Light Mission, and The Way.[6]

Myth Three

Both Christian and non-Christian groups can produce problems, but all of the people involved in the groups must have had prior psychological hang-ups that would have surfaced regardless of what group they joined.

I encountered this myth regularly among both Christian and secular psychologists. I suspect that it will achieve a status of near immortality. It seems that no amount of contradictory evidence can persuade some that "normal" people can get involved in such groups. Sometimes reminding my colleagues about Nazi Germany helps to dispel this myth for their thinking. I ask, "Were all those Germans suffering from individual pathology that made them vulnerable to the Nazi religion?" Or I ask, "How about Iran and the Ayatollah? Are all of his followers fanatical and sick people, or were they fairly normal people who got fanatical and sick because of following him?" There are more that a few illustrations from history which underscore the falsity of myth #3.

My own clinical research, along with a number of other studies, shows that not all cult members had prior psychological problems. In fact, the proportion of those with prior problems (about 1/3) to those *without* is only slightly above general population (about 1/4).

Levine, Singer, Maron, Clark, and Goldberg have all shown in separate studies that family or otherwise pre-existing psychological factors do not necessarily predict who will end up

---

[6]See also Flo Conway, James H. Sicelman, Carl W. Carmichael, and John Co'Vins, InformationC, Disease: Effects of Covert Induction and Deproramming, (parts one and two, *Update 10* (June 1986): 45-47, and *Update 10* (September 1986): 63-65.

in a cults.[7] And, of course, their findings concerning who joins cults could be consistent with the dynamics of large social movements such as the nazis, the fanatical Muslims, or communism. Simply put, individual psychopathology does not adequately explain the phenomena of large fanatical mass movements.

Nonetheless, there are a few variables that do help predict who will join a cult or cult-like group. Singer, Maron, and a number of other researchers have spelled out several of these factors, some of which are: 1) a stressful event within the past year; 2) a transition phase in life (between family and independence, between school and career, or between dating relationships); 3) a longing for community and caring friends; and 4) a desire to serve a great cause and be part of a movement that will change society.

Now, for those who *do* have pre-existing problems, cultic life can be extremely dangerous. At least on this point most researchers seem to be in substantial agreement. For those with pre-existing emotional problems cultic involvement may produce dissociation, inability to think or concentrate, psychosis, hallucinations, or extreme suggestibility.

Myth Four

While normal unbelievers may get involved with cults, born-again believers will not. And even if they did, their involvement would not affect them so negatively.

Myth #4 is perhaps the most dangerous of all because it prevents the provision of help of those who are really hurting. It is also an old myth, and was challenged as early as Old Testament times. Ezekiel warned that God's sheep *could* be abused by wicked shepherds (Ezek. 334:1-7). Regarding this, St. Augustine

---

[7]Levine Singer Neil Maron, "Family Environment as a Factor in Vulnerabiltiy to Cult Involvement," *Cultic Studies Journal 5*, 1 (1988): 23-43; John G. Clark, MD, "Cults," *Journal of the American Medical Association* 242, 3:279-80; Loma Goldberg and William Goldberg, "Group Work with Former Cultist," Social Work 27 (March 1982).

said: "The defects of the sheep are widespread. There are very few healthy and sound sheep ... But the wicked shepherds do not spare such sheep. It is not enough that they neglect those that are ill and weak, those that go astray and are lost. They even try, so far as it is in their power, to kill the strong and healthy."[8]

So it is obvious that bad shepherds can damage God's sheep, and no more obvious examples of "wicked shepherds" could be given than the leaders of destructive cults and aberration religious movements.[9]

Myth #4 is particularly dangerous to the Christian community because it ignores the fact, pointed out by several Christian cult watchers, that a sizable proportion of those involved in cults or extremist groups come from some type of evangelical church base. Of the cultists I have personally worked with, approximately 25% came from evangelical or fundamental churches and over 40% had backgrounds in the large, more liberal Protestant denominations.

Myth Five

Christians can and do get involved in these aberrational groups and they can get hurt emotionally but all they really need is some good Bible teaching and a warm caring Christian fellowship and they will be fine.

There is certainly a lot of truth to this statement. Unfortunately, half-truths are often the worst form of error. Myth #5 is false for the following reasons: First, many persons who have left cults do not want Bible teaching, or Christian fellowship. They are "once burned, twice shy."

Second, according to a recently published survey of about 3000 ex-cultists by Conway and Siegelman, the following essential non-religious activities proved to be very important for rehabilitation:

---

[8]Singer, John G. Clark, MA, *Testimony to Vermont Senate on Cults* (Pittsburg FAIF, 1979); Golberg and Goldberg 9

[9]Augustine of Hippo, *Sermons on the Old Testament*, no. 46, "On Pastors," excerpts entitled "Shepherds Who Kill Their Sheep" reprinted in *Pastoral Renewal*, January/February 1989, 23-24

- Love and support of parents and family members — 64%
- Insight and support of former cult members — 59%
- Professional mental health counseling — 14%
- Acting to recover lost money, possessions, etc. — 9%
- Going back to school or college — 25%
- Finding a job and establishing a new career — 36%
- Helping others emerge or recover from cults — 39%
- Establishing new friends unrelated to cults — 50%
- Getting as far away from cults as possible — 29%

Although many members of the extremist Christian groups return to evangelical churches, they often continue to suffer. These members will typically seek a church that is very similar tot he one they left. Such people have left their former group because they were incapable of submitting to its demands, but they still believe many of its tenets.[10]

For these people life can be a nightmare — they feel they have left "the apple of God's eye" because they were, in their own terms, "too fleshly" or "too worldly" to keep up the pace. The rigor of cultic life had produced in them all the symptoms of burnout — a state of spirituality. Mental, emotional, and physical.[11]

This prevents the hurting Christian form hearing Bible teachings and counsel that would free his or her mind from guilt-inducing teachings of the group. It is clear that Christian helpers often overlook or misunderstand the erroneous teachings, which serve as subtle control mechanisms. In certain fringe Christian groups, control mechanisms are frequently contained in their teaching on faction, slander. submission, or confession.[12]

---

[10]See, for examle, Dave Breese, "How to Spot a Religious Quack," *Mood Monthly*, June 1975, 57-60. J.L. William, *Identifying and Dealing with Me Cults* (Burlington, NC).

[11]Conway, Siegelman, Carmichael, and Coggoins. 64

[12]See Jerry Paul MacDonald, "Reject the Wicked Man-Coercive Persuasion and Deviance Production: A Study of Conflict Management." *Cultic Studies Journal 5* (1988): 59-121.

It is necessary, then, for the helper to be able to systematically refute a particular group's teaching on, for instance, faction, slander, submission, or confession. This will allow the ex-member an opportunity to open up his or her mind and entertain thoughts that may have been hitherto viewed as "slander" but now can be viewed as "sound doctrine" or even "reproof." I cannot underscore enough the importance of getting these ex-members to think, and to think critically.

Myth Six

Perhaps the best way for these ex-members to receive help is to see a professional therapist such as psychologist, psychologist or mental health counselor.

As with Myth #5, Myth #6 is only half-true and therefore also particularly dangerous. Being a professional therapist does not automatically confer expertise regarding cultic phenomena. Some therapists may be prone to subscribe to Myth #3. Therapists who operate according to Myth #3 may inadvertently play the "blame the victim" game; or they may commit what social psychologist call the "attribution error"[13] (i.e., the problem lies within the person and not within the *group*). Such therapy can make the ex-member even worse.

There is sufficient literature and research showing the deleterious effects of cultic or extremist group experience to forewarn those seeking counsel to be cautious when choosing, a therapist who subscribes to the "benign" view of cultic involvement.[14]

A small percentage of professional therapists, on the other hand, not only consider *cultic involvement* but also religious interest per se to be unhealthy, and will seek to help the ex-cultist look at life more "realistically." Others are explicitly hostile

---

[13]See K. Shaver, *An Introduction to Attribution Processes* (Cambridge, MA: Winthrop, 1975).

[14]An excellent discussion of these issues can be found in Stephen M. Ash, Psy. D., "A Response to Robbins' Critique of My Extremist Cult Definition and View of Cult Induced Impairment," *Cultist Studies Journal I* (Fall/Winter 1984): 172-35, See also Stephen Hassen , *Combating Cult Mind Control* (Rochester VT: Park Street Press, 1988).

toward Christianity. For example, N. Brandon declares that the Christian beliefs of sin and self-sacrifice are "as monstrous an injustice, as profound a perversion of morality as the human mind cans conceive. He encourages counselors to help their clients get free of such destructive doctrines. A. Ellis views the concept of sin as the direct and indirect cause of virtually all neurotic disturbances. Little comment is needed to point out the potentially disastrous effect of sending an ex-cultist to a therapist subscribing to such views. Counseling from such therapist could create a double sense of loss: 1) from the cultic group, and 2) from religious beliefs per se. The resulting confusion and spiritual disillusionment could last for years (not to mention the potentially eternal consequences of such counseling for the ex-cultist's soul).

SEVEN STEPS TO RECOVERY

What then is needed to help former members of these extremist groups? I recommend the following seven steps be taken.

Step One: Most importantly, find a helper that does not subscribe to these six myths and who knows how to counter them properly.

Step Two: Understand that cultic involvement is an intensely personal experience. Correspondingly, *therapy must be intense and personal.* The therapist, counselor, pastor must be able to relate to the ex-member's emotional needs for acceptance, belonging, friendship, and love.[15]

Harold Bussell notes that he *never* saw an evangelical who entered a cultic group for doctrinal reasons. Among the things he describes as factors which make a group attractive is the cult's emphasis on "group sharing ... community and caring.[16] In this connection a few notes of caution should be sounded when working with the ex-member. To begin with, the time-honored

---

[15]N. Brandon, *Honoring the Self* (New York: Bantam Books, 1983), cited in P.J. Watson, Ronald J. morris, and Ralph W. Hood, Jr. "Sin and Self-Functioning, Part 2: Grace, Guilt, and Psychological."

[16]"Adjustment," *Journal of Psychology and Theology* (Fall 1988): 270.

and effective method of doing a sound intellectual and theological refutation of the group's teachings is only one of the several crucial elements in the former member's recovery. In addition to theological and intellectual exposes, the group's ethics (e.g., its use of money, methods of thought reform, and practice of deception) need to be thoroughly examined (2 Cor. 4:2; Eph. 5:11; Psalms 24:3-4).[17][18][19]

Furthermore, the ethics and theology of the group need to be viewed in the context of the person's psychological needs (i.e., what was it about the group's teaching that drew him or her into it?). In recovering from cultic life, the issue that takes longest to resolve s typically the gnawing search for the love, fellowship, and caring experienced while in the group.

It is extremely important that a trusting relationship be established. The helper must work hard to accomplish this. One study showed that only one-half of cult members who sought help were able to engage in a successful relationship with a counselor.

Although the counselor, pastor, and church must provide warmth and care to the former member, they should not try to become a substitute or imitation of the intense "social high" experienced in the group. The tremendous fellowship and warmth that the ex-member longs for is often an "artificial high." Yes, the group experience felt great, but was it grounded in truth? Did the Holy Spirit always produce it, or might it have been more on the order of a drug-induced euphoria? True, the addict maintains there is no better feeling in the world. But look at the results — a most pitiable addiction that wrecks lives, health, career, and often kills.

---

[17]Brandon, *The Psychology of Self-Esteem* (New York: Bantam Books, 1969), cited in Watson, et al, 1988.

[18]A. Ellis, *Reason and Emotion in Psychoteraphy* (Secaucus, NJ: Lyle Stuart, 1962), cited in Watson, et al, "Sin and Self-Functioning, Part 1: Grace, Guilt, and Self-Consciousness," *Journal of Psychology and Theology*, 1, 16 (Fall 1988): 225

[19]Cultic involvement can produce serious psychological problems, though the problems of ex-cultists may not all be cult-related. Pastors are well advised to seek mental health consultation if they treat these people.

While the group member was on a "high," he/she may have — at the same time — unknowingly repressed or dissociated emotional pain, doubts, and the telltale signs that his/her health was being neglected. Such "highs" (which are not unique to professedly Christian groups) are psychologically and spiritually unhealthy.[20] The experience for the most part produces in the cults a strong sense of dependence on the group and its leaders. Consequently, the counselor must be very careful no to foster dependency towards him or herself. Dependency conflicts are typically a major concern for the ex-member. Good rehabilitation will seek to avoid unhealthy dependency while providing healthy group support.

Step Three: Most people who join cults have a powerful and highly commendable desire to serve God and their fellow man. Sadly, it has been my experience that the cults often get the "best" of our youth. The recovery process must *enable these individuals to see the possibility of a life of dedication to God free of cultic confines.* Churches need to show these people there are challenging, exciting, and fulfilling opportunities to serve God in a valid, non-cultic setting. At the appropriate time in his or her recovery process, summer team mission programs offered by several different church groups may be "just the ticket" for the ex-member.[21]

Research shows that non-theological explanations (i.e., those which do not not involve some divine purpose) can also be helpful. See Janoff-Bulman.[22]

Step Four: The ex-cult member has almost invariably suffered some rupture in family relations. *Family counseling is essential to produce health reintegration.* The typical concerns of the other family members are: 1) the tension between the ex-member's desire for independence (especially if the ex-member is between 18 and 25 years) and the parent's desire to protect;

---

[20]Lawrence Bennet Sullivan, Ph.D., Counseling and Involvement in New Religious Groups," Cultic Studies Journal I (Fall/Winter 1994): 178-95.

[21]Horowitz, "Psychological Response to Serious Life Events," in *Human Stress and Cognition,* ed. V.

[22]Hamilton and D. Warburton (New York: Wiley, 1980), cited in Janoff-Buman.

2) gaining information about the group; 3) how to reestablish communication with ex-member; 4) fear that their family member is seriously and/or permanently damaged by his or her cult involvement; and 5) guilt that somehow the parents were responsible for their child's entering the extremist organization.[23]

The nature of family concerns suggest that the Pastor and/or counselor need to provide information, be supportive, and lend assistance in finding other families with members in cultic groups.

Step Five: In attempting to understand what has happened to the ex-cultist it is quite helpful to employ the victim or trauma model. According to this model, victimization and the resulting distress are due to the shattering of three basic assumptions the victim held about the world and self: "the belief in personal invulnerability, the perception of the world as meaningful, and the perception of oneself as positiveness." The ex-cultist has been conned, used, traumatized, and often emotionally and, mentally abused while serving the group and/or a leader of the group. Like other victims (e.g., of criminal acts, war atrocities, rape, serious illness, etc.), ex-cultists often re-experience the painful memories of their group involvement. They also lose interest in the outside world, feel detached, and may show limited emotions.[24]

The ex-cultist's belief in a "just world" is shattered. He or she can no longer say "it won't happen to me." A need for meaning among these people is paramount. The victim must be helpful to regain a belief in self and the world that allows room for "bad things happening to good people."

He or she may also need to talk about and relive the trauma again and again, as do[25] the victims of other types of crises. Unfortunately, the process of talking about the trauma is

---

[23]Sullivan.

[24]Ronnie Janoff-Bulman, "The Aftermath of Victimizaiton; Rebuilding Shattered Assumptions," *Trauma and Its Wake: The Stud, and Treatment of Post-Traumatic Stress Disorders*, ed Charles R. Figle) Ph.D. (New York: Brunner/Maze).

[25]M.J. Horowitz, "Psychological Response to Serious Life Events," in *Human Stress and Cognition*, ed. V. Hamilton and D. Warburton (New York: Wiley, 198), cited in Janoff-Bulman, 23.

sometimes "short-circuited" by well-intended helpers who view such rumination as "unedifying" or "focusing too much on the past." Effective therapy must be very supportive and reaffirming, as self-esteem needs to be rebuilt.

Victims need to be freed from the view that they were somehow solely responsible for their plight. This task is especially problematic for those who had strongly believed in a version of "prosperity" teaching. Thus, theological reconstruction is often most helpful. For a sense of meaning to be restored victims must be helped to see their cultic experience in view of a benevolent God who truly loves them.[26]

Although it has been my experience that the majority of persons join and remain in cults for sincere reasons, my recommendation of the victim model is not to deny that for others the motives of power, pride, greed, and sex may have enticed and sustained their cultic involvement. In these cases effective rehabilitation must include an honest acknowledgment and forsaking of such sinful inclinations.

Behavior change is also very helpful. Pastors who work with ex-cultists should know that the chances for (and speed of) the ex-members recovery may in part depend on how similar the church's and pastor's style is to that of extremist group. If there is a marked similarity between the former group and the present church, there will be a great probability that the church setting will trigger traumatic memories. Consequently, the ex-member should seriously consider buying a new Bible translation and finding a pastor unlike his or her past leader in personality or teaching style. Along these lines, he or she would do well to seek out a church or fellowship providing a welcome contrast to the cultic milieu. Far too often ex-cult members drop out of good churches because they remind them too much of their group. It is tragic that these people are sometimes viewed as "backsliders" than as victims.

A support group or professional counseling can go a long way in helping by giving the ex-member strategies that will enable

---

[26]Research shows that non-theological explanations (i.e., those which do not involve some divine purpose) can also be helpful. See Janoff-Bulman, 26.

him or her to avoid future victimization by manipulative people. This allows the victim to regain some sense of his or her own strength and self-esteem. As with other victims, finding and talking with other former members (preferably from the same cultic group) is an essential step to recovery. Often through this process former members become close friends. This is a process similar to the "war buddies" phenomenon or the plethora of support groups that have arisen in recent years to help those who are victims of drug and alcohol abuse, divorce, cancer, or the like.

Step Six: *Education and support groups are essential.* The recovery process inevitably takes time. But, although many will eventually recover on their own, it is unwise to prolong the recovery process. I believe that one hour per week with a pastor or counselor is not the best approach. There are simply too many issues facing the ex-member that can be dealt with effectively on such a basis. What has been spelled out in this article hopefully underscores the need for special programs designed to aid the recovering member.

Dr. Ronald Enroth has emphasized the need for halfway houses or rehabilitation centers to treat ex-cultists.[27] After scores of successful rehabilitations at our Wellspring Retreat and Resource Center, I can certainly attest to the need for and effectiveness of such programs. But for various reasons some individuals find them either inconvenient or unworkable. For those not entering a rehabilitation center, then, a local program consisting of education, group support, and counseling would be most desirable.

Step Seven: It is essential to *help those coming from aberration Christian groups to rediscover the gospel.* It is my experience that all cultic or aberrant groups distort the gospel. This includes those that call themselves orthodox Christian as well. What is particularly disturbing is that many of these groups, could, with a clear conscience, subscribe to the most orthodox, fundamental, and evangelical statements of faith. But *practically*

---

[27]Ronald M. Enroth and J. Gordan Melton, Why Cults Succeed Where the Church Fails (Elain, IL: Brethern Press, 1985), 98-99

they are living a subtle but deadly religion of works righteousness, at least in regard to sanctification, if not justification. For this reason it is very liberating for former members to study the letter to the Galatians in a step-by-step fashion and contrast St. Paul's message with their group's practices.

Through the gospel, meaning to life is restored and self-esteem is regained. Ex-cultists can see, Joseph did, That "God meant it for good" (Gen.50:20). It has also been Harold Bussell's experience that a clear understanding of the gospel is the single most important issue in a cultist's recovery and future immunity from further cultic involvement.[28]

In conclusion, cultic involvement certainly entails more than theological aberrations. The existing published research demonstrates that psychological harm also occurs and that Christians are not immune. It is likely that there are several hundred thousand people in churches today who were once members of cults or other extremist organizations. This may be one of the largest unrecognized problems in the church today. It is recommended that specialized programs be established that can more effectively identify and help these individuals.

Paul R. Martin, Ph.D., a practicing psychologist, directs the Wellspring Retreat and Resource Center, New Athens, Ohio. Wellspring's mission is to help former cultist overcome the harmful effects of their experience. (740) 634-3007 and (740) 698-6277.

Permission granted by: Christian Research Institute, 1989, Winter/Spring, by Paul Martin DC 950, PO Box 7000 Rancho Santa Margarita, CA 92688-7000.

---

[28]Harold Bussell, *A Study on Justification, Christian Fullness, and Super Believers*, unpublished paper, see also Walter Martin, Essential Christianity (Ventura, CA: Regal Books, 1980), 71-81.

"THE CULTS ARE THE UNPAID BILLS OF THE CHURCH"
By Dr. Van Baalen

(Chaos of Cults, p. 14)

DANGERS OF THE NEW AGE: A SHADOW OF JONESTOWN

Jim Jones, minister in the Disciples of Christ denomination, led a large number of his church family to death by poison in the jungles of Guyana. This was sparked by his assassination of a sincerely inquisitive congressman and other numbers of the politician's party during their visit to the headquarters of the cult in Guyana.

Any serious analysis of the dangers of the New Age movement must take into consideration the tragic lesson of Jonestown, where 915 followers of Jones and a concerned senator investigating the cult became the victims of a fanatic influenced by New Age teachings.

This celebrated tragedy of cultic deception and murder in 1978 can be traced unerringly to the New Age doctrines of man's divinity and the relativistic world view of the New Age Cult.

This little known fact has been omitted by all studies of the New Age. It is, however, important and must be analyzed.

Let me hasten to add that Jones was the exception among cultists, not the rule. But he was significantly influenced by the New Age and sadly gave in to those ideas with awful consequences. Jones carried some of the teachings to terrifying illogical conclusions.

THE MISSING LINK: FATHER DIVINE AND THE PEACE MISSION MOVEMENT

In the aftermath of Jonestown, we discovered that Jim Jones had been an admirer and imitator of a Philadelphia-based cult leader who had proclaimed himself *Father Divine.*

Father Divine whose real name was George Baker, was born the son of slaves at a plantation on Hutchinson Island in Georgia. In 1914, in Valdosta, Georgia, George Baker was **arrested and jailed as a "public menace."** Since Baker refused to give his right name, the court Writ stated, *The people v. John Doe, alias God.*

The jury found Baker "not crazy enough to be sent to the state sanitarium, but crazy enough to be ordered to leave the State of Georgia." Thus the future god made a hurried exodus from the ungrateful state. From Valdosta, Baker led a little band of followers to New York City, where he arrived in 1915 and joined forces with a gentleman known as St. John the Divine Hickerson, who had a successful work called the Church of the Living God. Baker learned how to organize his group from Hickerson and, though terribly lacking in formal education, became an apt pupil in the art of "godhood."

After much deliberation, Baker bought a two-story frame house for $2,500 at 72 Macon Street in the all-white community of Sayville, Long Island, and proceeded to move in. The deed to this house carried the names of Major J. Divine and his wife Penniah.

George Baker, following Hickerson, believed quite literally in 1 Cor. 3:16, which refers to believers as the "temple of God"; so he reasoned that since God dwelt in him, he was God and entitled to divine authority. Baker became known as "the messenger," bearing the exalted title "God and the Sonship Degree."

To support and expand his work, Father Divine instituted communal living among his followers, taking the wages of the people of the commune to finance food and shelter for a growing number of people. After 1929, there were many empty stomachs that would willingly hail as divine anyone who would fill them. He moved from Sayville to Harlem and there, during the Great Depression, fed hundreds of thousands of people and rode the crest of the Harlem popularity wave. After Baker took the name "Father Divine," he accepted worship from his followers. It was common for his devotees to laud him with such words as "Bless your holy heart, Father Dear. Your children are happy knowing you are a god at hand and not a sky-god afar off." Father Divine's followers claimed that he bad died almost 2,000 years ago in the form of Jesus of Nazareth, and that the nineteenth century manifestation of God was not to be the return of Jesus Christ in power, as Scripture so clearly describes it (Rev. 1: 7-8), but in the form of a crusader against racial intolerance and false information about the true nature of God. Father Divine approved. He preached:

Why believe in something that they say can save you after passing from this existence to keep you living in poverty, debauchery, lacks, wants, and limitations while on this earth you are tabernacling. I will not only lift you as my true believers, but I shall lift humanity from all superstition and cause them to forget all about the imaginary God I am now eradicating and dispelling from the consciousness of the people. Baker blasphemously affirmed:

I shall fulfill the Scriptures to the letter and you may tell all the critics and the accusers and blasphemers when they speak maliciously and antagonistically concerning me that I am the Holy Ghost personified! Whether they believe it or not is immaterial to me, for all shall feel the results of thoughts they think and speak concerning me.

'This is the mission for which I came. It is written, "The government shall be upon His shoulders, He shall be call Wonderful Counselor, the Mighty God, the Everlasting Father."

Why do you call me Father? God Almighty! Thunders a response from thousands. Now isn't that wonderful! And Prince of Peace! Why do you say peace around here? Because the Prince of Peace has been recognized. (2) In a personal letter directed to Mr. Kenneth Daire, written on March 16, 1949, Father Divine stated:

Thus the greater the opposition, the more I advance, and the more my deity is observed the more I prove my omnipotence, omniscience, and omnipresence. And I prove my mastery over all flesh, for if I were not God I would have long since failed. His publications reveal that he found foundational basis for his teachings in the writings by the Unity School of Christianity. In some instances, the language of the Unity and Father Divine publications is identical. The Unity School (founded in 1891) was heavily influenced by Hinduism and Theosophy, teaching the New Age concept that man is essentially deity and needs only to recognize that fact in order to be freed from the limitations of this existence. Father Divine believed and taught the same thing, combining this with a genuine effort to feed, clothe, and shelter people during the Great Depressions of the 1930's. Social work was the great emphasis of Father Divine, but he also crusaded against racial prejudice, which he combined with the teaching that he was God. Concerning

¹The New Day, July 16, 1949. ²The Spoken Word, June 16, 1936. On racial prejudice he stated:

If the prejudiced and antagonistic employers refuse to have you in their service just because of your belief in me and your conviction of my deity, they will suffer even as Sodom and Gomorrah did, in whom righteousness was not found sufficient to save them....

So it is the same spirit, the same one you have been praying to that I am summed up and recognized in this body to reach them and to save them of every undesirable condition. That is such an expression as being termed different races and colors could be United together in the unity of the spirit of mind, of aim, and of purpose until I came personally! But I came to let you and all mankind know that "out of one blood God created all nations of men for to dwell upon the face of the whole earth." Jones was attracted by the communal lifestyle of Father Divine's Peace Mission movement and took busloads of his people there to observe how it functioned. He was impressed with Father Divine's capacity to provide funds by means of communal living and to carry out what he considered to be the Christian imperative of the Good Samaritan, taking care of one's neighbor. Surely no one can fault either Father Divine or Jim Jones for pursuing the

Christian ethic and doctrine of "loving our neighbor as ourselves" (Lev. 19:18). But as history has shown, it did not end there. George Baker affirmed his, divinity in terms of the New Age, and through his publications, he urged his followers to recognize themselves as his children. These are the things that Jim Jones absorbed and put into practice in San Francisco. Eyewitness accounts tell of how Jones would begin by quoting from the Bible in his hand. Later, as shifted emphasis from the Bible to himself as the messenger of God, he would throw the Bible on the ground and kick it because he considered his The New Day, July 1949.

In The New Day, Divine's propaganda newspaper, he spoke of his cooperation with the Communism, while at the same time affirms his uniqueness: "Every knee shall bow and every tongue confess that Father Divine is God, God, God."

By 1941, Father Divine's admiration for the Communism had worn rather thin. Their relationship came to an abrupt end in that year, and Father Divine described the Communism as un-American and ungodly. By the time the Korean war broke out in 1950, he freely declared himself "a righteous fighter against the forces of communism."

We now know that Jim Jones was intrigued with Marxism and even attempted to bribe the Russian ambassador to Guyana in a vain attempt to leave South America and place himself under Communist rule elsewhere. It appears that Father Divine, becoming aware of what the Communism was all about, had the good sense to jettison his support for them. Jim Jones, even when rebuffed by the Soviets, pursued his courtship with Marxism.

Permission granted for reprint by:

Bethany House Publishers
6820 Auto Club Road
Minneapolis, MN 55438
Copyright 1989, Walter Martin

HOW CULTS AFFECT FAMILIES
By Henrietta and Kurt Crampton

*This report was originally prepared for "Cultism: A confer-
ence for Scholars and Policy Makers," sponsored by the
American Family Foundation, the Neuropsychiatric Institute of
the University of California at Los Angeles, and the Johnson
Foundation of Racine, Wisconsin. The conference was convened
at the Johnson's Foundation's Wingspread facility in Racine from
September 9-11, 1985. The authors who live in Redondo Beach,
California, were among the founders of the Cult Awareness
Network, a nationwide affiliation of local groups that conduct
public education programs and offers information and referral to
the cult-involved.*

Our efforts to alert others to the nature of destructive cults
began in 1973 when our nine our nineteen-year-old daughter
joined a cult. Out of desperation we physically removed her,
under the scrutiny of national television. Although the coverage
was not sympathetic to us, we were deluged with phone calls and
letters from parents who identified their problems with ours.
Between the 1973 and 1983 we probably interviewed more
cult-affected families and former cult members and read more
letters from them than all of the academicians who were doing
research on cults. We did not compile family data as such.

In our opinion, it is an understatement to say that families are
adversely affected by destructive cults. Our own experience,
combined with the experiences of other families in similar
circumstances determined our early conclusion. The cults used
the role of the family and the cult leader becomes the surrogate
parent. Alienation of the cult members from the family is a direct
result. The effect this alienation has on families depends on the
family members or members involved. Of course, not all families
are affected the same way.

In the latter case, our knowledge was gleaned, for the most
part, from numerous letters and calls we received after our
address and phone number were given in an article about a cult.

Parents consider their offspring "children," and cannot sever that relationship on a child's eighteenth birthday. Many parents are providing financial aid for education to adult children in most cases, the adult children are still living at home or have only recently left. When such young adults become involved with cults, families feel the alienation very directly.

Initially the family is shocked to discover one of its own members is actually involved with a cult. The first clue is an abrupt personality change, which the parents usually are the first to notice. When they then discover that their family member has renounced his parents, family, friends and former values, stopped making his own decisions, and is totally devoted to the cult leader, they are appalled. They try to communicate with the new cult member and cannot do so, either because the cult forbids contact with families or because the cult's dogma defines familiar in alien ways so that language loses its common meaning. The family contacts their religious leaders and usually receives little help or understanding. After seeing psychologists, psychiatrists, or lawyers, the family learns that their is no ready made solution to bring the cult member back to his former self grief and frustration set in.

Just as families with handicapped children win search everywhere, grasping at straws, in their help seeking, so do families with members in cults. Disagreements arise within families regarding actions taken or proposed. Some try to place the blame on others. Bickering results. Guilt is felt. Parents see themselves as failures. Some siblings, feeling neglected because of the time and energy parents spend on cult related problems, often develop behavior problems. Great turmoil results. At this point families are in desperate need of help and do not know where to go. They must understand that they are not alone, that others have faced the same frustration, grief and guilt, and that there is hope. It is important to save the remaining family from destruction, avoid panic and try to keep communication open with the cult member.

Many families have lost a second child to a cult. In almost all these cases the second child visited the cult to inquire about a brother or sister and was recruited. We advise parents to instruct their children never to visit the cult alone.

Parents of a long-time cult members have much difficulty keeping a healthy perspective in their lives and maintaining their own physical and mental well being. At the death of a loved one, grief is severe, but with time becomes easier to bear. When children are cult members, families feel as though their children are hostages, held by terrorists, and often do not know where their children are or if they are dead or alive.

When parents learn their son or daughter has been married in the cult, they become more distressed and alienated. To them, the cult involvement has lost its temporary status, if there are grandchildren, the grief becomes even more severe. Adequate diet, medical care, and education are denied to children and adults alike in many cults. Reports of child abuse in cults often appear in the newspapers. Some cults abuse children sexually as well as physically. It is extremely difficult for non-member parents and grandparents to endure this knowledge.

In addition to concerns for health and safety families feel a deep regret over a lost of a family continuity.

Consider the emotional trauma for parents when they must alter wills to prevent cult leaders from becoming beneficiaries of their child's inheritance. When heirlooms can't be passed on, and family traditions are lost, parents feel deprived. Cult members sometimes don't even return when there is death in the family. One son wrote his mother upon his father's death: "Let the dead bury the dead."

We are seeing a second generation of cultists children who have lost their birthrights and roots. Some do not have birth certificates. Many will never know their ancestry, in some cases they will not know their legal names. Grandparents have occasionally been given visitation rights by the courts and have been able, if they can locate their grandchildren, at least to have some communication with them This, of course place additional stress on families, particularly if parents/grandparents are not in good health. Greater frustration is heaped upon these families when they read reports by intellectuals who expound against organizations of cult-affected parents and claim cult membership is temporary and a benign or even therapeutic experience.

We are hearing news from parents of long-term cult members who report that their children are in mental hospitals, suffering extreme depression or paranoia. There also seem to be a high incidence of cult-related suicides.

The fortunate families who see their members leave cults have the continuing burden of helping them reenter society. Parents who are older, and perhaps retired, find themselves financially burdened, needed to pay for medical attention or education which was terminated by the cults. Parents must exhibit great patience to help former cult members through moods of depression and loneliness. Families, whose endurance and resources have been stretched to the limits over the years, must be able to supply the tender loving care so necessary to a person recovering from the effects of cult membership. Sometimes there are grandchildren with special needs. Since some cults do not allow children to live with their parents within the cult unit, sometimes members cannot bring their children out with them when they leave. Later they try to find them to gain custody, and families are called upon them to help pay for private investigators and lawyers.

There are no public-supported facilities to assist these families. Those leaving cults usually have no personal belongings, money or employment prospects, and, in many cases, not even identity papers. to receive public assistance for children, there must be birth records. Families must come up with necessary records and interim financing. Drug and Alcohol abusers, children under eighteen, and battered wives, can usually find help in their communities. former cult members have told us that many more cult members would leave their cult if they had a place to go.

Members leaving cults after several years may be able to locate their families. In one case the parents had separated and moved, the mother had remarried, and the new married name was unknown. In another instance a psychiatrist called us from Alaska to see if we could furnish a surname of one of his patients who had been a member of our daughter's cult. His patient could remember only his cult name. Our daughter could not help as members seldom know the real names of fellow cultists. Unless his memory returned, that young man's true identity was permanently lost.

From September to October, 1981, as a result of an article in *Reader's Digest*, we received approximately 300 calls from people requesting information and assistance concerning cults and related problems. About two-thirds of the calls were from women who had cult involved husbands. They said that their husbands were attracted to the cult with expectations of personality improvement, better job opportunities, and other desired goals. As time passed the husband spent more time and money on cult-related courses and their attitudes toward their families changed. When the families complained about neglect and money spent on the group, arguments ensued. When money saved for cars, down-payments on homes, or even placed in children's banks accounts, was gone, the wives realized too late that their family was in deep trouble; divorce was the only alternative. Other calls stimulated by the Digest article were from separated spouses seeking custody of children. The non-cult parents were concerned that there would be placed in cult schools and indoctrinated. But having custody is no guarantee against child stealing, as there is documentation on missing children hidden in cults. A parental concern about kidnapping by the spouse who is a cult member is often justified. To make matters worst, the non-cult parent who maintain custody of the children is faced by the myriad problems of sin parenting with no financial assistance or shared responsibility.

We have read reports that cults are on the wane and observed that the largest groups do not seem to be recruiting as heavily as they did in the 70's. They still have followers, however. and new groups have emerged which also use sophisticated recruitment and indoctrination techniques. We do not expect the problems for families of cult members do disappear or diminish significantly.

HOW CAN THE YOUNG PROTECT THEMSELVES AGAINST CULTS?

Cope with stress —When stress is getting the best of us, we are more likely to be "seduced" by someone selling "happiness." If you are having difficulty coping, seek help from reputable, trustworthy persons.

NEVER be afraid to question.

ALWAYS be wary of anyone who tries to discourage or prevent you from questioning. Learn to recognize common cult recruitment tactics and situations.

BE WARY OF:

- People who are excessively or inappropriately friendly. Genuine friendships takes time to build.
- People with simplistic answers or solutions to complex world problems.
- People with invitations to free meals, lectures and workshops.
- People who pressure you to do something you don't really want to do. Don't be afraid to say "no!"
- People who are vague or evasive. If they are hiding something, it's usually because they don't want you to know!
- People who try to play on your basic human decency. You don't always have to reciprocate a kindness, for example, especially when it may have been a way to manipulate you.
- People who claim to be "just like you." This is often a device to disarm your vigilance.
- People who confidently claim that they can help you solve your problems, especially when they know little about you.
- People who make claims about "saving mankind," "achieving enlightenment," or "following the road to happiness." If their claims seem too good to be true, they are probably false!
- People who always seem "happy," even when common sense dictates otherwise.

- People who claim they or their group is really special." Arrogance is much more common than genuine superiority.
- People who promise quick solutions to difficult life problems.
- People who claim that "you need to destroy the mind to find God," or "the devil works through the mind," or otherwise disparage the critical mind.

Permission granted for reprint by AFF News, P.O. Box 2265, Dept. 0, Bonita Springs. FL. 34133.
Web Site: http://www.csj.org

REPAIRING THE SOUL AFTER
A CULT EXPERIENCE
By Jania Lalich

I was recruited into a cult in 1975 when I was 30 years old. The previous year I returned the United States after having spent almost four years in exile abroad, where I lived the most serene life on an island in the Mediterranean off the coast of Spain. If someone had told me that within a year I would be deeply involved and committed to a cult, I would have laughed derisively. Not me! I was too independent, too headstrong, a lover of fun and freedom.

I was told that we would be unlike all other groups on the Left because we were led by women and because our leader was brilliant and from the class. I was told that we would not follow the political line of any other country, but that we would create our own brand of Marxism, our own proletarian feminist revolution; we would not be rigid, dogmatic, sexist, and racist. We were new and different — an elite force. We were going to make the world a better place for all people.

The reality, of course, was that our practical work had little if anything to do with working-class ideals or goals. Our leader was an incorrigible, uncontrollable megalomaniac; she was alcoholic, arbitrary, and almost always angry. Our organization, with the word *democratic* prominent in its name, was ultra authoritarian, completely top down, with no real input or criticism sought or listened to. Our lives were made up of 18-hour days of busywork and denunciation sessions. Our world was harsh, barren, and unrewarding. We were committed and idealistic dreamers who were tricked into believing that such demanding conditions were necessary to transform ourselves into cadre fighters. We were instructed that we were the " " and that we take all guidance from our leader who knew all. We were never to question any orders or in any way contradict or confront our leader. We were taught to dread and fear the outside world which, we were told, would shun and punish us. In fact, the shunning and punishment was rampant within; but, blinded by our own belief, commitment, and fatigue, in conjunction with the group behavior-control techniques, I and the others succumbed to the pressures and quickly learned to rationalize away any doubts or apprehensions.

I remained in that group for more than 10 years. When I got out of the cult in early 1986, I had to begin life anew. I was a decade behind in everything. Both my parents had died, and I had lost touch with former friends. I had to play catch so to speak, culturally, socially, economically, emotionally, and intellectually. But most important of all, I had to repair my soul. Who am I? How could I have committed the many unkind acts while in the group? Where do I belong now? What do I believe in now? Will I ever restore my faith in myself and in others? These are the kind of questions and dilemmas that troubled me. Over time, and most recently through my contact and work with former members of many types of cults, I've come to see that the single most uniform aspect of all cult experiences is that it touches, and usually damages, the soul, the psyche.

I define a cult as a particular kind of relationship; it can be a group situation or between two people. Within that relationship there is an enormous power imbalance, but more than that, there is a hidden agenda. There is deception, manipulation, exploitation, and almost certainly abuse, carried out and/or reinforced by the use of social and psychological influence techniques meant to control behavior and shape attitudes and thinking patterns. A cult is lead by a person (or sometimes two or three) who demands all veneration, who makes all decisions, and who ultimately controls most aspects of the personal lives of those who are cleverly persuaded that they must follow, obey, and stay in the good graces (i.e., the grips) of the leader.

Cult leaders and cult recruiters capture the hearts, minds, and souls of the best and brightest in our society. Cults are looking for active, productive, intelligent, energetic individuals who will perform for the cult by fund-raising, by recruiting more followers, by operating cult businesses and leading cult seminars. In the 1960s and 1970s it was perhaps more typical for cults to recruit primarily young and old alike and everyone in between. With anywhere from three to five thousand cults active in the United States today, it is quite likely that a cult recruiter has been knocking on your door or that you have unwittingly answered a cult advertisement for a course, a workshop, a lecture, a book or tape, or some other product.

Today, cults are so sophisticated in their recruitment and indoctrination techniques that their methods go far beyond what anybody imagined in the 1950s when certain scholars and researchers were studying and writing about thought-reform programs and systematic behavior-control processes. Cults today have perfected their approach and refined their manipulations. They had to — after all, recruiting and retaining bright people isn't easy. And this is again where the soul comes in.

Cults appeal to that part of ourselves that wants something better; a better world for others or a better self. These are the genuine, heartfelt desires of decent, honest human beings. Cult recruiters are trained in how to play on those desires, how to make it look as though what the cult has to offer is exactly what you are interested in. Cults can be formed around almost any topic, but there are nine broad categories: religious, Eastern-based, New Age, business, political, psychotherapy/human potential, occult, one-on-one, and miscellaneous (such as lifestyle or personality cults).

All cults, no matter their stripe, are a variation on a theme, for their common denominator is the use of coercive persuasion and behavior control without the knowledge of the person who is being manipulated. They manage this by targeting (and eventually attacking, dissembling, and reformulating according to the cult's desired image) a person's innermost self. They take away you and give you back a cult personality, a pseudo personality. They punish you when the old you turns up, and they reward the new you. Before you know it, you don't know who you are or how you got there; you only know (or you are trained to believe) that you have to stay there. In a cult there is only one way — cults are totalitarian, a yellow brick road to serve the leader's whims and desires, be they power, sex, or money.

When I was in my cult, I so desperately wanted to believe that I had finally found the answer. Life in our society today can be difficult, confusing, daunting, disheartening, alarming, and frightening. Someone with a glib tongue and good line can sometimes appear to offer you a solution. In my case, I was drawn in by the proposed political solution to bring about social change. For someone else, the focus may be on health, diet, psychological awareness, the environment, the stars, a spirit being, or even becoming a more successful businessperson. The crux is that cult leaders are adept at convincing us that what they have to offer is special, real, unique, and forever — and that we wouldn't be able to survive apart from the cult. A person's sense of belief is so dear, so deep, and so powerful; ultimately it is that belief that helps bind the person to the cult. It is the glue used by the cult to make the mind manipulates stick. It is our very core, our very belief in our self and our commitment, it is our very faith in humankind and the world that is exploited and abused and turned against us by the cults.

When a person finally breaks from a cultic relationship, it is the soul, then that is most in need of repair. When you discover one day that your guru is a fraud, that there are no more magic tricks, that the group's victories and accomplishments are fabrications of an internal public-relations system, that your holy teacher is breaking his avowed celibacy with every young disciple, that the group's connections to people of import are nonexistent — when awarenesses such as these come upon you, you are faced with what many call a "rape". Whether your cultic experience was religious or secular, the realization of such enormous loss and betrayal tends to cause considerable pain. As a result, afterwards, many people are prone to reject all forms of belief. In some cases, it may take years to overcome the disillusionment, and learn not only to have trusted in your inner self but also to believe in something again.

There is also a related difficulty: that persistent nagging feeling that you have made a mistake in leaving the group — perhaps the teachings are true and the leader is right; perhaps it is you who failed. Because cults are so clever at manipulating certain emotions and events — in particular, wonder, awe, transcendence, and mystery (this is sometimes called "manipulation") — and because of the human desire to believe even after leaving the group. For this reason, many people go from one cult to another, or go in and out of the same cultic group relationships (known as "hopping"). Since every person needs something to believe in — a philosophy of life, a way of being, an organized religion, a political commitment, or a combination thereof — sorting out these matters of belief tends to be a major area of adjustment after a cultic experience.

Since a cult involvement is often an ill-fated attempt to live out some form of personal belief, the process of figuring out what to believe in once you've left the cult may be facilitated by dissecting the cult's ideological system. Do an evaluation of the group's philosophy, attitudes, and world view; define it for yourself in your own language, not the language of the cult. Then see how this holds up against the cult's actual daily practice or what you now know about the group. For some, it might be useful to go back and research the spiritual or philosophical system that you were raised in or believed in prior to the cult involvement. Through this process you will be better able to assess what is real and what is not, what is useful and what is not, what is distortion and what is not. By having a basis for comparison, you will be able to question and explore areas of knowledge or belief that were no doubt systematically closed to you while in the cult.

Most people who come out of cultic experiences shy away from organized religion or any kind of organized group for some time. I generally encourage people o take their time before choosing another religious affiliation or group involvement. As with any intimate relationship, trust in reciprocal and must be earned.

After a cult experience, when you wake up to face the deepest emptiness, the darkest hole, the sharpest scream in inner terror at the deception and betrayal you feel, I can only offer hope by saying that in confronting the loss, you will find the real you. And when your soul is heated, refreshed, and free of the nightmare bondage of cult lies and manipulations, the real you will find a new path, a valid path — a path to freedom and wholeness.

Jania Lalich, Education Director, Community Resources on Influence & Control — PO Box 1199, Alameda, CA 94501 — Tel: 510-522-1556. She is co-author with Margaret Singer of *Cults in Our Midst: The Hidden Menace in Our Everyday Lives* (Jossey-Bass, 1995), and *"Crazy" Therapies*, (Jossey-Bass, 1997.

ABOUT JANICH LALICH

Janich Lalich is a widely recognized expert on cults, totalist systems, and social and psychological influence. A former 10-year member of a political cult, Ms. Lalich has been working in this field since 1986. She has a master's degree in Human Development. After receiving a B.A. from the University of Wisconsin (1967), she did postgraduate work at Fulbright scholar.

Ms. Lalich is co-author of three highly acclaimed books — *Captive Hearts, Captive Mind: Freedom and Recovery from cults and Abusive Relationships; Cults in Our Mist;* and *"Crazy" Therapies* — and Editor of *Women Under the Influence: A Study of Women's Lives in Totalist Groups.* She also facilitates support groups for those who have had abusive group experiences.

She has lectured to civic, educational, religious, professional, and business groups; and has appeared in the media, including on *Meet the Press* and *Time/CNN* online. She has been a feature speaker and conference panelist. Speaking engagements have included Stanford University, UC-Berkeley, University of San Francisco, Arizona State University, Adams State College (Alamosa, Colo.), Queen's College (Charlotte), Wesley Monumental United Methodist Church (Savannah), and numerous public forums.

Ms. Lalich has served as a consultant to educators, mental health professionals, attorneys, law-enforcement officials, television and film producers, and the State of California Department of Education.

Permission granted for reprint by Janich Lalich, 2325 Clement Ave. Suite 235, Alameda, Ca. 94501. Tel: 510-522-1556, Fax: 510-522-1020, E-mail: janja @crl.com

COPING WITH TRANCE STATES:
THE AFTERMATH OF LEAVING A CULT
By Patrick L. Ryan

Trance states, derealization, dissociation, spaceyness ... What are they? What strategies can we use to cope with them?

Trance states: By trance states, we mean dissociation, depersonalization and derealization.

In the group we called it spacing out or higher/altered states of consciousness.

All humans have some propensity to have moments of dissociation. However, certain practices (meditation, chanting, learned processes of speaking in tongues, prolonged guided imagery, etc.) appear to have ingrained in many former members a reflexive response to involuntarily enter altered states of consciousness.

Even after leaving the group and ceasing its consciousness-altering practices, this habitual, learned response tends to recur under stress.

For some former members this can be distressing and affect their functioning. When this happens, it tends to impair one's concentration, attention, memory and coping skills.

Many former members coming from prolonged consciousness-altering groups find that the intensity, frequency and duration of the episodes decrease when they deliberately and consistently use the strategies outlined below.

It is important to note that when one is tired, ill, or under stress the feelings of spaceyness, dissociation, depersonalization and derealization may temporally return.

By developing the ability to immediately label these states and attempting the following strategies, one can return to consistent state of mental functioning.

DEFINITIONS from Diagnostic and Statistical Manual of Mental Disorders (DSM-III):

Dissociative Disorders: The essential feature is a sudden, temporary alteration in the normally integrative functions of consciousness, identity, or motor behavior. If the alteration occurs in consciousness, important personal events cannot be recalled. If it occurs in identity, either the individual's customary identity is temporarily forgotten and a new identity is assumed, or the customary feeling of one's own reality is lost and replaced by a feeling of unreality. If the alteration occurs in motor behavior, there is also a concurrent disturbance in consciousness or identity.

Atypical Dissociative Disorder (300.15): Trance-like states, derealization unaccompanied by depersonalization, and those more prolonged dissociated states may occur in persons who have been subjected to periods of prolonged and intense coercive persuasion (brainwashing, thought reform, and indoctrination while captive of terrorists or cultists).

Depersonalization Disorder (300.60): The essential feature is the occurrence of one or more episodes of depersonalization that cause social or occupational impairment.

The symptom of depersonalization involves an alteration in the perception or experience of the self so that the usual sense of one's own reality is temporarily lost or changed. This is manifested by a sensation of self-estrangement or unreality, which may include the feeling that one's extremities have changed in size, or the experience of seeming to perceive oneself from a distance. In addition, the individual may feel "mechanical" or as though in a dream. Various types of sensory anesthesia and feeling of not being in complete control of one's actions, including speech, are often present.

Associated Features: Derealization is frequently present. This is manifested by a strange alteration in the perception of one's surroundings so that a sense of the reality of the external world is lost. A perceived change in the size of shape of objects in the external world is common. People may be perceived as dead or mechanical.

Other common associated features include dizziness, depression, obsessive ruminations, anxiety, fear of going insane, and disturbance in the subjective sense of time. There is often the feeling that recall is difficult or slow.

Maintain a Routine: Makes change slowly: physical, emotional, nutritional, geographical, etc. Monitor health, including nutrition, medical checkups. Avoid drugs and alcohol. Daily exercise reduces dissociation (spaceyness, anxiety and insomnia). Avoid sensory overload. Avoid crowds or large spaces without boundaries (shopping malls, video arcades, etc.). Drive consciously without music.

Reality Orientation: Establish time and place landmarks such as calendars and clocks. Make lists of activities in advance. Update lists daily or weekly. Difficult tasks and large projects should be kept on separate lists. Before going on errands, review list of planned activities, purchases and projects. Mark items off as you complete them. Keep updated on current news. News shows (CNN, Headline News talk radio) are helpful because they repeat, especially if you have memory/concentration difficulties.

Reading: Try to read one complete news article daily to increase comprehension. Develop reading "stamina" with the aid of a timer. Increasing reading periods progressively.

Sleep Interruptions: Leave TALK radio/ television, news programs (not music) on all night. (Preferably not Rush, though.)

Don't push yourself. Dissociation is an acquired habit, so it will take time break.

INDIVIDUAL DIFFERENCES AFFECTING RECOVERY

Each person's experience with a cult is different. Some may dabble with a meditation technique but never get drawn into taking "advance courses" or moving to the ashram. Others may quickly give up all they have, including college, career, possessions, home, or family, to do missionary work in a foreign country or move into cult lodgings.

After a cult involvement, some people carry on with their lives seemingly untouched; more typically, others may encounter a variety of emotional problems and troubling psychological difficulties ranging from inability to sleep, restlessness, and lack of direction to panic attacks, memory loss, and depression. To varying degrees they may feel guilty, ashamed, enraged, lost, confused, betrayed, paranoid, and in a sort of a foe.

ASSESSING THE DAMAGE

Why are some people so damaged by their cult experience while others walk away seemingly unscathed? There are predisposing personality factors and levels of vulnerability that may enhance a person's continued vulnerability and susceptibility while in the group. All these factors govern the impact of the cult experience on the individual and the potential for subsequent damage. In assessing this impact, three different stages of the cult experience — before, during, and after — need to be examined.

Before Involvement

Vulnerability factors before involvement include a person's age, prior history of emotional problems, and certain personality characteristics.

During Involvement

Length of time spent in the group. There is quite a difference in the impact cults will have on a person if she or he is a member for only a few weeks, as compared to months or years. A related factor is the amount of exposure to the indoctrination process and the carious levels of control that exist in the group.

Intensity and severity, of the thought-reform program. The intensity and severity of cults' efforts at conversion and control vary in different groups and in the same group at different times. Members who are in a peripheral, "associate" status may have very different experiences from those who are full-time, inner-core members.

Specific methods will also vary in their effect. An intense training workshop over a week or weekend that includes sleep deprivation, hypnosis, and self-exposure coupled with a high degree of supervision and lack of privacy is likely to produce faster changes in a participant that a group process using more subtle and long-term methods of change.

Poor or inadequate medical treatments. A former cult member's physical condition and attitude toward physical health may greatly impact post cult adjustments.

Loss of outside support. The availability of a network of family and friends and the amount of outside support certainly will bear on a person's reintegration after a cult involvement.

Skewed or nonexistent contact with family and former friends tends to increase members' isolation and susceptibility to the cult's world view. The reestablishment of those contacts is important to help offset the loss and loneliness the person will quite naturally feel.

After Involvement

Various factors can hasten healing and lessen postcult difficulties at this stage.

Many are related to the psycho-educational process. Former cult members often spend years after leaving a cult in relative isolation, not talking about or dealing wth their cult experiences.

Shame and silence may increase the harm done by the group and can prevent healing.

Understanding the dynamics of cult conversion is essential to healing and making a solid transition to an integrated postcult life.

Engage in a professionally led exit counseling session.

Educate yourself about cults and thought-reform techniques.

Involve family members and old friends in reviewing and evaluating your cult experience.

See a mental health professional or a pastoral counselor, preferably someone who is familiar with or is willing to be educated about cults and common postcult problems.

Attend a support group for former cult members.

The following sets of questions have proven helpful to former cult members trying to make sense of their experience.

REVIEWING YOUR RECRUITMENT

1. What was going on in your life at the time you joined the group or met the person who became your abusive partner?
2. How and where were you approached?
3. What was your initial reaction to or feeling about the leader or Group.

4. What first interested you in the group or leader?
5. How were you mislead during recruitment?
6. What did the group or leader promise you? Did you ever get it?
7. What didn't they tell you that might have influenced you not to join had you known?
8 Why did the group or leader want you?

UNDERSTANDING THE PSYCHOLOGICAL MANIPULATION USED IN YOUR GROUP

1. Which controlling techniques were used by your group or leader: Chanting, meditation, sleep deprivation, isolation, drugs, hypnosis, criticism, fears. List each technique and how it served the group's purpose.
2. What was the most effective? The least effective?
3. What are the group's beliefs and values? How did they come to be your beliefs and values?

EXAMINE YOUR DOUBTS

1. What are your doubts about the group or leader now?
2. Do you still believe the group or leader has all or some of the answers?
3. Are you still afraid to encounter your leader or group members on street?
4. Do you ever think of going back? What is going on in your mind when this happens?
5. Do you believe your group or leader has any supernatural or spiritual power to harm you in any way?
6. Do you believe you are cursed by God for having left the group?

Excerpted from *Captive Hearts, Captive Minds: Freedom and Recovery for Cult and Abusive Relationships* by Madeleine Tobias and Jania Lalich (Hunter House Publishers, (800) 266-5892). © 1994. Reprinted with permission.

CULTS: WHAT CLERGY SHOULD KNOW
By Rev. Richard L Dowhower

A DUTY OF CARE

Given the unavoidable intrusion of cults and cultism into their pastoral lives, clergy ought to understand the nature of cultism in order to better serve those who come to them for support and guidance.

I suspect that the intrusions of cultic groups into my pastoral life is not unlike the experience of many other clergy. Consider the middle-aged woman who recently came into my office in tears because she did not know what to do about the progressive loss of her son and daughter-in-law to a group called Scientology. Or note the case of my own daughter who only a decade ago at a high school told me of the visit of a Hare Krishna speaker to her sociology class, now says that she had been invited to an informational meeting for a new personal development workshop which allegedly uses cultic techniques.

Even I have been the object of such approaches. Not long ago a pleasant female voice called to ask if I had received her organization's invitation to a special Christian anti-Communist meeting for local clergy sponsored by CAUSA, which I later learned is a Unification Church front actively promoting the politics and religion of Rev. Sun Myung Moon.

My point in noting these episodes is to emphasize the fact that cults and cultic behaviors are all around, that clergy and us have a duty of care toward their congregants in this area of concern. They ought, therefore, to know something of the problem in general, be able to recognize its appearance, and above all, they ought to know how to help its victims.

THE PHENOMENON

A host of new religious, therapeutic, and New Age self-improvement groups now vies with more traditional institutions for spiritual commitments. New prophets and self-styled messiahs providing new revelations and new sacred scriptures challenge our mainstream practices. From in Lutheran religious perspective, these unorthodox new "ways" are spurious and be denounced and combated. They are modem manifestations of the ancient Gnostic heresy, which is to say salvation by special enlightenment.

But even from a nontheological perspective, these cultic manifestations of our troubled time can be seen to be harmful. They induce persons made anxious by the common ills of modern life, the spiritually and theologically immature, and especially those who are simply at a vulnerable point in their lives to abandon traditional and complicated approaches to problems in favor of unrealistically simple and unambiguous ones. And this is frequently destructive, for cultic groups intentionally deceive and defraud while violating basic human and civil rights. Typically, such groups exhibit:

> a great or excessive devotion or dedication to some person, idea, or thing, and employ unethically manipulative techniques of persuasion and control designed to advance the goals of the group's leaders, to the actual or possible detriment of members, their families, or the community. Unethically manipulative techniques of persuasion and control include, but are not limited to isolation from former friends and family, use of special methods to heighten suggestibility and subservience, powerful group pressures, information management, suspension of individuality or critical judgment, promotion of total depends "on the group and fear of leaving it."

The results of such methods are, all too often, family schisms, mental breakdown, financial disaster, loss of individuality and personal initiative, child and spouse abuse, lives of manipulation, deception, even criminal activity, and quite literally, enslavement. Two questions confront us. How do we help parishioners who have — despite any preventive educational measures we may have instituted — become involved in groups that produce such effects? How do we "inoculate" those who haven't become involved but who are, or might become vulnerable?

PASTORAL CARE STRATEGY

The first duty of pastoral care is to offer a patient and willing ear to the relatives or friends of the cult-involved. The initial appeal for help may well come hard on the heels of the caller own hysteria-inducing discovery that a loved one has cut his or her social moorings and gone off with a group suspected of being a "cult." On the other hand, the call may come from family members who have witnessed their loved ones' gradual alienation from friends, family, old values, and goals. In either case the pastor must listen and understand the situation, thus providing essential comfort while setting the state for a rational assessment of the issues. The congregant must be reassured — if the evidence is supportive — that the problem is a real one and that concern for the cult-involved person is justified (rather than simply being, for example, the unreasonable concern of overprotective parents). The congregants must also be reassured that the situation is not hopeless, that help is available, and that a rational plan can usually knit sundered relationships and draw loved ones out of destructive associations.

The pastoral counselor must then direct his congregant to sources of information likely to help achieve this. Certainly, the pastor himself can provide some of the needed information by learning, in anticipation, about both cults and counseling the cult-involved. He can turn not only to his own denomination — many pastors are not aware that such resources exist so close to home — but to agencies that specialize in providing such information, whether about the psychological and social dimensions of the phenomenon, or about particular troublesome groups — how they work, the nature of their appeal, the defenses they erect, and their weaknesses. Such knowledge is vital to effect the reassessment of relationships and attachments both the cult-involved person and those concerned about him, a reassessment that must precede a happy resolution of the problem. Knowledge like this may also be important if some appeal to the law is made.

Finally, remember that there are unique pastoral care opportunities in working with individuals and families once somebody has left a cultic group. In many cases, ex-members are still dealing with theological and other spiritual issues that may have been central to their original involvements. Here, you can assist the ex-member to clarify for himself healthy forms of faith and religious commitment as distinct from those with which he was involved in the cult.

In addition to the obligation to help victims of cultic groups, clergy also have a duty to forewarn potential victims, especially the naive young people who come of age every year. Churches and synagogues should make cult education programs, especially those that teach potential victims how to resist cultic sales pitches, a regular part of their work with congregants. An indispensable resource in this endeavor is the International Cult Education Program (PO Box 1232, Gracie Station, New York, NY 10028; 212-533-5420), a program of the American Family Foundation (AFF).

The intrusions of the cult phenomenon into a clergyman's life can be ill timed and frustrating, but they present great opportunities, if we are prepared, to fulfill the calling to which we have committed ourselves.

Rev. Richard L Dowhower is a Lutheran clergyman and author of articles on cults for his denomination's journal for church professionals. A member of AFF's Clergy Education Committee, he has counseled cult victims and their families and done cult-?education work with church youth assemblies, high schools and colleges, and other clergy, as well as radio and TV He is currently pastor of All Saints Lutheran Church in Bowie, MD.

ACKNOWLEDGMENTS

This publication was made possible in part by the gifts of Mr. Michael F. Royal and Mr. and Mrs. Leon Hagler.

Cults. Questions and Answers. M.D. Langone, Ph.D. American Family Foundation (Western, MA), 1988, p. 1.

AFF (American Family Foundation) is a non-profit; tax-exempt research center and educational organization founded in 1979. AFF's mission is to study psychological manipulation and cultic groups, to educate the public and professionals, and to assist those who have been adversely affected by a cult experience. AFF, PO Box 226S, Bonita Springs, FL 34133. 941-514-3081; 941-514-3451, e-mail. aff@worldnet.att.net; Web site: http://www.csj.org.

CULTS: QUESTIONS AND ANSWERS
By Michael D. Langone, Ph.D.

This article is a major revision of a 1982 publication, *"Destructive Cultism: Questions and Answers."* © Copyright 1988 by the American Family Foundation.

CULTS: QUESTIONS AND ANSWERS
By Michael D. Langone, Ph.D.

Q. What is a Cult?

The term cult is applied to a wide range of groups. There are historical cults, such as the cult of Isis, nonwestern cults studied by anthropologists, such as the Melanesian cargo cults, and a host of contemporary cults that have caught the publics attention during the Past fifteen Years. Webster's Third New International Dictionary (unabridged, 1966) provides several definitions of cult, among which are:

A religion regarded as unorthodox or spurious... a minority religious group holding beliefs regarded as unorthodox or spurious...

A system for the cure of disease based on the dogma, tenets, or principles set forth by its promulgator to the exclusion of scientific-experience or demonstration...

A great or excessive devotion or dedication to some person, idea, or thing...

a. the object of such devotion...

b. a body of persons characterized by such devotion, for example, "America's growing cult of home fixeruppers".

These broad definitions do not accurately reflect the concerns generated by contemporary groups often regarded as cults. The following definition focuses these concerns.

Cult a group or movement exhibiting a great or excessive devotion or dedication to some person, idea, or thing, and employing unethically manipulative techniques of persuasion and control designed to advance the goals of the group's leaders, to the actual or possible detriment of members, their families, or the community. Unethically manipulative techniques of persuasion and control include but are not limited to. isolation from former friends and family, use of special Methods to heighten suggestibility and subservience, Powerful group Pressures, information management suspension of individuality or critical

280

judgment, promotion of total dependency on the group and fear of leaving, etc. (See -What is Mind Control? — page 2.)

Contemporary cults, then, are likely to exhibit three elements to varying degrees: members' excessively zealous, unquestioning commitment to the identity and leadership of the group, exploitative manipulation of members: and harm or the danger of harm to members, their families and/or society.

Because cults tend to be leader-centered, exploitative, and harmful, they come into conflict with and are threatened by the more rational, open, and benevolent of members' families and society., at large. Some gradually accommodate to society by decreasing their levels of manipulation, exploitation, harm, and opposition. Others, however, harden their shells by becoming totalistic elitist, and isolated. These groups tend to:

- dictate sometimes in great detail how members should think, act, and feel;
- claim a special, exalted status (for example, occult powers, a mission to save humanity) for themselves and/or their leaders; and
- intensify their opposition to and alienation from society at large.

Because the capacity to exploit human beings is universal, a cult could arise in any kind of group. Most established groups, however, have accountability mechanisms that restrain the development of cultic subgroups. Some religious cult leaders, for example, began their careers in mainstream denominations from which they were ejected because of their cultic activities. Cults, then, are generally associated with newer, unorthodox groups, although not all new or unorthodox groups are cults.

According to this perspective a "new religious" "new psychotherapeutic," "new political," or other "new movement differs from a cult in that the use of manipulative techniques of persuasion and control to exploit members is much more characteristic of the latter than the former "new movements." This distinction, though unfortunately ignored by many students of the subject, is important in order to avoid **unfairly labeling** benign new groups as cults and conversely, giving bona fide cults the undeserved respectability of terms such as "new religious movement".

The perspective put forth here focuses on the psychological processes, in contrast to some religiously based perspectives which focus on the doctrinal deviations of cults. According to this statement, a group may be deviant and heretical without necessarily being a cult.

Q. What Types of Cults Exist?

Many systems for classifying cults have been advanced. A straightforward breakdown has been suggested by Dr. Margaret Singer, who observes the following types of cults: eastern religious Christian abberational satanic occult/w itchcraft/voodoo spiritualist, racist Zen and Sino/Japanese philosophical-mystical flying saucer and outer space psychotherapy mass therapy or transformational training political new age commercial communal/self-help.

Q. How Many Cults Exist and How Many Members Have They?

Cult educational organizations have compiled lists of more than 2,000 groups about which they have received inquiries, The frequency with which previously unheard-of groups may be new religious, Political, psychotherapeutic, or other kinds of movements, Experience suggests, however, that a significant number, perhaps more than 1,000, are cults. Although the majority are small, some cults have tens of thousands of members.

. Several research studies lend support to informal estimates that five to ten million Americans have been at least transiently involved with cultic groups. A study which randomly surveyed 1,000 San Francisco Bay Area high school students found that 3% of students reported that they were members of a cult group, while 54% reported at least one contact with a cult recruiter. Another study, which analyzed survey data from Montreal and

San Francisco, found that approximately 20% of the adult population had participated in 'new religious and para-religious movements," although more than 70% of the involvements were transient. Other data in this study suggest that approximately two to five percent of the subjects had participated in "new religious and para-religious" groups that are commonly considered cults.

Q. Are Cults Limited to the United States?

Absolutely not. Grassroots cult educational organizations exist in more than 15 countries. Government sponsored inquiries into cult activities have occurred in at least five countries. International Congresses on cultism have been held in Germany, Spain, and France. And in 1984 the European Parliament passed the "Cottrell Resolution," which called member states to pool their information about the "new organizations" as a prelude to developing "ways of ensuring the effective protection of Community citizens.

Q. What is Mind Control?

Mind control (also referred to as "'brainwashing," "coercive persuasion," "thought reform," and the "systematic manipulation of psychological and social influence") refers to a process in which a group or individual systematically uses unethically manipulative methods to persuade others to conform to the wishes of the manipulator(s), often to the detriment of the person being manipulated.

Such methods include:

- extensive control of information in order to limit alternatives from which members may make .choices,
- deception,
- group pressure,
- intense indoctrination into a belief system that denigrates independent critical thinking and considers the world outside the group to be threatening, evil, or gravely in error;

- an insistence that members' distress — much of which may consist of anxiety and guilt subtly induced by the group — can be relieved only by conforming to the group;
- physical and/or psychological debilitation through inadequate diet or fatigue; the induction of dissociative (trance-like) states (via the misuse of meditation, chanting, speaking in tongues, and other exercises) in which attention is narrowed, suggestibility heightened, and independent critical thinking weakened;
- alternation of harshness/threats and leniency/love in order to effect compliance with the leadership's wishes;
- isolation from social supports;
- and pressured public confessions.

Choice-respecting techniques can be further broken down into educative and advisory techniques, while compliance-gaining techniques can be broken down into techniques of persuasion and control. A cult environment differs from a non-cult environment in that the former exhibits a much greater proportion of compliance-gaining techniques of persuasion and control.

In rearing children, it is often necessary and proper to use control and persuasion to protect them from danger and to help them grow up. As children grow into adults, however, they develop an identity and a sense of personal autonomy that demand respect. Parents learn to surrender control as their children learn to assume responsibility. When this process of normal development breaks down, as when an adult becomes suicidally depressed, relatives and/or helping authorities will tend to become compliance-oriented and step into a "caretaker" role (possibly, in this case, commitment to a psychiatric hospital). When the crisis has passed, however, unwritten ethical rules require that the influencer return to a choice?respecting mode of relating to the adult.

In certain special situations, such as joining the army or joining religious orders, individuals choose to relinquish some of their autonomy. Unlike cult situations, these situations entail informed consent, do not seek to "transform" the person's identity, and are contractual, rather than dependency-oriented

Furthermore, most of these situations involve groups that are accountable to society.

Cults, on the other hand, answer to no one as they flout the unwritten ethical laws by deceptively establishing a compliance-gaining relationship with individuals whose autonomy and identity they disregard. Hence, any similarities between a cult environment and boat camp, for example, are psychologically superficial.

Some cult apologists maintain that mind control doesn't exist because most cult recruits don't become members. These apologists often cite a study which reported that 10% of those completing a two-day workshop offered by a controversial group became members, while 5% remained members after two years. Those who did join, however, made major and rapid changes in their lives, for the group in question demands the total commitment of members' time. In contrast, in the typical Billy Graham crusade, only 1% of attending unbelievers (who have been personally evangelized to for months) come forward during the altar call, let alone modify their lives radically. And Billy Graham is considered to be one of the most effective evangelists in history! Persuading 10% of a group of people, who are largely recruited from the street, to become full-time missionaries within a matter of weeks reflects an astounding level of psychological influence!

Q. Who Joins Cults and Why?

Contrary to a popular misconception that cult members are "crazy," research and clinical evidence strongly suggest that most cult members are relatively normal individuals, although about one-third appear to have had mild psychiatric disorders before joining (it should be noted, however, that a recent study by the National Institute of Mental Health found that approximately 20% of the general population has at least one psychiatric disorder).

Cult members include the young, the old, the wealthy, the poor, the educated, and the uneducated. There is no easily identifiable "type" of person who joins cults. Nevertheless, clinical experience and informal surveys indicate that a very large majority of cult joiners were experiencing significant stress (frequently related to normal crises of adolescence and young adulthood, such as romantic breakup, school failure, vocational confusion) prior to their cult conversion. Because their normal ways of coping were not working well for them, these stressed individuals were more open than usual to recruiters selling "'roads to happiness".

Other factors that may render some persons susceptible to cultic influence include:

- dependency (the desire to belong, lack of self -confidence);
- unassertiveness (inability to say no or express criticism or doubt);
- gullibility (impaired capacity to question critically what one is told, observes, thinks, etc.);
- low tolerance for ambiguity (need for absolute answers, impatience to obtain answers);
- cultural disillusionment (alienation, dissatisfaction with status quo);
- naive idealism;
- desire for spiritual meaning; susceptibility to trance-like states (in some cases, perhaps, because of prior hallucinogenic drug experiences); and
- ignorance of the ways in which groups can manipulate individuals.

When persons made vulnerable by one or more of these factors encounter a group which practices mind control, conversion may very well occur, depending upon how well the group's doctrine, social environment, and mind control practices match the specific vulnerabilities of the recruits. Unassertive individuals, for instance, may be especially susceptible to the enticements of and authoritarian, hierarchical group because they are afraid to challenge the group's dogmatic orientation.

Conversion to cults is not truly a matter of choice. Vulnerabilities do not merely "lead" individuals to a particular group. The group manipulates these vulnerabilities and deceives prospects in order to persuade them to join and, ultimately, renounce their *old lives*.

Government/Law — Infiltration of government agencies, political parties, community groups, and military organizations for the purpose of obtaining classified or private information, gaining economic advantage, or influencing the infiltrated organization to serve the ends of the cult.

Tax evasion — Fraudulent acquisition and illegal disposition of public assistance and social security funds.

Violation of immigration laws — Abuse of the legal system through spurious lawsuits, groundless complaints to licensing and regulatory bodies, or extravagant demands for services (such as those provided by the "Freedom of Information Act") as part of "fishing expeditions" against their enemies.

Pursuit of political goals while operating under the rubric of a nonpolitical, charitable, or religious organization.

Business — Deceptive fund-raising and selling practices. Organizational and individual stress resulting from pressuring employees to participate in cultic management training and growth seminars.

Misuse of charitable status in order to secure money for business and other non-charitable purposes.

Unfair competition through the use of underpaid labor or "recycled salaries."

Education — Denial of, or interference with, legally required education of children in cults.

Misuse of school or college facilities or misrepresentation of the cult's purposes, in order to gain respectability.

Recruitment of. college students through violation of their privacy and/or deception.

Religion — Attempts to gain the support of established religions by presenting a deceptive picture of the cult's goals, beliefs, and practices, and seeking to make 'common cause' on various issues.

Infiltration of established religious groups in order to recruit members into the cult.

Cults also harm society in important indirect ways. Cults violate five interrelated values that sustain free, pluralistic cultures: human dignity, freedom, ethics, critical thinking, and accountability. Because they "cheat," cults are able to gain power far beyond their numbers. Furthermore, the majority seek the protection guaranteed by the Bill of Rights, even though their ultimate goal is to eliminate the very freedom they claim for themselves. They thus pose a serious challenge.

How does a free, constitutionally-based society protect itself against the totalistic impulses and practices of cults and other groups of zealots without becoming closed and repressive? Simply put, how does the constitutional center hold together?

This question is especially important today because the American cultural identity has fragmented.

The once-dominant Judeo-Christian tradition has been challenged, some say supplanted, by a secularism which, although consistent with the American Constitutional heritage, rejects many major tenets of traditional Judeo-Christian morality.

While these two camps have been battling, a third value system or world view, rooted in eastern mysticism and issuing from the humanistic psychology movement, has worked itself into the American consciousness. Commonly called the New Age movement, this world view's fundamental tenet is that men are blind to the fact that they are all one, that they are all God, and that they are all capable of developing superhuman capacities.

Most proponents of these three world views tolerate disagreement and respect their opponents, even as they compete — knowingly or not — for dominance within the changing American identity. But on the fringes of each world view, zealots, many of whom belong to well organized cults, seek to remake the culture in their own image.

If cultic zealotry is not ethically restrained, American culture will lose its ethical moorings and the values that have for so long undergirded constitutional guarantees. The hundreds of thousands of families whom cults have torn apart and the millions of individuals whose rights and integrity they have violated testify to the gravity of this threat.

Q. Why Do People Leave Cults?

People leave cults for a variety of reasons. After becoming aware of hypocrisy and/or corruption within the cult, converts who have maintained an element of independence and some connection with their old values may simply walk out disillusioned. Other members may leave because they have become weary of a routine of proselytizing and fund-raising. Sometimes even the most dedicated members may feel so inadequate in the face of the cult's demands that they walk away, not because they have stopped believing, but because they feel like abject failures. Still others may renounce the cult after reconnecting to old values, goals, interests, or relationships, resulting from visits with parents, talks with ex-members, or counseling.

Q. Is Leaving a Cult Easy?

Persons who consider leaving a cult are usually pressured to stay. Some ex-members say that they spent months, even years, trying to garner the strength to walk out. Some felt so intimidated that they departed secretly.

Although most cult members eventually walk out on their own, parental alarm should not be discounted. First, many, if not most, who leave cults on their own are psychologically harmed, often in ways which they do not understand. Second, some cultists never leave, and some of these are severely harmed. And third, there is no way to predict who will leave, who won't leave, or who will be harmed. Consequently, to dismiss parental concern out of hand is analogous to dismissing concerns about youthful marijuana smoking because most youths who try marijuana do not become substance abusers.

Q. What is Exit Counseling and How Does It Differ from Deprogramming?

Exit counseling and deprogramming both involve talking to cult members (sometimes in long sessions spread over many days) in order to help them recognize manipulative, deceitful, and exploitative cult practices, reconnect to pre-cult personal attachments, beliefs, values, and goals, and reestablish the ability to think independently and critically. But they differ in a least one very significant way.

Deprogramming, unlike exit counseling, is traditionally associated with a "rescue" process, in which family members (usually parents) hire a deprogramming team to force the cultist to "listen to the other side of the story." During the early and mid-1970's, dozens of newspaper stories and at least a half-dozen books described dramatic tales of deprogrammers "snatching" adult children of parents desperately concerned about their children's cult involvement.

Although cult-supported propaganda depicted deprogramming as a lurid, violent process, the overwhelming majority of deprogrammings were, other than the initial "snatching," quite peaceful. Many deprogrammed ex-members have remarked that they were surprised by the respect and genuine concern shown them.

Deprogramming was, of course, controversial. Many observers, including large numbers of cult critics, opposed it because:

- they believed it violated cultists' civil rights (although some legal scholars put forth arguments supporting deprogramming as a necessary remedy to cults' destruction of individual *autonomy*);
- it sometimes resulted in lawsuits against parents and deprogrammers, some of whom were successfully prosecuted;
- it was sometimes attempted on individuals who did not belong to cults and, therefore, were not "programmed" in the first place;
- it was psychologically risky in that irreparable harm to the parent?child bond could sometimes result from a failed deprograrnming, which occurred about one?third of the time;

- its high cost ($10,000 being a conservative estimate for deprogrammers, travel, lodging, security, etc.) was sometimes financially devastating for parents who turned to it because they did not realize other options existed.

I have used the past tense in describing deprogramming because it rarely occurs today, partly because of legal risks, but mostly because workers in this field have become more skilled at helping family members persuade cult-involved relatives to participate voluntarily in exit counseling. Exit counselors, who have begun to organize in order to become more effective and professional, have begun work on a code to guide their behavior. Their growing professionalism is a significant development for cult-affected families.

Q. What Can Parents of Cultists Do?

There is much they can do, but all intelligent alternatives involve considerable uncertainty, anxiety, and effort. Parents should realize that

- there is hope for parents;
- not all new or unorthodox groups are cults (see Question 1: "What is a cult?");
- troubling behavior in a young adult or adult child can sometimes have little or nothing to do with involvement in a cult or "new" movement;
- "rescuing" cultists or persuading them to leave a cult is not always possible or even advisable, because, for example, the group may provide a refuge for a psychologically disturbed person;
- a "'recipe" for persuading a person to leave a cult does not exist — each case must be treated individually;
- hence, collecting valid information bearing on the group's destructiveness to their child is vital.

After parents understand these points. they can then try to conduct — with professional assistance when appropriate — an informed, reasoned investigation of their possible courses of action, which include the following:

- accept a child's involvement,
- persuade the child to make an informed reevaluation of his commitment to the group,
- set up a deprogramming "rescue",
- disown the child.

Although space permits only a superficial analysis, consider briefly each of these alternatives:

Alternative One: Acceptance. Parents may accept, even approve of a cult involvement because they respect their child's autonomy and deem his group to be psychologically benign. If parents believe the group is destructive to their child, they may reluctantly accept his involvement because they are not able to pursue a course of action that would lead him to reevaluate. Such reluctant passivity can sometimes be very trying to parents, who may benefit from professional assistance designed to help them cope with the grief, anger, fear, and guilt that cultists' parents often experience.

Alternative Two: Promote Voluntary, Informed Reevaluation. Parents who choose this alternative must:

- devise an ethical strategy for maximizing their influence over the cultist and
- develop the self-control and awareness needed for implementing, evaluating, and revising the strategy as needed.

Although the former task is difficult, the latter is usually even more trying, as well as easier to neglect. Parents following this course are advised to seek help from a variety of resources, including other parents of cultists, ex-members, reading material, exit counselors, and professionals with expertise in this field. The American Family Foundation's book, *Cults: What Parents Should Know*, explores this option in detail.

Alternative Three: "Rescue." Although many former members of cults have publicly supported deprogramming as a necessary means of freeing people from cult bondage, the procedure, as noted earlier, is legally and psychologically risky. One-third of deprogrammings fail, and often lead to parent-child estrangement, or even law suits. Furthermore, many individuals who leave cults after a deprogramming might have been persuaded to leave voluntarily, without the risks inherent in a "rescue." Therefore, the American Family Foundation does not recommend deprogramming.

Alternative Four: Disown Child. Some parents who cannot persuade their child to leave a destructive group are psychologically unable to make the best of a bad situation. They may feel a strong impulse to "disown" their child, to shut him out of their lives completely.

Disowning a child is a form of "blocking out" an unpleasant reality. Although many persons are able to function adequately while denying "bits" of reality, the depth of the parent-child bond makes this alternative impossible to follow without paying a severe and emotional penalty, even when disconnection seems less distressing than intense, continuous, and unresolvable family conflict. Hence, parents who seriously consider this alternative are advised to seek professional assistance.

Q. How Can Parents and Others Help Cultists Voluntarily Reevaluate Their Cult Involvement?

Because cults discourage open and honest analysis of their beliefs and practices, parents and other concerned relatives or friends must exercise imagination and tact to help cultists voluntarily reevaluate a cult involvement.

The ultimate goal is to help cultists make an informed reevaluation of their cult involvement, that is, to help them carefully examine critical information which their group does not make available to members, and to talk calmly and at length about the reasons for and consequences of their commitment to the group. Helpers should try to avoid emotional harangues about theology, "brainwashing," the corruption of cult leaders, and the like. Such tactics squander opportunities to gather important information about the group and the cultist's relationship to it. Furthermore, emotional attacks may be offensive and unwarranted if the person belongs to a benign group, And, in the case of bona fide cults, emotional attacks confirm cult stereotypes of the "satanic" outside world and raise fears of deprogramming, which may cause cultists to withdraw deeper into the group.

Helpers should try to be active listeners and should ask questions designed to open up the cultist's mind. In being active listeners, helpers not only gather information, but also model the openness, rationality, and patience that cultists need to reevaluate their commitment to the group.

Helpers should:

- Stay calm and keep the lines of communication open. One cannot have any constructive influence without communication.
- Respectfully listen to cultists' points of view. Inquire into their beliefs, feelings, and thoughts about life in the cult and outside the cult. Find out if they have doubts or unanswered questions about the group — but don't pounce on them as soon as these are uncovered.
- Be patient.
- Be more inclined to calmly ask questions, rather then proffer opinions.
- Find out if they miss aspects of their old lives (friends, recreational activities, school, relatives, music, etc.) Open their minds to their own memories.
- Find out what they believe and why.
- Question their beliefs or try to get them to question them, but do so in a calm, respectful manner so as not to push them into a defensive corner. Timing is critical.
- Calmly express your point of view, but don't insist that they agree. Respect their right to disagree. Sometimes it is more effective simply to plant "thought seeds."
- Demonstrate one's love and concern, but do not make this contingent upon agreement or obedience, for doing this will

rightly be perceived as a bribe. Instead, show love and concern even when disagreement is substantial,

- When possible, neutralize anger by analyzing its source, for anger begets anger. But do not artificially stifle anger, for the cultist will most likely sense the insincerity inherent in stifling emotion. Instead, show the sorrow, pain, and anxiety which are usually the root causes of anger.
- Let cultists know that their actions hurt or worry you, but simultaneously respect their right to do as they see fit, however manipulated they may seem to you.
- Communicate love and help the cultist reconnect to his "old" life by talking about old times and encouraging him to write, call. or visit relatives and old friends. Also, when appropriate, encourage relatives and friends to contact the cult member.

Patiently listening, expressing one's love, and modeling calmness and rationality help create a climate of trust. If cultists trust a helper, they will be more willing to discuss their cult involvement, even, perhaps, with ex-members, exit counselors, or professionals knowledgeable about cults. Once this step is reached, an informed reevaluation of a cultist's commitment to a group is much more easily achieved.

Unfortunately, following this advice doesn't always produce the desired results. Sometimes the cult refuses to let members talk at length with parents or others from the "old world." Indeed, it is not uncommon for cults to send members to distant states of foreign countries without telling parents where they are. *Sometimes* cultists' minds are so taken over by the cult's world view that a rational dialogue is impossible. Sometimes the old world is so full of problems, pain, and insecurity for cultists that — no matter how unhappy they may be in the cult — they are too frightened even to consider returning to their old lives. Sometimes cultists may honestly and intelligently reevaluate their commitment to a group and decide to stay in it because they believe it is better for them. And sometimes achieving the requisite self-awareness and self-control is simply too demanding for parents and other helpers. Nevertheless, those who can successfully follow this path of sharing and reevaluation often discover that they have become closer to the cult-involved person than they ever dreamed possible.

Q. What Can Educators, Clergy, and Others Do to Protect Young People Against Cultic Recruitment?

Educators and clergy interested in preventive education regarding cults can join the International Cult Education Program (ICEP), a joint program of the American Family Foundation and the Cult Awareness Network a grassroots organization composed largely of parents and ex-cult members. Joining ICEP will enable educators and clergy to communicate with others who share their interest, purchase tested educational materials, obtain videos, and speakers for educational programs, and keep abreast of developments in this new and exciting educational area. If you are interested in obtaining more information about ICEP, contact AFF.

The cultic danger to young people is decreased when:

- outside criticism causes cults to decrease the level of manipulation in their environments,
- young people develop resistance to cultic sales pitches by learning about how groups in general (not just cults) can influence one's thoughts, feelings, and behavior, and
- young people learn to cope with stress and recognize and try to overcome personal vulnerabilities, such as dependency, low tolerance of ambiguity, and naive idealism — seeking professional help when appropriate.

Consequently, educators and clergy can help protect youth by not being afraid to criticize cult abuses, but teaching youth about cultic manipulations, and by helping youth cultivate three values that will make them less vulnerable to cultic enticements:

- personal autonomy — the individual's capacity to determine his life with minimal pressure or manipulation from without,

- personal integration — the individual's continuing attempt to order his memories, values, beliefs, heritage, etc., into a unified whole; and
- independent critical thinking, without which autonomy cannot be maintained or integration achieved.

CONFRONTING CULTISTS VICTORIOUSLY

One must know what God's word is and what it says. One must be able to "rightly divide" it, or use it properly. It is far more important to have an intelligent, comprehensive grasp of the Scriptures than to know the details about any cult or groups of cults. An illustration here may be of help.

Once there was a young woman who was to be employed as a teller in a bank. She was told that one of her responsibilities was to be on the lookout for counterfeit currency. In order to prepare her to detect such fraudulent bills, she was not given piles of many different counterfeits to study and analyze. Rather, she was taken to a room near a vault and there was huge stacks of genuine currency to count repeatedly and study. After this process had gone on for sometime, a few counterfeit bills were mixed in with a pile of genuine ones. Without difficulty she was able to pick out or spot the bogus money. It had a different look and feel from the real thing.

In a similar way, if one studies and meditates on the truth of God as contained in the Bible, one will be able at once to detect teachings and emphases that do not square with genuine Christianity. To know God's truth and to be saturated with the understanding of the authentic Christian message is the best cure for cultism. This course is offered, then, not as a substitute for the best answer to cults — comprehensive Bible study — but as an aid to help Christian workers to be able to lead newer Bible students away from error and to provide sufficient material to enable one to answer persistent cultists who may be bothering one seek one's friend or one's family.

TESTIFY TO THE TRUTH

One of our problems in contemporary Christianity is that those who are in the possession of the authentic Christian message tend to remain silent while those seeking to promote some exotic variant are vocal and demonstrative. If we know that Jesus is God's Son, if we enjoy the sweet fellowship of His church, if we trust in His redemption, delight in His service, and look forward to His coming and His kingdom, we should make this known. We may well testify in a world of pessimism to the One who can make "all things new"; in a world of ethical confusion and base behavior we can witness to the One who speaks "as never *man* spoke" and, in a world of tears and death, we can point to the One who came 'to comfort all who mourn" and to be the living among the dead."

LIVE THE TRUTH

This has been developed earlier in this chapter, but it cannot be emphasized too strongly that an active, wholesome constructive Christian life is both the best answer to and the best antidote for cultism in all of its forms. Most cultists begin with a "pitch" that goes something like this: "Are you satisfied with what you know about the Bible?" "Don't you wish you knew more about God's plan for the future?" "Do you know that great things are being done in missions and education by Seventh Day Adventists?" "Here's how you can have peace, prosperity and health." If a person can reply that he is doing God's will now, and has a responsibility to know Christ better and to make Him known, the cultist will usually look for an easier task. Further if one is learning more of God's peace and care constantly, as one does His will, there is little temptation to uncover strange and mysterious Bible "secrets."

When the secret of life is being revealed to us in a life of service we have no need of soothsayers that peep and mutter. When we are filled and thrilled with the all-sufficiency of Jesus as the New Testament presents Him, we shall not need to turn to Joseph Smith, Emanuel Swedenborg, or Mary Baker Eddy for future light. As Paul says in Colossians 3:11 (Phillips Translation): "In this new man of God's design there is no distinction between Greek and Hebrew, Jew or Gentile, foreigner or savage, slave or free man. Christ is all that matters, for Christ lives in them all."

Permission granted for reprint by Standard Publishing Company. Cincinnati Ohio. 45202 CULTS Challenge the Church, pages 126-128 copyright 1963: Standard Publishers.

RELIGION VERSUS CULT[1]

Religions respect the individual's autonomy.
Cults enforce compliance.

Religions try to help individuals meet their spiritual needs.
Cults exploit spiritual needs.

Religions tolerate and even encourage questions and independent critical thinking.
Cults discourage questions and independent critical thinking.

Religions encourage psychospiritual integration.
Cults 'Split "members into the "good cult self" and the "bad old self."

Conversion to religions involves an unfolding of internal processes central to a person's identity.
Cultic conversion involves an unaware surrender to external forces that care little for the person's identity.

---

[1]From "Guidelines for Clergy" by Rev. Richard L Dowhower, in *Recovery From Cults*, edited by Michael D. Langone, Ph.D. and published by W. W. Norton and Company. Reprinted with permission.

Religions view money as a means, subject to ethical restraints, toward achieving noble ends.

Cults view money as an end, as a means toward achieving power. Or the selfish goals of the leader.

Religions view sex between clergy and the faithful as unethical.

Cults frequently subject members to the sexual appetites of the leaders.

Religions respond to critics respectfully.

Cults frequently intimidate critics with physical or legal threats.

Religions cherish the family.

Cults view the family as an enemy.

Religions encourage a person to think carefully before making a commitment to join.

Cults encourage quick decisions with little information.

THE AUTHORITY OF THE BELIEVER

At the center of the cult, either openly or disguised as an "angel of light", is Satan. Peter exhorts believers concerning our chief foe when he writes, "Be of sober spirit, be on the alert. Your adversary, the devil, prowls about like a roaring lion, seeking someone to devour" (1 Peter 5:6, NASB).

Christians often have the tendency to "blame it all on the devil", when in fact it was their own carelessness or fleshly nature which led to the sin or error. It can also be said, however, that even when it is our fleshly nature or the world which draws us from the Lord — and not the devil directly — it is nevertheless true that Satan and his army of demons desire that we be drawn to the world's standards.

Satan is the one who ultimately desires that we pursue the lust of the flesh, and it is he who sits as the "god of this world" (Ephesians 2:1-10). Though not always directly involved, Satan's prime objective is the defeat of God, and for us that means our defeat.

The authority of the believer spells out the authority a believer has over Satan and his efforts to thwart God's desire for our lives and his attempt to defeat us.

For the rest of your life, one of the most important Scriptural messages you'll ever consider is found here.

The authority of the believer is a possession that belongs to every true child of God. And it gives so much authority over the enemy that Satan has tried to blind most believers to the authority they have.[2]

Now, to point out what the authority is, let's look at Luke 10: 19: "Behold, I give you power to tread on serpents and scorpions, and over all the power of the enemy: and nothing shall be any means hurt you" (KJV).

Two separate Greek words are used for *power* here, but one English translation. The first one should be translated authority, not *power*. The Lord is saying, "Behold, I give you authority over the power of the enemy," The Christian does not have power over Satan; he has authority over Satan.

Second, let's examine the source of this authority. Paul writes, "And what is the surpassing greatness of His Power toward us who believe. These are in accordance with the working of the strength of His might which He brought about Christ, when He raised Him from the dead, and seated Him at His right hand in the heavenly places, far above all rule and authority and power and dominion, and every name that is named, not only in this age, but also in the one to come. And He put all things in subjection under His feet, and gave Him as head over all things to the church, which is His Body, the fullness of Him who fills all in all."

When Jesus Christ was raised from the dead, we see the act of the resurrection and the surrounding events as one of the greatest workings of God manifested in the Scriptures. So powerful was the omnipotence of God that the Holy Spirit, through the Apostle Paul, used four different words for power.

---

[2]Ibid. 196

First, the greatness of his power — in the Greek — is *dunamis*, from which comes the English word *dynamite*. Then comes the word *working-energios*, where *energy* comes from — a working manifestation or activity. The third word is *strengthkratous* — meaning the exercise strength. Then comes might, or *esquai* — a great summation of power.

These four words signify that behind the events described in Ephesians 1:19-23 are the greatest workings of God manifested in the Scriptures — even greater than creation. This great unleashing of God's might involved the resurrection, the ascension and the seating of Jesus Christ. "When He made a public display of them, having triumphed over them through Him" (Colossians 2:115, NASB). Satan was defeated and disarmed. All of this unleashing of God's might in the resurrection, the ascension and the seating of Jesus Christ was for you and me — that we might gain victory right now over Satan. The source of our authority over Satan is rooted in God and His power.[3]

Third, what are the qualifications you must have to be able to be consistent in exercising the authority of the believer?

First, there must be knowledge, a knowledge of our position in Christ and of Satan's defeat. At the moment of salvation we are elevated to a heavenly placement. We don't have to climb some ladder of faith to get there. We are immediately identified in the *eyes* of God — and of Satan — with Christ's crucifixion and burial, and we are CO-resurrected, CO-ascended and CO-seated with Jesus Christ at the right hand of the Father, *far above* all rule and power, authority and dominion and above every name that is named.

The problem is that, though both God and Satan are aware of this, most believers are not. And if you don't understand who you are, you will never exercise that authority which is the birthright of every true believer in Jesus. So the first step is knowledge.

The second qualification is belief. A lot of people really don't comprehend one of the primary aspects of belief, which is "to live in accordance with". This is not merely mental assent, but it leads

---

[3]Ibid. 197-198

to action. You could say it like this: That which the mind accepts, the will obeys. Otherwise you are not really a true believer. Do we actually believe that we've been CO-resurrected, CO-ascended, CO-seated with Jesus Christ? If we do, our actions will be fervent.

We should wake up each morning and say, "Lord, I accept my position. I acknowledge it to be at the right hand of the Father, and today, through the Holy Spirit, cause it to be a reality to me, that I might experience victory." You talk about space walking! A Christian who is filled with the Holy Spirit and who knows his position with Christ is walking in the heavenlies. I put it this way: Before you can be any earthly good, you have to be heavenly minded. Your mind should be set at the right hand of the Father, knowing who you are.

The third qualification is humility. While belief introduces us to our place of throne power at the right hand of the Father, only humility will ensure that we can exercise that power continuously. Let me tell you, ever since Mr. & Mrs. Adam occupied the Garden of Eden, man has needed to be reminded of his limitations. Even regenerated man thinks he can live without seriously confederating his total dependence upon God.[4]

The next qualification, the fourth one, is boldness. Humility allows the greatest boldness. True boldness is faith in full manifestation. When God has spoken and you hold back, that is not faith, it is sin. We need men and women who have set their minds at the right hand of the Father and who fear no one but God. True boldness comes from realizing your position in Jesus Christ and being filled with the Holy Spirit.

The fifth and final qualification is awareness, a realization that being at the right hand of the Father also puts you in the place of the most intense spiritual conflict. The moment your eyes are open to the fact that you are in that place, that you have been CO-resurrected, CO-ascended and CO-seated with Christ, Satan will do everything he possibly can to wipe you out, to discourage you. You become a marked individual. The last thing Satan wants is a Spirit-filled believer who knows his throne rights. Satan will

---

[4]Ibid. 198-199
[5]Ibid. 200

start working in your life to cause you not to study or appropriate the following principles, which show you how to defeat him.[5]

The author stated that he learned to exercise the authority of the believer and then to walk by faith and to wait. Sometimes he had to wait six months or a year, but in the long run, when I looked back on a situation and saw how God has been glorified, it was beautiful.

The author stated that he never repeated the exercise of the authority of the believer in a given situation. Satan only needs one warning. God will take care of it from there. Jesus said, "All authority has been given to me in heaven and earth. Go therefore, and make disciples of all nations.[6]

---

[6]Ibid. 202. Permission granted for reprint by Don Stewart, *Handbook of Today's Religions — Understanding the Occults.* Copyright 1982, Here's Life Publishers, Inc., PO Box 1576, San Bernardino, California 92402

MESSAGE TO THE CHURCH[7]

The existence of an evil, supernatural realm, led by Satan and supported by his legions of demons, is reality. Satan's devices are many, and his methods are as varied as his devices. We as believers never are called to investigate all of these occult phenomena. Preoccupation with Satan's methods is not the best means of approaching our foe, our enemy, and the accuser of the brethren. However, this does not mean we are to do nothing.

Rather, as believers, we are exhorted in three major areas. First, we are called to *understand* — understand that Satan has already been defeated. Christ's death and resurrection sealed Satan's fate and destruction. That fact became reality for us when we trusted Christ.

Second, we are called to *know* — know Satan's strategy. Not to know all his methods, but rather his means of operation. This includes his being disguised as an angel of light. Satan's *modus operandi*, aside from a direct assault of lies, also includes the more subtle and often used art of deception. He seeks to lure through the things of the world and the temptations of the flesh. Satan's desire is to replace God's plan with his counterfeit, just as he attempted to do in the Garden of Eden.

Third, besides having a good defense of knowing our position in Christ and recognizing Satan's strategy, we must be on the offensive in what we do. This means knowing God and making Him known. When we get closer to our Lord and share the gospel with others, it pierces Satan as with a knife — the Lord uses us to advance His Kingdom and bring Satan's domain to ruin. For our mastery over Satan is not in our power, but in God's power and through His plan — sharing the gospel. This is why Jesus said in Luke that we should not rejoice because we have power over demons but because our names are in the book of life (Luke 10:17-20).

---

[7]*Handbook of Today's Religions*, Don Stewart. Here's Life Publishers, Inc., PO Box 1576, San Bernardino, CA 92402

Paul clearly states, "For I am not ashamed of the gospel, for it is the power of God for salvation to everyone who believes" (Romans 1:16 NASB). Communicating the gospel is our goal, even amid all the conflicts that Satan and the world attempt to throw at us. The command to believers is to grow in the gospel and to share it with others.

This is graphically and clearly illustrated in chapter six of Paul's epistle to the Ephesians. The whole point of this chapter is often overlooked, as the emphasis is usually placed in the "armor of God". That is not Paul's point. The whole reason for Paul's emphasis on the armor to stand against the powers of darkness is the need to get the gospel out (Ephesians 6:18-20 NASB).

In this section, Ephesians 6:10-20, Paul points out that the true battle stems from the evil forces in the heavenlies, and that his purpose for the life is to spread the gospel. His very prayer at the end of the book, which comes in the context of this section on the armor of God, is for him to be able to *make known the gospel*. He places that prayer there by design and not by accident. As Paul saw fit to end his discussion of the forces of darkness in that way, so do we:

Finally, be strong in the Lord, and in the strength of His might. Put on the full armor of God, that you may be able to stand firm against the schemes of the devil. For our struggle is not against flesh and blood, but against the rulers, against the powers, against the world forces of the darkness, against the spiritual forces of wickedness in the heavenly places. Therefore take up the full armor of God, that you may be able to resist in the evil day, and having done everything to stand firm. Stand firm therefore, having girded your loins with truth, and having put on the breastplate of righteousness, and peace; in addition to all, taking up the shield of faith with which you will be able to extinguish all the flaming missiles of the evil one. And take the helmet of salvation, and the sword of the Spirit, which is the word of God. With all prayer and petition pray at all times in the Spirit, and with this in view, be on the alert with all perseverance and petition for all the saints, and pray on my behalf, that utterance may be given to me in the opening of my mouth to make known with boldness the mystery of the gospel, for which I am an ambassador in chains; that in proclaiming it I may speak boldly, as I ought to speak (Ephesians 6:10-20 NASB).

SUMMARY

The summary is the author's view on why young African American people join such groups, what they derive by joining such groups and how the group is benefited by the addition of new members. It attempts to analyze the rise of non-Christian/ nontraditional religious sects and studies in the United States and comment on them in general. This concludes the work.

The author also wants to thank all those persons with whom she came in contact in the course of work in order to put this study together. They were very cooperative, helpful and frank. That experience between author and young people was very helpful.

The growth of religious groups and charismatic leaders that draw young African Americans into its folds has been astronomical in the last two decades. Contributing to this growth is the free environment provided under freedom of religion guarantees by the constitution and also the tax exemption status for religious organizations and work. It takes little investment to set up an organization or to embark upon such a program. Growth of groups is dependent upon the dynamic quality of their leaders. Many groups flourish and many fall by the wayside.

The groups and individuals studies in this work have thus far flourished. The Jehovah Witnesses have grown for years and are now respectable in the African American community as is the case with Buddhism, Baha'i Faith, Nation of Islam, Jehovah Witness, and popular religious studies which include the Hebrew Israelites Amon-rah and Kwanzaa.

One of the features that these groups and individuals share is that they have something valuable to offer their members that other bodies or individuals do not have. They have all the right answers. Thus they offer their members the Good Life. By following and structuring one's life in line with the guidelines of the group or individual then one will secure for himself the Good Life. All employ tactics for recruiting new members. Included are personal contact, the passing of leaflets and literature, members bringing family and friend in the fold, television and radio exposure, etc. It is the support of members — their free labor in enterprising, e.g., distributing literature and leaflets; in persuading friends, relatives, and others in joining, in donating food, money and clothing as well as other material goods that feed life into the organization sustaining it while allowing it to further grow and continue a more rapid rate of growth.

Some groups cater strictly to the poor, e.g., the Jehovah's Witness. They do most of their work in the poorer sections. Others seek to attract the middle class, e.g., the Black Muslims.

It appears from the groups and individuals under consideration and from the groups that were observed but not part of the study, that the poor look more for organization or leader whom is grounded in fundamentalism. Others want simple and pure religion and pursue the Bible vigorously in their preparing for doomsday as is exhibited by the Witness.

Middle class African Americans are more subtle and prefer more subtle religious doctrines in that they do not see reality as a struggle between godly and demonic forces fighting for the soul of folk. They prefer the Black Muslims and other exotic groups, e.g., Nichren and Zen types of Buddhism. The Nation of Islam gives to the African American middle class youth his own natural religion replenished with geography, language, philosophy, and literature. Others go into Hindu and Buddhist sects, which have been modified to meet their needs. Thus groups and individuals who attract young African Americans generally have varying doctrines, practices, and tenets ranging from fundamental to very liberal upon which their rationale is predicated. They also range from being individual to communal oriented. All youths seems to be in search for some authority or disciplinarian on which to structure and transact their lives.

Some groups and individuals use various techniques in their recruitment efforts. Included are personal contact, friends and relatives converting members, television and radio exposure, the mail, personal appearances, literature, buttons, bumper stickers and leaflets. Motives for joining include escapism, dissatisfaction with present life style, search for identity, search for meaning, need for stability, need for a sense of dignity and personal worth, need for a purpose, and need for some authority. Benefits which befell members include economic, culture, social and psychological benefits accumulated as result of being a member.

Tactics employed for keeping members include involving them in scriptural and doctrinal studies at church and in homes, holding rap sessions, giving them work to do for the group or individual, providing some type of distance or isolation from the larger society, and impressing upon them that they are among the righteous and the saved. They must feel superior to someone and somehow be right.

As was pointed out, what these groups and individuals offer their members is all the right answers. The member is saturated with these right answers. There is some evidence that members may become psychologically dependent upon the group or leaders to the point where they lose all control over themselves. They come to adopt only the referent point of the group or leader as their own. The pressure to conform and accept within the body is so overwhelming that members conceivably can submit their will and life to the group or leader as was the case with Jim Jones followers in Guyana. Isolation further intensifies this dependency the greatest danger of groups and leaders to the individual. In groups where psychological dependency heightened by isolation is most evident, members tend to be very rigid. They only see in black and white. Those outside their pale are always wrong while the only righteous are those within their pale. Members tend to think that everyone who is different are enemies and are out to destroy them. They become highly agitated and suspicious.

It appears that in an age of rapid change and uncertainties that young African Americans are looking for something which offers them security and stability. Religiously oriented groups and leaders offer them this stability. Provided is an authority figure who is desperately needed for direction and to give order to new life. Finding this stability and order in a sea of chaos many escape the world of reality in which their lives are transacted especially if they follow an authority figure or doctrine in which their energies are spent in preparing themselves for the coming of the Kingdom or in fighting a war of saints aligned against sinners. They become intolerant of others and often forget 1 John's injunction to love, not only in tongue, but in word, thought, deed and action.

The study was very interesting. It brought into question and suggested ways in which the more established, traditional bodies can best serve young minorities. It suggested the neglect of these bodies in ministering to the young. It raised the question of how does one guard against extremism. It showed benefits members derived from leaders and groups and how these leaders and groups benefited from the induction of new members.

By understanding what it is that cause young African Americans to join non-Christian/nontraditional religions, cults and sects of follow a charismatic leader, it is hoped that the established bodies can better deal with their young African Americans.

MY STATEMENT OF
DOCTRINAL CONVICTIONS
By: Dr. Joyce T. Henderson

I believe in God who is creator and Sustainer of all that exists. I also believe that God is one, eternally coexisting as Father, Son and Holy Spirit.

I believe in Jesus Christ, the full expression and revelation of God to humankind, consequently, I believe that Jesus is the center of history — and that all historical events before "the word became flesh" (John 1:14a) point to his birth life, teachings, death, resurrection and ascension. I also believe that all historical events since "He lived for a while among us" (John 1:l4b) is defined by and given witness to Him as we await His coming again. I also believe that Jesus Christ entered human history, fully God and fully human, to proclaim the good news of the Gospel. That even though we are living in a broken relationship with God, the Father has sent his "only begotten" son to die on a cross and be raised to live that we might enter into a holistic relationship with him.

I believe in the Holy, the comforting, convicting, counseling, and challenging presence of God, who introduces us to Jesus Christ and bears witness to his Lordship. I believe the Holy Spirit, through His indwelling presence, empowers Christians to live joyous lives of love and purity. I also believe the Holy Spirit enables Christians to build up the Church, and the Body of Christ through the giving of spiritual gifts.

I believe in the authority, inspiration, integrity, and trustworthiness of scripture from Genesis to Revelation. The Bible is the written revelation of God to His people, relevant for all people in all places, at all times. It is the standard by which our lives, faith and prospective are measured.

I believe the church is the community of the redeemed. It is the flock of God (John 10), His family (Eph. 3:15), His building (Eph. 2:21-22), and his bride (Eph. 4). Entrance into the church is through faith in Christ alone; it is He who adds us to the church as we are saved by grace.

I also believe in the mission of God's church is to reconcile all persons to Jesus Christ and therefore to each other and us.

I believe in the Kingdom of God as a present spiritual reality of God's rule and reign in the lives of Christians. I believe Christians will experience the blossoming of this reality in all its fullness when Jesus Christ returns to raise the dead. At that time in the not-too-distant future, I believe that all people who have ever lived will be rewarded or punished according to Christ's righteous judgment. The righteous, through their faith, will enter into eternal glory with Christ, and the unrighteous will enter into eternal separation from God.

Because of these doctrinal convictions, my goal in life is to extend the Kingdom of God by making certain that my calling and elections is sure.

I thank God for His call upon my life and for new opportunities to respond to His call.

ABOUT THE AUTHOR
Dr. Joyce T. Henderson

I made the monumental decision to follow Jesus Christ as my Lord and Savior 50 years ago, at the age of 8 while attending Miles Chapel Christian Methodist Church in Little Rock, Arkansas. Shortly afterward, I was baptized as a testimony to my being buried with Christ in His death and raised to new life with Him. In 1959, I enrolled as a student at Lane College in Jackson, Tennessee where I was awarded the BS Degree in 1962.

Following graduation, I relocated to Los Angeles, California. I later became a member of Phillips Temple Christian Methodist Episcopal Church where I married John W. Henderson Sr. I recall experiencing a deeper desire to know God more intimately and to acquire a more in-depth study of the Word of God.

My mother's membership was also in the C.M.E. Church. However, she attended the Greater Victory C.O.G.I.C. mainly because she loved the worship experience, the Word of God and the location of the church in proximity to her home. Following the close of our worship service at 12:30 p.m. on Sundays at Phillips Temple C.M.E. Church, I would drive over to attend my mother's church. One night while praying, I was engulfed by the presence of the Lord. In those hours, I encountered an incredible dimension of the presence and power of the Holy Spirit.

In 1977, I enrolled in Fuller Theological Seminary in Pasadena, California. In December 1979, I received my MA Degree in Theology; becoming the first African American woman to graduate from the "Black, Asian, Hispanic Program."

In 1980, I served as an Associate Pastor at Amos Christian Methodist Church in Los Angeles. Shortly afterwards, I was assigned as an Associate Pastor at Lewis Metropolitan C.M.E. Church. Several years later, I founded and organized the Carson C.M.E. Church in Carson, California.

In 1987, I served as Pastor of the Harper Chapel C.M.E. church in Cerritos California. During my tenure in the Christian Methodist Episcopal Church, I was ordained a Deacon and Elder. I am very grateful for the love, training, and leadership skills I received while being a member in the C.M.E Connection. I will always be grateful to the church and the Fathers in Zion!

In 1989, I united with the First Church of God in Inglewood, California under the pastorate of the late Bishop Benjamin F. Reid. I was ordained several years later in the Church of God. In January 1997, I received my Doctor of Ministry Degree from Carolina University of Theology, and later became a Certified Christian Marriage and Family Therapist. Presently, I serve as an Associate Pastor at the First Church of God, where Dr. Gregory L. Dixon is Senior Pastor. I serve in the areas of Director of Pastoral Counseling, Instructor of Women's Ministers, and Prayer and Deliverance.

I also serve as an Instructor in the Southern California School of Ministry in Inglewood, California.

I have been married for 35 years to John W. Henderson Sr. and we have one young adult son, John W. Henderson Jr.